BETWEEN PSYCHOLOGY AND EDUCATION

David E. Hunt
Edmund V. Sullivan

ONTARIO INSTITUTE FOR STUDIES IN EDUCATION
UNIVERSITY OF TORONTO

THE DRYDEN PRESS
901 NORTH ELM STREET
HINSDALE, ILLINOIS

to Janice and Patricia

Library of Congress Catalog Number: 73–927
ISBN: 03–089047–0
Printed in the United States of America
45678   038   98765432

Preface

Because so many books have been written about psychology and education, the first question is why another one is necessary. Educational psychology textbooks typically provide specific information such as procedures for educational measurement or implications of learning theory for instruction written by psychologists to educators, and such content is important, especially in teacher training. This book presents a *way of thinking* about such content, a system for organizing these ideas that makes it possible for psychologists and educators to communicate more effectively.

If one picture is worth a thousand words, then one model is worth a thousand pictures. *Between Psychology and Education,* therefore, presents models or ways of thinking about psychological ideas, educational problems, and the application of psychological ideas to educational practice. The purpose of this book is to provide a system for organizing and thinking about the content of educational psychology. This is not a traditional educational psychology text, but it provides a model or way of thinking about such content that hopefully will make it more meaningful. Its purpose is to take seriously the question of understanding the needs of the child and their relation to environmental requirements. Put in educational terms, its purpose is to coordinate student characteristics with educational approaches.

The model was initially proposed almost forty years ago by the psychologist Kurt Lewin in his classic formula "Behavior results from both the Person and Environment," or B = P,E. This book describes the BPE way of thinking as a model or paradigm; thus B-P-E stands not only for Behavior, Person, and Environment but also for Between Psychology and Education. Such a new way of thinking, or paradigm (Kuhn 1964), affects what is observed, what methods are used, how observations are interpreted, and how generalizations are stated.

How can a new way of thinking help psychologists and educators in their work? We have found in using an early draft of this book with teachers that the BPE way of thinking provides a systematic way of considering what goes on in the classroom. Translated into the classroom, the BPE paradigm becomes "Learning (B) results from both the student (P) and the educational approach (E)." This is the framework within which a teacher can consider why a specific approach "worked" or failed with a specific student or group of students. The BPE model does not in itself answer the question, but it puts the problem in a form that makes it potentially answerable. For example, a teacher might be puzzled by a student's failure to learn from lectures, and when considering the specific student in B-P-E terms, the teacher might realize that the student was very independent and learned more effectively with a less structured approach.

Many experienced teachers already intuitively use differential ways of thinking. For them, the BPE model simply articulates what they have known, but it also should help them communicate with other teachers and teacher trainees. Similarly, the B-P-E way of thinking provides a possible solution to questions such as "Is a discovery approach better than a lecture approach?" by adding to this question, "for whom and for what purpose?" Adopting the B-P-E model requires that principles be stated in a different form so that, rather than general recipes, they will indicate the students and purposes to whom they apply.

Educators who attempt to sift through various psychological theories and ideas for their practical value are likely to be frustrated and confused because almost every psychological theory is presented as "the answer" or the best general approach. How can the educator decide between the relative merits of Piaget and Skinner or Ausubel and Rogers if he must accept one and reject the other? The B-P-E model provides a basis for putting these ideas into more specific form by emphasizing the particular students and purposes to which they apply. Thus, the educator can identify those features of the approach most likely to be valuable in a specific situation. In this sense, the B-P-E paradigm is a way toward a synthesized eclecticism.

For the psychologist, the B-P-E approach emphasizes the necessity for including the person, or individual differences, in designing research and in drawing conclusions from such research. Psychologists can make a special contribution to educational practice by taking seriously the cliché, "to understand and meet the needs of the child." To do so requires that researchers take individual differences into account in the design of their investigations as well as in the statement of their conclusions. Psychologists concerned with educational research will likely view the B-P-E model as a version of what has been called "Aptitude-Treatment-Interaction" (ATI), which studies how students with different aptitudes (P) learn or have difficulty (B) when they experience different educational treatments (E). The B-P-E approach is similar to ATI in a sense but is based on a general paradigm rather than on statistical results alone. The B-P-E model insists that the person be included in principles or generalizations because learning and development occur within the person, and the principle must be qualified in relation to individuals if it is to be useful. The BPE model also provides the psychologist with a basis for estimating the educational relevance of his theories and research.

Finally, if both psychologists and educators adopt this way of thinking, they should be able to communicate more effectively. The BPE model presented here is *not* a theory but a way of looking at theories. Neither do we propose it as original since it was proposed by Lewin and revitalized by Cronbach (1957). We use the term educator intentionally because we have found that the book is useful not only for teachers but also for educational decision makers, curriculum developers, and others involved in the educational process.

Because we believe that the BPE way of thinking will make for better communication between psychologists and educators, the book is written for both groups. It assumes some basic knowledge of psychological concepts and research, but no more than would be acquired in an introductory course in psychology. This approach was first used in our educational psychology program with first-year graduate students who have considerable background in psychology. It has also been used successfully in an M.Ed.-level course with teachers, principals, and curriculum developers, some of whom had a very limited background is psychology. We believe that it would also be appropriate for use in teacher training programs as a complementary text to one of the traditional books in educational psychology. Additional readings are included at the conclusion of each chapter to extend the material.

Ways of thinking do not change quickly or easily. In using early versions of this book, we found that most students required some time before they grasped this new paradigm and were able to apply it. In some cases, teachers did not see its full implication until they returned to the classroom after experiencing the BPE model during the summer. If our book achieves its purpose for the graduate student in psychology interested in conducting educational research, then it will affect his conception of research. For the teacher, it will affect how he views his teaching and how he considers ideas that may help him improve it. For both, the world will look different. However, such a change does not occur immediately. At first, most students react in one of two extremes: either the paradigm is self-evident or it is impossibly complex.

We base our book on another idea of Kurt Lewin, "There is nothing so practical as a good theory." In this case, the B-P-E model is what is practical. Therefore, we ask the reader to consider the ideas sufficiently so that he can try them out for himself. We believe that using the paradigm will prove demonstrably valuable to psychologists and educators in their work. What we ask is that you give it a try.

The first part of the book contains five chapters which outline the B-P-E model by describing each of the three components—Person, Behavior, and Environment—and their interaction. Our purpose in these five chapters is to get the reader thinking about the issue of how to describe these components, not to provide a summary of how each has been described. For example, in Chapter 2 on the Person, the focus is on what psychologists refer to as individual differences and what teachers consider student characteristics. The idea in this chapter is to get both groups thinking about how to describe differences among persons in terms that are compatible with an interaction view, that is, ways of describing persons so that they can be stated in person–environment terms. Also, this chapter is intended to bring psychologists and educators closer together in their ways of thinking about how persons differ. It is not intended as a survey of individual differences, developmental theories, or systems of personality, and therefore, very little of such traditional content is included. We refer very selectively to a few individual differences as examples. The same point is true of Chapters 3, 4, and 5. Those chapters are in no way attempts to include a survey of what has been written about behavior, environment, and concepts of interaction. Unless this point is understood, some readers may be disappointed that certain ideas about the educational environment have been omitted. At the end of the first five chapters, the reader should have a general grasp of this way of thinking and some idea of how it might apply to the analysis of a psychological theory, a classroom observation, or an educational research report.

The second part of the book applies the B-P-E model to several psychological theories and describes its implications for the application of such theories to educational practice. Five psychological approaches are described in some detail: Piaget's, Skinner's, Ausubel's, the Conceptual Level, and the humanistic approaches, such as those of Rogers and Maslow. In addition, the theories of Bruner, Gagné, and Vygotsky are considered. These five chapters are intended to give enough of a selection of the application of the B-P-E model so the reader can himself apply it to other theories (in fact, this has typically been our major assignment in the course). Therefore, like Part 1, Part 2 is not intended as a survey or comprehensive review of theories but rather as a sample of how a B-P-E model may be applied to such theories. In this section, our emphasis is in part on identifying the strong features of the theory by stating those persons and purposes for whom it seems most appropriate as well as assessing its potential educational relevance, in short a critical evaluation in B-P-E terms. However, equally important is a consideration of how a particular approach might be made even more valuable by giving more attention to one of the three B-P-E components. For example, we note how Skinner's "empty organism" theory might be made more valuable with more explicit attention to individual differences, and how these differences interact with various reinforcement patterns. By the end of Chapter 10, therefore, the reader should have some idea of the differential value of the approaches discussed as well as an understanding of how to apply a B-P-E analysis to a psychological theory.

Chapter 11 is a dicussion of the application of theory to practice. This discussion should give the reader some criteria for judging the relevance of theory to practice as well as more concrete examples of how the B-P-E paradigm helps implement psychological ideas in educational practice. At the conclusion of the text, the reader should be able to evaluate the usefulness of the model by applying it to his own work: if a psychological researcher, to the evaluation of journal articles and to the design of experiments; if a teacher, to the analysis of what happens in his classroom and to the evaluation of new teaching strategies suggested by various psychological theories; if an educational administrator, to the most useful planning of educational programs.

We very much appreciate the valuable feedback provided by our students with whom we have been using this approach during the past three years. We also appreciate the constructive suggestions from many of our colleagues, especially those of Bruce Joyce and Raymond Wolfe.

Toronto, Ontario   D.E.H. and E.V.S.
September 1973

Contents

chapter 1

COORDINATING PSYCHOLOGY AND EDUCATION

How Disciplines Are Coordinated

To coordinate the disciplines of psychology and education requires facing problems similar to those encountered in coordinating other disciplines, such as biology and chemistry. It is easy to label the interdisciplinary effort—educational psychology, biochemistry, physiological psychology—but it is much more difficult to understand how one discipline can communicate and work effectively with another. Some disciplines, like biology and chemistry, have synthesized their concepts and language into a bridge discipline (biochemistry); some disciplines are on speaking terms with one another but translate with difficulty; a few cannot or do not communicate with each other at all. Successful interdisciplinary coordination, therefore, requires a system of communication.

Disciplines also vary in the nature of their relation to one another: for some,

1

like biology and chemistry, the relation is interdependent in that each contributes to and receives from the other; for others, like physiology and psychology, the relation is unilateral, that is, psychology must be reducible to physiology. Interdisciplinary coordination also requires agreement about the nature of the working relation. Before assuming that educational psychology provides a bridge between psychology and education similar to that of biochemistry, let us consider some of the problems facing any effort to develop a system that will link two disciplines in their communication and working relation.

Interdisciplinary activity, like interpersonal relations, requires a mutually agreeable communication system compatible with the language, frame of reference, concepts, and ideas of each party. To communicate with an educator, a psychologist should begin by clarifying his own language. Next, he should try to understand the language of the educator so the two parties can arrive at a decision on how they will communicate, for example, "psychologese," "educationese," or a third language. Finally, they must decide how they will structure their working relation—will they work reciprocally so that each depends on the other, will one set goals and the other develop means to achieve them? Successful coordination of two disciplines like psychology and education therefore depends on how well each of these problems is handled.

To compare the relations between two disciplines with the relations between two persons is oversimplified, but instructive, because similar problems occur. If you are about to begin talking and working with another person whom you have just met, then you should deal with these problems: (1) clarifying your own language, frame of reference, and ideas so he will be better able to understand you; (2) attempting to understand the other person's language and viewpoint; (3) deciding on a means for communication which may require that one or both of you modify your language; and (4) agreeing on what kind of working relation you will establish, or some ground rules for your working together. Like disciplines, people vary in how effectively they communicate with each other and work together.

Relation Between Psychology and Education

Psychology and education are presently on speaking terms, but the language is "psychologese," and the ear of the educator is often tuned out. Their working relation, as would be expected from their one-sided communication pattern, is not very well balanced: psychology often prescribes with insufficient attention to the language and concepts of education, and education often disregards the prescriptions because of their perceived irrelevance. Psychology and education can probably never evolve a synthesized subdiscipline like biochemistry, but their coordination can be improved.

Nonconstructive criticism ("Only a handful of the 75,000 studies in the psychology of learning have had educational implications") and rationalization ("Rather than focusing its efforts after World War II in the clinics and mental hospitals, psychology should have centered its work in the schools") are not particularly helpful. We agree with its critics that educational psychology has been less effective than it might in its attempt to coordinate psychology and education. Therefore, we take as our basic assumption the idea that the relation between psychology and education can be improved to the mutual benefit of both disciplines. As stated in the Preface, the reader who feels that the psychology-education relation need not or cannot be improved will not likely be interested in what follows. It may help us get on with our major purpose of constructing guidelines for improving the nature of the communication and working relation between these disciplines if we consider the problems in terms of the four steps proposed.

CLARIFYING THE LANGUAGE OF PSYCHOLOGY

In 1957, Cronbach described "The two disciplines of scientific psychology"—experimental psychology which studied environmental effects upon "persons-in-general" and the psychology of individual differences which studied variations among persons while ignoring environmental effects. He presented a logical and persuasive argument for the necessity of coordinating these two approaches within a unified discipline. The point is that psychology itself must be coordinated before it can relate meaningfully to another discipline.

For example, to the layman who is well aware "You can count on John to be cool in a pinch, but don't trust Henry. Incidentally, Henry's just great when things are calm, and it's hard to tell whether John gives a damn," it must be hard to believe that, after one hundred years, psychologists are still arguing about whether or not to include a statement about the person in the principles that they develop. The language of psychology, especially its definition, is not easily changed by logic, persuasion, or common sense, and Cronbach's appeal to study person-environment interaction has produced only grudging acceptance, for reasons we consider later in more detail. How well psychology has combined environmental effects with individual differences can be debated, but we maintain, and will provide evidence for the belief, that there is much more lip service being paid to person-environment interaction than there is serious action being taken on it in theory, experiment, and practice.

Psychologists may construe the educator's question "How can we meet the needs of the child?" as vague and fraught with emotional overtones, but dismissing the educator's language does not dispose of the question. Teachers are well aware of differences in students' reactions to the same way of teaching (even though they may not always be able to do something about it). Their reaction to general psychological principles will be qualified because these principles take no account of variation among individual students. Psychological principles stated for persons-in-general will never answer educational questions such as how to adapt educational approaches to different students. Therefore, an adequate system for coordinating psychology and education will require that the language, definition, and concepts of psychology be clarified before any form of communication or working relation is developed.

UNDERSTANDING THE LANGUAGE OF EDUCATION

Like psychologists, educators also disagree on the definition of their field. For the psychologist who is attempting to understand a specific educator's view, the most central issue is likely to be the educator's philosophy of education— what he values and what he sees as the objectives of education. Next is the question of how he thinks education works or how such aims are accomplished. In short, what is his definition of education? Which of the following views of education proposed by Thelen best describes his personal definition of education: learning specified content, participation in classroom activities, engagement in inquiry, socialization for a position in society, an interactional transaction with the teacher, or strengthening the student's ego outside the classroom (Thelen 1967, pp. 15–40)? Other definitions focus on the academic, social, or personal domains (Joyce 1969) and on a curriculum that is knowledge-centered, skill-oriented, or provides individual fulfillment (Gill 1971).

To understand how a teacher thinks of education does not mean simply giving him a multiple-choice test with the alternatives listed in the preceding paragraph. Eliciting such information requires more subtlety both because the conventional view of education as defined by most school boards says that all these objectives (and others) are equally important, and because teachers may have only implicit awareness of such belief systems. Later in this chapter we will suggest that the educator must find out how a psychologist defines psychology in order to understand his work, and the same point applies here for psychologists to educators. An example of how psychologists and teachers can come to understand each other's belief systems is described in Chapter 11.

Much of education's rejection of psychology's prescriptions stems from disagreement between the educator and the psychologist on how learning occurs or what constitutes evidence of such learning. A teacher whose implicit theory of learning consists of the belief that a generally stimulating environment will provide the conditions for the child's natural abilities to mature is unlikely to be influenced by a psychologist's recommendations that reflect a view of education as the "stamping-in" of responses.

We do not believe that a system for coordinating psychology and education can ever enforce a synthesis of such value orientations (and this is one reason why psychology and education can never be completely integrated), but such a system should provide the basis for understanding the nature of the disagreements and making it explicit. Therefore, an adequate system should provide the basis for considering educational objectives, theory of instruction, and the role of individual differences so that they may be appropriately coordinated with related psychological constructs.

ESTABLISHING A MEANS OF COMMUNICATION BETWEEN PSYCHOLOGY AND EDUCATION

In 1965, Sanford asked the question, "Will psychologists study human problems?" He observed that the major restriction was the psychologist's preoccupation with "basic research." If psychologists are to communicate meaningfully with educators they will have to be willing to adopt more flexible attitudes about basic research. Sanford suggests that psychologists study many trivial problems described as basic research, and there is a need to detect such trivial, unproductive work. Certainly teachers do not accept a finding simply because it is basic research. Therefore, the establishment of a psychology-education communication system will provide a rigorous testing ground for psychological principles. As previously suggested, we agree with Kurt Lewin that "There is nothing so practical as a good theory." Thus, to test a theory's applicability as well as to obtain evidence on its utility, a system of communication is required. This is not to say that utility is the only criterion for psychological ideas or experimental results, but it is to say that work in psychology should be considered in terms of its direct relevance to human problems.

Communication does not necessarily mean that the psychologist must accept the problem as given in educational terms—for example, "How do we meet the needs of the child?"—but it does mean that the psychologist should understand the problem well enough to redefine it for analysis and investigation. The following list of needs as seen by a school superintendent gives some indication of how school people view problems on which they would like assistance from psychologists:

1. Evaluation of concepts; team teaching, modular scheduling, group dynamics, open concept, individual timetables, continuous progress, nongradedness.
2. Optimum sizes for study groups; for classes in elementary schools and secondary schools.
3. Evaluation of second-language programs.

4. Help for school systems to determine the importance, significance, and relevance of a testing program in our schools, particularly at the intermediate and senior levels. What are the pros and cons of examinations? Are weekly tests sufficient, or is there a place for term- and year-end exams?
5. Thorough examination of vocational educational programs. Are they worthwhile?

Psychologists may be shocked at these imprecise, general questions, but they will need at least to listen to them, if for no other reason than to indicate why the question is unanswerable in that form, to establish communication with the educator. A language of communication between the disciplines will likely be different from the traditional languages of psychology and education, but it should be translatable into each discipline. Therefore, an adequate communication system should permit an interchange of concepts from both disciplines that would be translatable into psychological analysis and into educational implementation. The B-P-E system described in the next section is suggested for this purpose.

DEVELOPING A WORKING RELATION BETWEEN PSYCHOLOGY AND
EDUCATION

An adequate system of communication should provide the basis for at least the beginning of a reciprocal, interdependent relation between psychology and education. Part of establishing a working relation is an agreement about who will determine what is studied and how such decisions will be made.

A specific working relation between a psychologist and a group of school people will require, for example, an agreement on how to deal with questions such as those listed above. Cronbach and Suppes (1969) describe decision-oriented research in which "the investigator is asked to provide information wanted by a decision-maker. . . . The decision-maker believes that he needs information to guide his actions and he poses the questions to the investigator" (p. 20). By contrast, conclusion-oriented research "takes its direction from the investigator's commitments and hunches. The educational decision-maker can, at most, arouse the investigator's interest in a problem. The latter formulates his own question, usually a general one rather than a question about a particular institution" (pp. 20–21).

The working relation, therefore, may involve synchronizing the decision-oriented work suggested by the educator and the conclusion-oriented work initially suggested by the psychologist. The better the means of communication, the more likely the psychologist and educator are to synchronize their efforts. Two examples of working relations are described in Chapter 11.

In summary, a system of coordination should provide a basis for:

1. Clarifying the language, definition, and concepts of psychology.
2. Understanding the language, philosophy, and theory of instruction of education.
3. Establishing a means for communication.
4. Defining the nature of the working relationship

B=f(P,E): A Coordinating System

B=f(P,E) is the formula version of Kurt Lewin's classic statement, "Behavior (B) is a function of the Person (P) and the Environment (E)" (1936). We will use the B-P-E formula as the coordinating system (1) for considering psychological theories and investigations and (2) for coordinating psychological concepts with educational practice. The B-P-E paradigm reminds us that the statement of a psychological principle should include references to the person and to the kind of behavior to which the principle applies. The potential value of the B-P-E paradigm can be seen by considering it in terms of the four criteria above.

CLARIFYING CONCEPTS OF PSYCHOLOGY

The B-P-E paradigm clarifies the language of psychology by forcing attention upon the differential nature of all psychological principles and the psychological experiments on which they are based. We observed earlier the common-sense quality of including the nature of the person in any principle or generalization. Thus, when considering a conclusion from the psychological literature such as "Praise facilitates learning more than criticism," we should ask first, "For whom?" Inclusion of the person in the principle might lead to a statement such as "Praise is more effective than criticism for introverts while criticism is more effective than praise for extroverts" (Thompson and Hunnicutt 1944). Viewed in B-P-E terms, this statement includes the person (introvert or extrovert) and the environment (praise or criticism) but does not specify the behavior. Therefore, the next question is, "For what?" The final form is "Praise (E) is more effective for facilitating cancellation test scores (B) than criticism for introverts (P), while criticism (E) is more effective for extroverts (P)." The principle then is a specification of the *differential* effects among the three components: behaviors, persons, and environments as shown in the following diagram:

Results of a Psychological Experiment
Classified in B-P-E Terms

Behavior	Person	Environment
Cancellation test score	Introverts	Praise
	Extroverts	Criticism

(From Thompson and Hunnicut 1944)

One's first reaction to the B-P-E way of thinking may be either that it is too simple or that it is too complex. For those who feel that it is too simple, we repeat that, despite its commonsense and logical quality, the person-environment interaction approach has not been taken seriously by many psychologists.[1] For those who feel that the B-P-E paradigm is too complex, we note that there is no way of analyzing without a system of categories, and the B-P-E paradigm provides the minimum number of categories for a psychological analysis of the educational process.

UNDERSTANDING THE LANGUAGE OF EDUCATION

The B-P-E way of thinking provides a basis for understanding the language of education by classifying objectives, educational approaches, and students. A teacher planning a course, or one period of that course, must deal with objectives (B), the nature of the students (P), and the form and content of the educational approach (E). For example, for a particular period, a teacher may plan to divide the students (P) into two groups according to their previous knowledge of the topic, municipal elections, giving a lecture (E) to one section and holding a discussion (E) with the other to increase their understanding of municipal elections (B) as summarized in the chart on page 9.

Of course, these variations in behavior, person, and environment must also be organized in their differential or interactive form. For example, "For students with little previous knowledge of the topic (P), a lecture (E) was used, while for students with considerable previous knowledge (P), a discussion (E) was used." From the teacher's viewpoint, the B-P-E formula is usually thought of as E:P ⟶ B, or an environment directed to a person produces a behavior.

---

[1]Educational psychologists have recently become interested in the educational version of B-P-E —Aptitude-Treatment-Interaction (ATI)—but as we elaborate in Chapter 5, ATI unfortunately is less a way of thinking than it is an arbitrary statistical definition.

A Teacher's Plan Classified in B-P-E Terms

Behavior	Person	Environment
Increased understanding of municipal elections	No knowledge of topic	Lecture
	Some knowledge of topic	Discussion

(Note that the educational environment here refers primarily to ways of teaching or educational approaches rather than to elements of the physical environment, such as color of walls or seating arrangements.) Although the B-P-E paradigm applies in this example to a specific lesson (E) presented to an individual learner (P) to produce a particular immediate objective (B), it can also apply to longer educational interventions, for example, one-year curriculum; to environmental influences beyond the classroom, for example, peer group influence; or to more enduring behavioral effects, for example, becoming proficient in solving problems.

ESTABLISHING A BASIS FOR COMMUNICATION

The B-P-E way of thinking provides a basis for communication between psychologists and educators by casting the activities of the psychologist and the educator in comparable terms as shown in the following diagram:

Comparison of Psychological Experiment and Classroom
Situation by Classification in B-P-E Terms

Viewpoint	Behavior	Person	Environment
Psychological researcher	Criterion measure —speed of performance	Subjects— college sophomores	Experimental treatment— reward, stress
Teacher	Student performance and attitude— specific response to question in class or answer on a test	Students	Variations in content and mode of presentation— lecture, discussion, question–answer

Psychological researchers and teachers are similar in that both may vary the environments that persons experience to produce behavioral change—again a very simple observation, but nonetheless potentially valuable. For the psychologist and teacher to view their activities in the same B-P-E terms should serve to acquaint the psychologist with the real world of educational practice in terms that are potentially translatable into psychological analysis and should make the activities of the psychological researcher less mysterious and more comprehensible for the teacher. In B-P-E terms, the educational value of psychological idea will depend on (1) the degree to which it coordinates behaviors, persons, and environments, and (2) the degree to which it can be translated into educational practice.

Educational relevance is a term frequently used but rarely defined in specific terms (cf. Hilgard 1964). In B-P-E terms, one indication of relevance can be obtained by considering the degree of correspondence between psychological experimentation and the actual educational practice as indicated in the following example:

B-P-E Model for Estimating Potential Educational Relevance

Degree of relevance	Behavior	Person	Environment
Low	Observed behavior	Subjects	Experimental treatment
High	Educational objective	Students	Educational approach or way of teaching

We realize that this relevance yardstick is not likely to be accepted by those psychologists who consider their experiments as miniature versions, or analogs, of the real world, regardless of how closely the world is represented. However, the analog experiment that studies, for example, the effects of punishment or electric shock (E), upon response acquisition or the learning of nonsense syllables (B) by students in their second year of college (P) is not likely to be especially relevant to educational practice. One index of this lack of educational relevance is the lack of similarity between the behavior, person, and environment studied in the experiment and those in the actual educational situation. In this case, the environmental effect of electric shock is dissimilar to those environmental influences that a teacher can exert; the behavior of memorization of nonsense syllables is dissimilar to most educational objectives; and the subjects are different from the younger students to whom these results would likely be applied.

To use B-P-E dimensions as a potential relevance index has the advantage of detecting work of little value to the teacher (as in the above example), but the disadvantage of possibly downgrading work that might lead to greater understanding and ultimately to practical applications. We will discuss these issues in more detail in Chapter 11, but for now we note that much of what passes for basic research in personality and social psychology is possibly the result of a game of duplicity between the experimenter and his subjects (Argyris 1969; Bakan 1965; Kelman 1968).

DEFINING THE WORKING RELATIONSHIP

The B-P-E way of thinking provides a basis for establishing a working relation between psychology and education. Using B-P-E models similar to those above, a psychologist and educator could discuss more meaningfully the reciprocal relation they wish to establish. A psychologist can explain the necessity for controlling variables in a classroom experiment while an educator can point to his questions about the significance and implication of special features of certain experiments or principles.

B-P-E AS A WAY OF THINKING

B-P-E is *not* in itself a formula to explain behavior but rather a means of classification; it is *meta*theoretical—a way of thinking about and considering theories—rather than theoretical.[2] The reader whose theoretical persuasion is behavioristic can use the Stimulus-Organism-Response, or S-O-R, paradigm just as well. In other words, the B-P-E paradigm states the problem but does not solve it. Its primary value is as an analytic tool—a means for considering reports of both psychological experiments and classroom activities. The B-P-E way of thinking is used as the basic organizing feature throughout the book to compare various theories, to consider the relevance of work, to view unexplored educational problems, and to consider why psychological ideas are put into educational practice. We hope that applying the B-P-E way of thinking to a diversity of areas will persuade the reader of its potential value for coordinating psychology and education so that he can use it himself in analyzing problems of theory, research, and practice.

[2]Thus, although Lewin first suggested the B-P-E idea as a way of thinking, this should not be confused with Lewin's field theory. Put another way, the B-P-E emphasis does not necessarily advocate Lewin's theory as such, but his B-P-E way of viewing all theories.

In the remainder of this chapter, we will consider conceptions of psychology and conceptions of education within the B-P-E framework.

Conceptions of Psychology

To understand a particular psychological theory or investigation requires asking the question, "What *definition of psychology* lies behind this work?" This apparently obvious question is important because a psychologist's definition of psychology will influence his choice of observation, choice of method, choice of analysis, and choice of conclusion (Kessen 1966). Equally important, his definition of psychology will affect his definition of education and his selection of conclusions from his work for their educational implications.

Most people who have taken a course in psychology would be likely to say that its definition is "the prediction and control of behavior." Such a definition is usually associated with the belief that this objective will be accomplished by discovering, or verifying, general laws of behavior, for example, laws of learning, and it takes the physical sciences as its model. This conception of psychology has produced a highly organized belief system that implicitly specifies what will be studied and how. This "psychology-as-science" conception gives rise to a search for a set of general laws, such as "Reinforcement increases the likelihood of response," that pays no attention to the differential applicability of these laws to persons and little attention to differences in behavior.

Defining "mastery" in psychology as the prediction and control of behavior, Bakan summarized (1965) the features of the "mastery-mystery complex" as follows, and they are appropriate as features that characterize "psychology-as-science":

1. The scientist-subject distinction
2. The definition of psychology as the study of behavior
3. The choice of lower animals, particularly domesticated animals, as subjects of choice in research
4. The specification of the aim of research as the discovery of "laws"
5. The cultural norm that research consists of the testing of preconceived hypotheses (p. 187)

To these, one might add the belief that laws are discovered through the "randomly-assigned-to-treatments" design that mimics the physical sciences and explicitly attempts to eliminate variation between persons. In these designs, persons are randomly assigned to different experimental groups in an effort to eliminate individual differences, a prime example of how the "psychology-as-science" definition avoids person-environment interactions. However, as Vale and Vale (1970) observed:

> What we cannot imitate is the manner in which Newtonian physics treated
> its "subjects" in arriving at those laws. Organisms are far more complex,
> and differ from one another in far more numerous and profound ways than
> do the "subjects" of Newtonian variety. (p. 1098)

The psychologist who defines his goal solely in terms of the prediction and control of behavior quickly focuses his study on those behaviors he *can* predict and control, and when drawing educational implications from his work, emphasizes controllable behaviors as educational objectives. For example, work in behavior modification to be discussed in Chapter 7 provides some basis for controlling certain behaviors, but thus far it applies primarily to simple behaviors that can be controlled.

The "psychology-as-science" conception has led, therefore, to experimentation with fairly simple behaviors that can be predicted and controlled, to the almost total exclusion of concern for variation between persons. There is nothing wrong in aiming ultimately for prediction through psychological constructs, but it is questionable whether psychological constructs should be immediately evaluated by use of the rigorous yardsticks employed by the physical sciences. All we learn is that we know very little when our constructs are judged by these rigorous criteria, and we learn nothing about how to extricate ourselves from our ignorance.

A second conception of psychology might be called "psychology-as-understanding," in which psychology is defined as the attempt to understand the underlying processes of the behavior of persons in a particular environment. As Lewin (1951) stated,

> One of the basic tasks of psychology is to find scientific constructs which
> permit adequate representation of psychological constellations in such a
> way that the behavior of the individual can be derived (p. 62)

Bakan's comments are also relevant to "Psychology-as-understanding":

> The psychologist is not intrinsically different from other people. All people
> seek to understand themselves and others in the course of their lives; and
> all people continually attempt to bring to bear such generalizations in the
> management of their lives. The special character of the psychologist inheres only in the intensity and systematic nature of his search. (p. 191)

Such an understanding is not expected to produce precise prediction immediately but to give some comprehension of the interplay of environmental and personal factors in determining various behavioral reactions. We find this second definition or conception more useful because it is more congruent with a differential approach. If the only gauge of usefulness is immediate payoff in prediction, then a psychological viewpoint that insists on taking account of person-environment interactions is easily dismissed as being too complex. However, when viewed within the framework of the "psychology-as-understanding" conception, then such a complex position can be seen as potentially useful. "Psychology-as-understanding" aims at underlying processes that should eventually permit more comprehensive prediction.

PSYCHOLOGICAL CONCEPTIONS OF ENVIRONMENTAL EFFECT

Because of the influence of the "psychology-as-science" definition, most psychological principles are stated in the general E-B (Environment $\longrightarrow$ Behavior) form. It is a curious tribute to the overwhelming impact of stimulus-response theory that when psychological principles are stated, they are almost always presented in a form that omits the person, or persons, to whom they apply. No doubt other influences such as dogmatic operationalism and blind imitation of the physical sciences have played a part, but it is nonetheless ironic that psychology, of all disciplines, should attempt to express what little accretion of knowledge has occurred through principles that are presumed to apply to "persons-in-general" but frequently do not apply to any person or group of persons in particular.

What do we mean when we say that a law about persons-in-general may not apply to any specific person? An example is found in a classic experiment by Hovland (1937) who investigated the degree to which a conditioned response could be produced by tones that varied in their frequency from the original conditioned stimulus.

Table 1 presents the galvanic skin responses to four tones for each of the twenty subjects in the experiment. For example, Subject #1's response to the original stimulus was 16.2. As the tone became less similar, this subject's response first decreased (11.3), then increased (12.6), and finally decreased again (11.4).

When the scores for all twenty subjects were averaged, as is customary in such an experiment, Hovland noted that the mean, or average, score decreased systematically as the tone became increasingly different from the original tone (mean scores decrease from 18.2 to 14.9, 13.6, and 12.9). Based on these systematically decreasing average scores, he therefore concluded that the results supported a principle of stimulus generalization: the less similar the stimulus, the weaker the response.

Razran (1949) later noted, in inspecting the results subject-by-subject, that the "principle" of systematic decrease, that is, reading across the four numbers for each subject, applied to only one of the twenty subjects (#11), and for this one subject, the effect was very slight. The reader should inspect Table 1 carefully to note this point.

Table 1. Generalization of Excitatory Tendencies

Amplitudes of galvanic responses (in mm.) to conditioned tone (0) and to tones 25(1), 50(2), and 75(3) j. n. d.'s removed in frequency.			
	Tonal Stimuli		
Subjects	Original Stimulus (0)	1 Unit Removed	2 Units Removed	3 Units Removed
1	16.2	11.3	12.6	11.4
2	22.4	18.1	25.4	20.9
3	13.5	6.7	11.2	6.3
4	15.3	6.4	3.3	7.6
5	19.2	18.5	22.8	15.3
6	16.2	18.5	11.9	13.9
7	23.7	17.1	18.0	16.5
8	11.5	14.1	9.6	13.8
9	13.8	10.3	13.4	9.9
10	22.4	18.7	10.7	15.3
11	23.7	21.3	21.1	10.2
12	16.5	20.6	13.9	12.4
13	17.7	18.4	15.2	13.7
14	18.6	13.9	14.3	12.5
15	15.9	15.5	13.8	14.2
16	18.8	12.3	14.6	9.7
17	21.3	9.7	10.5	12.3
18	23.2	17.8	13.9	14.5
19	13.8	16.8	9.3	11.8
20	19.9	12.3	6.9	15.6
Mean	18.2	14.9	13.6	12.9

(Abridged from Hovland, 1937)

Those readers not familiar with the psychological literature may think that this example is farfetched; however, many of the general principles found in introductory psychology textbooks ignore individual differences (regarding such variation as "error") in just this way. Table 1 illustrates that the conception of psychology that aspires to general laws uses statistical procedures that ignore the applicability of the laws to individuals. Rather than compare the mean differences for their degree of significance, one could equally well ask, "Was there a significant number of subjects to whom the principle applied?" or better still, "To whom does the principle apply?" For example, the results of Table 1 could be analyzed statistically to find whether the principle applied to a significant proportion of persons (1/20).

It is impossible to divorce the psychologist's conception of the environment from his conception of the person. If he assumes an "empty organism" position then he is likely to assume that the environment automatically stamps-in its effects. On the other hand, if he assumes that the person is an active, seeking, organized processor of information, then he is more likely to be concerned with the person's interpretation of the environment and its differential effect. (Differences between the environment as objectively and subjectively conceived are discussed in Chapter 4.) Finally, we note that some environmental effects *may* apply to persons-in-general, but such generality must be demonstrated for a variety of persons before its general effect can be asserted. There are very few psychological generalizations drawn from experiments that could not be shown to be inapplicable if particular persons were selected for another experiment.

PSYCHOLOGICAL CONCEPTIONS OF THE PERSON

Not only should variation between persons be included in psychological principles, but these variations should coordinate with the variations in the environment. As Lewin (1951) stated:

> A law is expressed in an equation which relates certain variables. Individual differences have to be conceived as various specific values which these variables have in specific cases. In other words, general laws and individual differences are merely two aspects of one problem: they are mutually dependent on each other and the study of one cannot proceed without the study of the other. (p. 243)

While "psychology-as-science" has restricted the study of person-environment interaction by ignoring individual differences, the psychology of individual differences has also restricted coordination by ignoring environmental effects. Individual differences were traditionally thought of as general characteristics of a person which held for all situations, for example, an aggressive person was aggressive in all situations. Therefore, a trait was evaluated by how well it characterized a person's behavior over a variety of environmental settings. Such nonsituational descriptions of individual differences are as useless as the principles of environmental effects for persons-in-general since they do not apply to the behavior of a person in a situation.

Like environmental effects, some individual differences or traits *may* be general across environments, but much more effort must be devoted to characterizing persons in terms of their differential reaction to various environmental influences before such a generality can be asserted. Consider which statement is more valuable for a teacher: "Johnny is an outgoing, active type" or "Johnny is likely to react more favorably to a structured situation than to one in which he must make the decisions." To describe Johnny in the latter form requires constructs that link a person's differential reaction to environmental variation.

We do not propose a complete specificity of individual description as some have done (for example, Mischel 1968), but we do propose that persons be described in relation to dimensions of the environment (to be discussed in more detail in Chapter 4). When one receives a psychological report on a student or looks at a test profile, he should ask the question, "How much does this description tell me about this person's differential reaction to environments?" A psychological test that provides information about a person's likely response to different environments is more valuable than one that does not. To be specific, when a teacher refers a child for psychological assessment, he does not need to be told that the student is an "underachiever" or an "aggressive type" since knowledge of these characteristics has probably led to the referral; what he wants to know is what to do to help the student function better and develop.

If one accepts the position that there is interaction between person and environment, then the person must be described in terms that give some understanding of his differential susceptibility to different kinds of environmental treatment. In educational terms, this means that the student should be described in terms of his reaction to those different environments that the teacher or decision-maker can vary. Clinical psychologists working in mental hospitals after the Second World War often wrote elaborate psychodiagnostic reports about the patient's intrapsychic conflicts without tying their assessments to action; often as not, the only decision to be made was whether to administer electroshock treatment or not.

The psychologist concerned with education should attempt to extend the boundaries of what is assumed possible in the kind and amount of learning a person can do. He should be concerned, therefore, with the child's potential, and he should focus on characteristic individual differences that shed light on such potential. Measures of fixed intelligence will continue to be used, but we need more knowledge about persons that will point to those experiences most likely to facilitate their learning, growth, and development. The idea of viewing persons in terms of "accessibility channels," or how they can be reached, is presented in Chapter 2 as a basis for such description of persons.

PSYCHOLOGICAL CONCEPTIONS OF BEHAVIOR

A generalization about environmental effects should include reference to what kind of behavior is being affected; however, psychological principles or conclusions rarely distinguish between different kinds of behavior. The psychological investigator who finds that an experimental treatment, such as stress, affects one behavior (for example, speed of performance) but not another (for example, errors) may feel frustrated and think that such a difference represents some error in measurement. However, such differential effects may be valuable in a study of the nature of effects.

If learning is defined as the acquisition of specific, correct responses, this definition has enormous implications for the conduct of psychological research and the educational practices based on such work. For example, most of the numerous studies on the effect of praise or positive reinforcement vs. criticism or negative reinforcement indexed these effects by how quickly and accurately the person learned. Until recently (Cronbach and Snow 1969), learning rate, or the number of trials required to learn to a specified level, was the unquestioned behavioral measure in learning experiments. In addition to the psychometric shortcomings described by Cronbach and Snow, learning rate tells nothing about what is going on in other aspects of the person's behavior. What are his attitudes toward the work? Is he learning to make any differentiations in this material compared with others? Is he acquiring skill in problem solving? A particular experimental treatment may produce "learning" in terms of immediate recall of factual information, but the subject may know nothing of how these facts are related to one another.

Psychological experiments derived from learning theory have influenced educational practice of course, but the influence has not always been maximally constructive. Until recently, psychologists have not paid attention to the distinctions made in the taxonomy of cognitive objectives (Bloom 1956) between recall, comprehension, and synthesis in designing their investigations. With recent improvements in multidimensional analysis, research psychologists can index a variety of cognitive outcomes as well as affective reactions.

When considering any general psychological principle, it is important to ask, "For what kind of behavior?" The form of the generalization almost always ignores behavioral distinctions: "X leads to better performance than Y" or "X produces better learning than Y" or "X is more effective than Y." Our question should be, "For what behavior?"

Behavior resulting from person-environment interaction usually refers to immediate, short-term responses. The term is also generally applied to more enduring, pervasive effects described in Chapter 3 and, in these cases, change in behavior is synonomous with a change in the person.

Psychological Conceptions of Person-Environment Interaction

One reason that person-environment interaction is poorly understood is that psychologists have not discussed strategies for dealing with this problem, or as one author (Carlson 1971) puts it, "Where is the person in personality research?" Recently, Vale and Vale (1969) stated some general guidelines:

> The key to the place of individual differences would seem to be the lawful-ness with which organisms interact with environments. That is, the test of the effect of individual differences lies in the extent to which it matters *which* individuals are being used in the search for relations between environmental treatments and responses. (p. 1096)

Cronbach and Snow (1968) have viewed the person in terms of aptitude measures and the environment in terms of treatment variations, using an Aptitude-Treatment-Interaction (or ATI) paradigm for considering person-environment interactions. They described ATI as follows:

> For a given task one can find alternative methods of instruction, one treatment being superior for learners having one aptitude pattern and another treatment being superior for those having a second pattern. That is to say, aptitude-treatment interactions (ATI) exist. Once ATI are identi-fied, aptitude measures can (in principle) be used to choose the method of instruction for the individual. (p. 2)

Another formulation is that of "matching models" (Hunt 1971, and an example in Chapter 9) in which person-environment combinations that produce the desired change are considered matched, while those that do not are considered mismatched. In educational terms, a matching model specifies an objective and then prescribes a specific educational approach that is most likely to accomplish the objective with a particular student. To derive the match, the student must be characterized in terms that bear some relation to the characteristics of the educational approach. The ultimate form of a matching model, therefore, is a set of "if . . . then . . ." conditional statements that specify the approach most likely to be effective for a specific student.

Differential effects analysis in education cannot be dismissed just because it has not yet "paid off." Considering the review of ATI results reported by Cronbach and Snow (1969), there have been few instances of significant ATI effects reported, and even fewer that have been replicated. This dearth of significant ATI effects should not be taken to mean that a differential approach is unpromising and should be abandoned. As mentioned earlier, ATI investigators limit the interactive way of thinking entirely to the occurrence of results conforming to an arbitrary statistical procedure. The occurrence of statistically significant results from controlled experiments is one source of evidence, but as discussed in Chapters 5 and 11, it is only one of several ways of evaluating the differential approach. ATI, like B-P-E, is not a theory but simply a way of setting forth problems with which theories must deal.

Learning occurs within a person, and different persons learn different things in different ways. Psychologists have not been very successful in accumulating knowledge about such differential processes, but this should not lead us to return to the study of general principles that do not apply specifically to anyone. Rather, we must try to deal with this complexity by gradually generating differentially applicable principles without being overwhelmed by our ignorance.

The investigation of person-environment interaction forces attention on the *process* of interaction. Not only must the person and the environment be represented in comparable terms, but the effect of their relation to one another on performance and satisfaction must be spelled out. The relation between person and environment may be described in terms of matched, optimal, or best-fit. This matching depends upon the behavioral objective, as the following quotation from Stern (1961) indicates:

> But what *is* an optimal environment—one that satisfies, or one that stimu-
> lates? While it may be true that pearls come from aggravated oysters, you
> can only get milk from contented cows. Pearls and milk each have their
> uses, and people will continue to exercise their preference for one or the
> other, but it would be a pointless exercise of freedom to insist on milking
> oysters. (p. 728)

Conceptions of Person-Environment Interaction in Education

Although the interaction view has not been sufficiently clarified in psychology to be applied explicitly to education, there have been some efforts to conceptualize the educational process in terms of the interaction between a particular educational approach and the individual student. The history of education in North America during the past century could be seen as a succession of attempts to improve educational programs by handling the problem of individual differences in different ways. The following overview describes some of these implicit attempts and indicates how psychological theory affected them.

AGE-GRADING

One of the earliest educational attempts to take account of individual differences was age-grading which was designed to restrict the amount of pupil variation that a teacher would encounter. Before 1850, elementary schools were ungraded (Woodring 1964). Age-grading was introduced because of efficiency rather than because of any psychological principle. The little red school-house was the place where children of various ages came together to receive a somewhat common education. As schools became larger as a result of urbanization, a graded system along the dimension of age became an increasingly common practice. Although age-grading procedures are currently criticized for their insensitivity to individual differences, their initial intention was in fact to take serious account of differences among students. When grouping students by age was first begun, school superintendents spoke hopefully of the time when class size could be reduced to sixty students per teacher (Cremin 1964).

Age-grading led to the belief that every child ought to climb the educational ladder at the rate of one grade per year, and that not doing so constituted failure. Educational achievements were sequenced in some fashion as shown in the following diagram, and it was expected that children at a certain age level would learn a particular slice of knowledge. For example, children, age 6, were expected to be accomplished in computation, and the Grade 1 curriculum reflected an emphasis on these skills. More advanced skills for older children (for example, seven-year-olds learning multiplication) saw the Grade 2 curriculum focusing on these skills.

Age-Grading in B-P-E Terms

Behavior	Person	Environment
Computational skills	6 years	Grade 1 curriculum
Multiplication skills	7 years	Grade 2 curriculum

Therefore, as knowledge of individual differences increased, it became apparent that age-grading and its related "one grade per year" rate were appropriate primarily for students of average ability (Woodring 1964). At the beginning of the twentieth century, the number of students of below-average ability increased because of pressure for universal education. The wholesale attack on the abuses and evils of child labor was the theme of the day, and the practice of raising the terminal age of compulsory schooling was one result (Hofstader 1963). This increase in students made it even more difficult for the school to deal with students on an individual basis. Therefore, the graded classroom of today encompasses a wide variety of individual differences (Goodlad and Anderson 1963). As shown in Figure 1, children entering first grade differ in mental age alone by about four full years. This difference increases as the children advance in grade so that by the time children complete the fourth grade, the range in mental abilities is about four times the range in the first grade. It is apparent in contemporary education that the grade level designation means little. This conclusion is reinforced when other dimensions of individual difference are added to mental age differences. As can be seen from Figure 1, the range in certain achievement areas follows the same pattern as that of mental age in general with few exceptions. Thus, this earlier curriculum innovation of age-grading has become entrenched and works opposite to its original intention. The eventual outcome of an educational innovation cannot be predicted, and it is to some of these earlier innovations that we now turn.

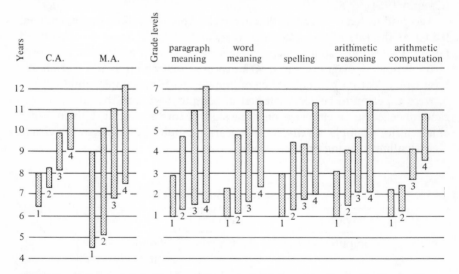

Figure 1   Range in Age by Years and Range in Achievement by Grades for Grades One Through Four (Goodlad and Anderson 1963, p. 14)

DEWEY AND THORNDIKE

At the turn of the century, the schools were much in need of reformers. It would be historically inaccurate to say that only two men were contenders for this position around the turn of the century, but a reading of Cremin's *Transformation of the Schools* leaves one with the impression that the philosopher Dewey and the psychologist Thorndike were certainly two of the more salient figures providing impetus for the changes in educational theory and practice that were about to take place. Both Dewey and Thorndike responded to the needs of a newly industrialized and increasingly urbanized society. Dewey's reform commentaries were ordinarily addressed to those involved in elementary education, whereas Thorndike's suggestions were geared to those in the emerging secondary level (Cremin 1964).

Probably the most explicit philosophical statement in support of the interactionist position is found in some of Dewey's writings at the beginning of the twentieth century (Dewey 1902; 1916). In his book *The Child and the Curriculum,* he stated that:

> The fundamental factors in the educative process are an immature, undeveloped being, and certain social aims, meanings, values incarnate in the matured experience of the adult. The educative process is the due *interaction of these forces.* Such a conception of each *in relation to the other* as facilitates completest and freest interaction is the essence of educational theory (1902, p. 4; italics added)

At that time, there were insufficient psychological constructs to concretize Dewey's interaction recommendations. Today, Dewey might have described the child in terms of Piaget's stages of development and the curriculum in terms of more recent conceptualizations of the educational environment. At that time, however, his ideas were not and could not be implemented in educational research and practice because of lack of specification.

The psychologist Thorndike, in contrast, allied his theoretical positions with vigorous empirical research. It is interesting that many of the proponents of progressive education, as well as Thorndike himself, saw Thorndike's theory and research as consistent with Dewey (Mayer 1961). Thorndike's psychology was in fact the antithesis of Dewey's interactionist position. Dewey's position was much more consistent with the Gestalt psychological tradition (McDonald 1964). Thorndike's educational psychology was a general effects model based on "psychology-as-science." Thorndike was quick to extrapolate educational prescriptions from his animal experiments to persons-in-general. However, the person in the person-environment interaction was virtually ignored.

He seemed to proceed on the assumption that his laws of learning were applicable across all persons or, for that matter, across species. Thorndike's viewpoint, in contrast to Dewey's, was much more compatible with S-R behaviorist psychology.

It would seem that the psychological research generated by Thorndike lent its support to many practices in North American schools throughout this century. His law of exercise and his related belief that there is no learning that is not *behaviorally* demonstrated were compatible with many school practices. His view did not differentiate behavioral effects but aimed exclusively for the behavioral objective of knowledge acquisition as indexed by recall. Thorndike's position was most consistent with curriculum methods that emphasized drill and repetition. This fostered:

> ... the rush of tests and examinations and weekly quizzes, of workbooks and homework, of recitations and catechisms by which children every-where—but especially in America—are made to prove that they have learned their lessons. If the child cannot give back on demand what he had been taught, it is assumed that he has not learned it. Behavior alone counts, and academically the required behavior is verbal. (Mayer 1961, p. 87)

It is clear that this emphasis on theory, research, and educational practice is incompatible with a differential or interactive perspective since it not only ignores variations in persons but specifically disregards variations in behavioral effects. It is much more in keeping with a general effects model as illustrated by behavioristic psychology.

Thorndike's vigorous empiricism also attracted his interest to the educational testing movement that was booming in the 1920s. Like many other psychometricians, he embarked on an elaborate program of testing and classification of learners. Although this kind of psychological approach has frequently been called individual difference psychology, it dealt with only variation according to ability, which was not usually linked to a best-fitting educational environment. The general thrust of the movement was not specifically geared to treating the individual differences found in terms of person-environment interactions. The educators were at the same time trying to find the single *best* curriculum and teaching method for each field of enquiry, and the testers did not tell them otherwise (Cronbach and Suppes 1969).

Surprisingly, the progressive-education movement initially joined forces with the testing movement, a liaison that had an unmistakable impact on the school. There was a considerable increase in the flexibility of grouping of students, most commonly on the basis of intelligence and achievement (Cremin 1964). The coalition of the educational testing movement with the progressive educators was short-lived because these two groups had incompatible aims. Specifically with regard to the IQ testing movement in education, a peculiar and restricted form of interaction procedure resulted from the assumption, held by many testers, that the measurement of intelligence was the assessment of a fixed capacity or skill (J. McV. Hunt 1961).

ABILITY GROUPING

The interactive approach associated with a fixed intelligence conception led to the ability mode of thinking in educational practice. Intelligence as expressed by the IQ measure was essentially a measure of the student's potential rate of skill acquisition as assessed by the test. The intelligence quotient was furthermore correlated with skill acquisition measured in the school's achievement tests. Those of the ability or skill mentality saw the IQ as a good predictor of a person's success and speed in school achievement. Ability grouping viewed in B-P-E terms held that behavior (school achievement) was a function of the person (for example, high-low intelligence) and the environment (for example, fast-slow pacing of teaching methods) as shown in the following diagram:

Ability Grouping in B-P-E Terms

Behavior	Person	Environment
Skill acquisition	Low ability	Slow rate
	High ability	Fast rate

The fact that a person had a low IQ did not bring about any qualitative changes in the teaching methods (environments). Rather, the low-ability student (slow learner) received the same material but at a slower pace than the high-ability student (fast learner). Thus, the only differences in educational environments between slow and fast learners (as measured by IQ) was the *rate* of presentation of materials. The low-ability student could "get there" (achieve), but it would take longer. Skill-grouping or tracking was supported for its potential practical effectiveness in the classroom as well as its gloomy congruence with the psychological assumption that intelligence is fixed and unmodifiable by experience. Although this orientation has been attacked by educational critics, its assumptions are still rather pervasive in contemporary education. The coalition between the testing movement and the progressive educators was broken in the thirties because the educational arrangements it generated were ultimately at odds with some of the tenets of the progressive philosophy (Cronbach and Suppes 1969).

EDUCATION FOR ADJUSTMENT

The period from 1930 to 1950, in contrast to the earlier period of diligent fact-finding and confident measurement and evaluation of pupils, could be considered a relatively shallow period for educational research and critical enquiry. The depression and World War II put a strain on most educational institutions, many of which were forced to abandon their research bureaus (Cronbach and Suppes 1969). With the lack of intellectual leadership in the progressive movement, education became more insular in relation to the academic disciplines (Cremin 1964). Educational psychologists during the later forties and early fifties adopted the slogan of schooling for "life adjustment" (Hofstadter 1963), which was essentially conservative in character and, when carefully analyzed, implicitly counter to an interactionist viewpoint. Education for adjustment aimed to mold the child to fit the environment. Dewey's ideas were thus ultimately distorted since life adjustment was heralded by the progressive advocates. It was unfortunate that Dewey's seminal contributions, especially those emphasizing the matching of curriculum to student characteristics, were lost in the attack made on life adjustment, because he never propounded the latter position. The more recent educational renaissance following the Russian Sputnik in 1957 has not taken advantage of Dewey's initial perspectives on the interaction of the child and the curriculum. This was not unexpected because Dewey's views on interaction were never taken too seriously, even during the heyday of progressivism.

Two circumstances are quite important in their effect upon present educational policy: (1) the U.S. Supreme Court decision of 1954 which made segregation in the schools a legal and moral issue for American society, and especially for educators, and (2) the 1957 launching of Sputnik by the Russians. The Supreme Court decision focused on the deleterious effects that segregation in the schools had on the growth of Negro children, while Sputnik led to soul-searching about American schools in general. This soul-searching produced strong condemnation of the schools and the educators responsible for them. The American schools were held responsible for Russia's apparent lead in the cold war.

The past decade has witnessed demands on the educational system that seem to exceed even the demands made on progressivism in its prime years, since the schools were now linked with the problems of the cold war, racial integration, crime eradication, and poverty elimination and with the goals of health, prosperity, and peace (Goodlad 1969). As a result of these demands, more money has been allotted by government to education to encourage the development of innovative solutions to these pressing problems.

The demands made on education after Sputnik forced a movement toward discipline-centered education (Goodlad 1969). The attack on the schools was that, in their "child-centeredness," they had forgotten there was valuable subject matter to be learned. The rash of new subject-matter specialists led to the development of many new programs, especially in the sciences and mathematics. In many instances, these new programs were devised and developed with the help of expert scholars from the disciplines, such as mathematics and physics. However, the programs maintained the old dichotomy between the child and the curriculum:

> We must take the learner into account in teaching and planning for teaching. This platitude covers up the complexity of the problems involved, however. The learner, obviously, is not the only data-source to which one turns in making curricular decisions. Awareness of this fact, when coupled with an inadequate conception of the total context of educational decision-making, leads us to scream, "You've forgotten the children" when someone attempts to analyze the place of the subject matter, and "You've forgotten the subject matter!" when someone seeks to analyze the place of the learner. Thus, a sterile debate arises out of our inability to see two quite different parts as essential to a larger whole as well as unique within themselves. (Goodlad 1966, p. 157)

It is interesting to observe that Goodlad's critique is almost a replica of Dewey's analysis made at the turn of the century.

From the Civil Rights movement that gathered momentum after the 1954 Supreme Court decision came the insistent demand that education be an equal opportunity for both black and white students. One of the arguments was that equality of educational opportunity was impossible for blacks, or, for that matter, for any children coming from lower-class environments. A lower-class background was thought to prevent children from competing equally with children coming from middle-class backgrounds. The lower-class child starts out below his middle-class counterpart and remains below, unless special intervention procedures eliminate these initial deficits. The period from 1960 to 1970 saw the initiation of special programs to deal with the problem of the lower-class, culturally deprived, or disadvantaged child. Special programs did not appreciably change the general course of education but were a tactical step to maintain the status quo. As Cronbach (1967) observes:

> Most tactics the school uses are intended to minimize the nuisance of individual differences so that it can go on teaching the same unaltered course. This is true also of remedial instruction which adds onto the common program rather than redesigning it. Remedial work takes it for granted that the classroom work is largely a fixed program. Many a pupil needs help that a standard program does not give him, and supplementary instruction is therefore provided, with the intention of repairing the gaps in skill and putting him back on the pace. That is to say, remedial instruction attempts to erase individual differences. (p. 27)

This way of thinking is reminiscent of the skill-acquisition mentality previously discussed. The special programs for culturally deprived children (assessed on the basis of IQ, social class, or race) attempted to give the children the skills to rise to the average track. For example, the Head Start prekindergarten is designed to get the culturally deprived child up to the skill level necessary to start him out on pace. If the program was devised for the student when he was already attending school, it was to get him back into pace. Most of these remedial programs claim as one of the main criteria of their success an increase in IQ (see Jensen 1969).

NONGRADING, OPEN SCHOOLS, AND TEAM TEACHING

Following the recommendations of Goodlad and Anderson (1963), the use of age-grading has been relaxed so that students might be considered in more individualized ways. The increased adoption of nongrading procedures has been frequently accompanied by open-space schools and teaching teams. The net effect of these more flexible arrangements has been to create the *possibility* of meeting the needs of each child more adequately. These new arrangements challenge psychologists to provide guidance for the most effective allocation of resources in these more flexible circumstances, a role that is illustrated by a case example in Chapter 11.

Concluding Comments

If one reads the recent reviews of research in educational psychology (Gagné and Rohwer 1969) and instructional psychology (Anderson 1967), he sees few *interaction* studies. Individuality in education remains within the domain of contemporary schooling procedures that are geared to deal with groups (McDonald 1964). As McDonald observed (1964), "A vague, unanalyzed feeling persists that the individual must not be sacrificed." Taking account of individual differences has become even more important at present because the products of our schools are revolting against the system. The poor minorities who do not enjoy the fruits of their education are not only ones expressing dissatisfaction with the school. Suburban runaways, college activists, and others normally thought to benefit most from modern education are attacking the system's dehumanizing and homogenizing aspects and are demanding reform.

We are aware that the present educational arrangements may not be suited to the interactive orientation we are advocating; in some ways, the interactive approach is probably even more likely to fail now than it was in Dewey's time (see Carroll 1967). Certainly, the school's lockstep programs are not conducive to individualized instruction (Goodlad 1969). However, we proceed on the optimistic assumption that the schools will alter their structure in the future because of social pressures.

In our view, education is much more than simply what teachers do to or for groups of children (Joyce 1969). Reflective use of advancing technology should make it possible to prescribe for each child the learning materials and teaching strategies that match his achievements, ability, and learning style (Joyce 1967). If carefully planned, computer-assisted instruction can incorporate interaction ideas that will enable this instructional medium to absorb the attention and encourage the involvement of children at all ages and grade levels (Alpert and Bitzer 1970). Our own goal in this book will be to elaborate B-P-E as a way of thinking in educationally relevant terms so that it can be incorporated into future innovations. We agree with the statement by William James (1958):

> I say moreover that you make a great, a very great mistake, if you think that psychology, being the science of the mind's laws, is something from which you can deduce definite programs and schemes and methods of instruction for immediate schoolroom use. Psychology is a science, and teaching is an art; and sciences never generate arts directly out of themselves. An intermediary inventive mind must make the application, by using its originality. (pp. 23–24)

Perhaps the intermediary can also be assisted by the way of thinking that is presented in the following chapters. This is our hope.

Summary

The B-P-E model (Behavior is a result of the Person and the Environment) was introduced as a way of thinking to coordinate the relation between psychology and education. Such coordination requires: (1) clarifying the language of psychology, (2) understanding the language of education, (3) establishing a means of communication, and (4) developing a working relation between psychology and education.

Application of the B-P-E model helps clarify the language of psychology, first by showing that when psychology is thought of as a science based on general principles about the prediction and control of behavior, many of these principles are of limited usefulness because they do not apply to specific individuals. Similarly, data on individual differences would become much more valuable if they were studied in conjunction with environmental differences. A differential model also emphasizes the importance of specifying the kind of behavior involved and distinguishing between different outcomes produced by different person-environment interactions. "Psychology-as-understanding," in B-P-E terms, therefore, involves taking account of differential person-environment effects, differential behavioral outcomes, and their interactions. The B-P-E model provides a paradigm for considering such complex relations.

Psychological theories stated in B-P-E terms provide the basis for understanding such educational arrangements as age-grading, ability grouping, and nongraded schools in a more systematic fashion. If both psychological ideas and educational problems are analyzed in B-P-E terms, the relevance of the psychological idea for educational practice can be considered. Finally, stating both viewpoints in comparable terms should facilitate communication and the establishment of a reciprocal working relation between psychology and education.

SUGGESTED READINGS

Bakan, D. "The Mystery-Mastery Complex in Contemporary Psychology." *American Psychologist* 20 (1965):186–191.

Cronbach, L. J. "The Two Disciplines of Scientific Psychology." *American Psychologist* 12 (1957):671–684.

Vale, J. R., and Vale, C. A. "Individual Differences and General Laws in Psychology: A Reconciliation." *American Psychologist* 24 (1969):1093–1108.

chapter 2

CONCEPTS OF THE PERSON:

Developmental and Individual Differences

> The child's present experience is in no way self-explanatory .... It is ...
> just a sign or index of certain growth tendencies .... What we need is
> something which will enable us to interpret, to appraise, the elements in
> the child's puttings forth and falling away, his exhibitions of power and
> weakness, in the light of some larger growth-process in which they have
> their place. (Dewey 1902, p. 13).

To describe what a person is like, how he is different from others, and to
predict how he will develop and change are probably the most difficult problems facing psychologists, but unless psychologists can cope with these problems, psychology has little to offer education. Therefore, we begin specific
discussion of the B–P–E model by talking about concepts of the person rather
than concepts of behavior or environment. We believe that the person occupies
the central role in any psychological theory and that educational planning

31

should begin with the student rather than with objectives or teaching methods (which are discussed in Chapters 3 and 4).

Every person differs in certain ways from every other person. However, psychologists and educators disagree among themselves about which individual differences to consider and how such differences have come about. What are *your* beliefs about human nature? How much do *you* believe people can change and under what circumstances can they change? What characteristics of other persons are most important to *you?* These are not issues that will be solved any more than the questions of how psychologists define psychology and how educators define education were solved in the last chapter. However, for the same reason, it is essential to understand one's concept of the person —beliefs in human nature, human characteristics, and developmental change. We raise these questions especially for psychologists and educators, but we hope that each of you will consider your own personal reactions to them. There should be advantages in trying to become more aware of one's own beliefs, as well as in illustrating how these beliefs influence communication and understanding between psychology and education.

Why Psychologists Have Difficulty Conceptualizing Persons

Apart from the fact that many psychologists consider the term human nature too vague to discuss, there are several reasons why psychologists have experienced difficulty in conceptualizing persons, a difficulty which, in turn, has limited their contribution to educational practice. The first stumbling block is using the rather awkward phrase "conceptualizing persons," rather than some more familiar phrase, such as individual differences or developmental stages. Most psychologists are too specialized in their study of persons (Kessen 1962): one group is concerned with current individual differences (states or types); another group studies personality development (stages); while a third group studies how states and stages change (transitions). Such compartmentalization of types, stages, and transitions limits understanding of human characteristics and how they change.

This compartmentalization not only restricts understanding, but also occasionally misrepresents what is known. Some psychologists have drawn unwarranted conclusions about how much a person can change based on evidence that does not coordinate development with environmental differences (for example, Bettelheim 1964; Bloom 1964). There is simply no way to address the enormously complex problem of how much, and under what conditions, a person can change without doing so from the standpoint of a psychological theory that simultaneously considers existing individual differences, the development of such differences over time, and the environmental conditions associated with such development. In short, a developmental-interactionist theory is required.

Sanford's question "Will psychologists study human problems?" (1965) also incorporated a plea for studying personality development, since it is only when behavior is seen in developmental perspective (as the Dewey quotation at the beginning of this chapter states) that any kind of comprehensive understanding about change can emerge. Psychology has not contributed to education in the way Dewey envisioned because most psychological descriptions of a person's present state have not been coordinated into developmental perspectives (stages) that specify the environmental conditions needed for development.

As the Jensen controversy (1969) illustrated, most psychologists still conceptualize the issue of why change occurs in terms of a percentage attributable to heredity or to environment, an attitude that is no more productive than the more categorical heredity vs. environment version of forty years ago. The vital question of why people change is not illuminated by formulas describing what percentage of cause is attributable to heredity and what percentage to environment because this way of thinking is basically wrong. Persons *interact* with environmental influences with resulting change or lack of it, and our concept of the change process must take account of this interaction. Generalizations about human capacity for change made at this time are merely statements of how persons have been influenced by those (often quite unsatisfactory) environmental conditions that they have experienced. Not only are such statements unwarranted from a scientific standpoint, but as Cronbach observed (1969), teachers must try to produce as much change as possible regardless of what they are told about potential for change.

The psychologists' way of thinking about human characteristics has been strongly influenced by enthusiastic public acceptance of the concept of intelligence as measured by the early IQ tests. On the basis of the psychometric stability and consistency of the tests, psychologists considered IQ scores to be stable, even immutable, and the public believed what they were told. Unfortunately, psychological thinking has not yet developed much beyond this notion of fixed intelligence (J. McV. Hunt 1961), so the same static model is still used when considering the question of human potential for change.[1]

So we see that there is a lack of concepts and methods for understanding how much persons can change. Such ideas are most likely to come from a fusion of personality theory with developmental theory. This chapter provides a paradigm for coordinating the person's present state (contemporaneous indi-

---

[1]It is possible that one reason that ATI (Aptitude-Treatment-Interaction) approach has not yielded better results is that most conceptions of aptitudes are static and not related to developmental change.

vidual differences) with his stage (developmental differences) and the conditions required for change (environments for transition).

Why Teachers Have Difficulty Conceptualizing Persons

First, psychologists have not helped teachers very much in understanding student differences. Courses in individual differences and child development are often required study for teachers, but the subject matter may be irrelevant because student differences are not described in terms of what teachers do with students. In a similar way, the millions of ability and personality tests administered annually are not used by teachers because test scores do not give them any useful information about student needs. For the most part, teachers tend to view the information provided them about individual differences and stage differences as inapplicable to their day-to-day work with children. What teachers need are descriptions of student characteristics that are clearly coordinated with teaching, for example, the relation of the student's learning style to teaching method.

Second, teachers are probably reluctant to consider differences between students for fear that they can do nothing about these differences, that is, we may know the student's needs but be unable to meet them. Even if a particular individual difference were demonstrably relevant to differential educational practice (goes the argument), it is unlikely that the overworked teacher could use such information. Part of teacher skepticism or reluctance has probably been occasioned by the overwhelming surplus of information about student characteristics—needs, motives, traits, types, stages, abilities, and aptitudes. It may well be that teachers are not able to utilize all the information about student characteristics that is provided for them, but psychologists should nonetheless continue to seek person characteristics relevant to educational approaches, in part because future educational settings may permit more adaptation to individual differences (Joyce 1967).

A final source of difficulty is characterized by the feeling that any kind of description of students is "dehumanizing," pigeonholing, and stereotyping. To emphasize differences among students may produce adverse effects (as with any procedure), but this will depend on the teacher who uses the information about students. The information may be helpful as an initial guide to the teacher working with a student, or it may serve to reaffirm a stereotype in the teacher's mind. The stereotyping comes from how the teacher thinks, not from the information about student characteristics.

Distinguishing Type and Stage

Consider what explanations might account for a person behaving in a dependent way. An individual difference psychologist might say that his behavior means that he is a dependent *type,* that is, compared with other persons, he has stronger tendencies toward dependent behavior. A developmental psychologist might say that the person is in a dependent *stage,* that is, he has a stong tendency toward dependent behavior now, but not necessarily in the future. There is a third explanation, that the behavior results from the *environment* that "pulls" dependent behavior, which is of less immediate concern, but to which we return after settling the distinction between type and stage.

This example is oversimplified to draw attention to the distinction between two kinds of individual differences: contemporaneous (type) and developmental (stage) (D. E. Hunt 1971; Sullivan 1972). Before distinguishing these further, one should stop to consider why such a distinction is important. Commonsense psychology favors explanation in terms of the type of person.

Understanding the distinction between viewing a person as a dependent type (contemporaneous) and viewing him as in a dependent stage (developmental) is essential because the two views lead to different expectations about the possibility of the person's changing. To account for a student seeking assistance by characterizing him as a dependent type is quite reasonable if the analysis is restricted to the contemporaneous, or immediate, situation. The difficulty comes with the excess meaning carried by a type description that implies a fixed, nonmodifiable state. By contrast, characterization of the person's same behavior in the same situation as resulting from a dependent stage does carry a different expectation, namely, the *possibility* of change.

To describe a person as a type need not imply a fixed, nonmodifiable state. However, individual differences were originally evaluated and accepted on the basis of their *stability* and nonchanging quality; traditional procedures for evaluating such measures usually emphasize the stability of the measure over time and consistency across situations. Such procedures make it difficult to evaluate how well a personal characteristic helps explain the pattern of change, or the behavioral variation, in different environments. We are not maintaining that all individual differences be limited to stage descriptions, since these also have limitations. Rather, type descriptions should not be taken to be unchanging without evidence that such types cannot be changed.

Despite the logic of Dewey's appeal in the initial quotation and throughout his essay on "The Child and the Curriculum," taking a developmental perspective is difficult. When observing a student seeking assistance from a teacher and from his peers, one is much more likely to form an impression of a dependent type than to think of the behavior in relation to developmental growth. The tendency is toward classification of the person as a type (whether we admit it or not) because of time demands and the relative difficulty of thinking in stages rather than in types. Consider your own perceptions of your friends or, if you have taught, of your students. Chances are your concepts will be in terms of types rather than stages. Because taking a developmental perspective is so essential in educational practice and so difficult, let us consider what it means to think in terms of developmental stages.

Taking a Developmental Perspective

To regard a child in developmental perspective is to see his present behavior in relation to past changes and to future growth. Thus, "a characteristic is said to be developmental if it can be related to age in an orderly or lawful way" (Kessen 1960, p. 36). Attempts to conceptualize these changes over age have led to the use of *stage* descriptions, or as Kessen (1962) puts it:

> Men seem always to have felt a need to impose segmentation on the complicated course of human development. Although it has usually been argued that development is continuous and without discrete shifts, more often than not the arguer has early called on the notion of stage or level to help him understand the speed and fluidity of change in children. (p. 55)

Dewey (1902) has stated the value of developmental stages most eloquently:

> Of what use, educationally speaking, is it to be able to see the end in the beginning? How does it assist us in dealing with the early stages of growth to be able to anticipate its later phases . . . ? To see the outcome is to know in what direction the present experience is moving, provided it moves normally and soundly. The far-away point, which is of no significance to us simply as far away, becomes of huge importance the moment we take it as defining a present direction of movement. Taken in this way it is no remote and distant result to be achieved, but a guiding method in dealing with the present . . . .
>
> Interests in reality are but attitudes toward possible experiences; they are not achievements; their worth is in the leverage they afford, not in the accomplishment they represent. To take the phenomena presented at a given age as in any way self-explanatory or self-contained is inevitably to result in indulgence and spoiling . . . Its genuine meaning is in the propulsion it affords toward a higher level. It is just something to do with. (pp. 12–15)

Taking a developmental perspective for a psychologist, therefore, means focusing on age-related structural changes, and for a teacher, it means viewing a student's present behavior in terms of indications of future growth and how it can be fostered.

DEVELOPMENTAL STAGES

Let us begin with a simple example of a stage theory that describes interpersonal development on a continuum consisting of three stages: Stage A (unsocialized) $\longrightarrow$ Stage B (dependent) $\longrightarrow$ and Stage C (independent). Details of this developmental theory will be provided in Chapter 9, but for now it will illustrate some characteristics of a developmental stage theory. It may be diagrammatically represented as follows:

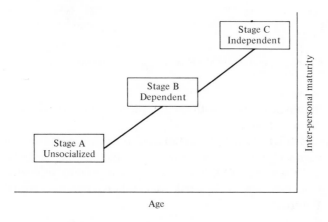

Figure 2   Stages of Interpersonal Maturity

Figure 2 characterizes the nature of developmental differences in stage terms. The A–B–C sequence is seen as invariant in that every person progresses through every stage, though each may do so at a different rate and in a different pattern.

For example, one person may remain at Stage A for a long time, while another may be there for a much shorter time, as indicated in Figure 3.

As you can see, there is no perfect correlation between stage and age. Figure 3 also illustrates how a teacher working with Tom and Dick in Grade 3, when both were age 8, would find one of them at Stage A and the other one at Stage B. As Dewey recommends, this information should help the teacher see how

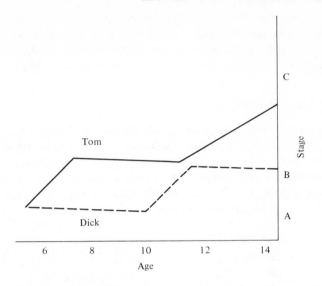

Figure 3   Patterns of Development of Two Persons

he might work most effectively with each to promote growth. However, at age 11, they are similar in stage.

Let us consider Figure 3 in more detail as it illustrates the earlier distinction between a dependent type and a dependent stage. At age 8, Tom is more independent (B) than Dick (A), but at age 11, there is no difference. If only cross sections in time were considered, their relative maturity would look as indicated in Figure 4.

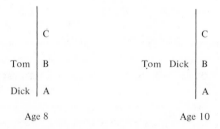

Figure 4   Cross-sectional Comparison of Two Persons at Two Times

If Dick is described as an unsocialized "type" at 8, then his growth to dependence at 11 would be seen as error because types are not expected to change. However, viewed according to Figure 3 in terms of stages, the two patterns make some sense.

One may wonder, of course, why these two boys progress in a different pattern, which raises the issue of what determines growth.

Conceptions of Growth

The question of how persons develop is one aspect of one's conception of human nature, and a psychologist's conception of development and change is probably the most central feature in his theoretical outlook.

Conceptions of development may be considered in relation to their emphasis on person, environment, or the interaction of person and environment (Ausubel and Sullivan 1970). If the major factors in development are the person (internal) and the environment (external), the various concepts of growth and development may be seen as (1) theories that locate the source of development *within* the person, (2) theories that locate the source of development *outside* the person in the environment, and (3) theories that view development as jointly determined by the *interaction* of internal and external factors.

These three concepts are not categorically distinct, because no internal conceptions completely disregard external factors, but they do differ in the emphasis placed on one or both factors.

INTERNAL CONCEPTS OF DEVELOPMENT

Developmental theories that emphasize the person as the source of change have been called "organic growth" conceptions (Scheffler 1960) or "organic lamp" theories (Langer 1969). They include strict maturational theories, such as Gesell (Gesell 1933; Gesell and Ilg 1934), as well as humanistic theories (Erikson 1958; C. R. Rogers 1969). For example, C. R. Rogers (1964) wrote:

> The inner world of the individual appears to have more significance upon
> his behavior than does the external environmental stimulus. (p. 125)

The environment prescribed by these internal conceptions to facilitate growth is a generally accepting, "nourishing" environment. For example, Rogers' suggestion of nondirective therapy specifies a *general* environment of acceptance that relies on forces within the patient to produce change (see Chapter 10).

Humanistic theories rarely make specific environmental prescriptions or view the person in terms of differential effects. Their lack of discrimination between various environmental influences is in sharp contrast to their insistence that every person is uniquely different from every other person. There-fore, internal conceptions do not provide guidelines for deriving the specific environment most likely to facilitate development in a person. A good example is found in Erikson's "eight stages of man," summarized in Figure 5.

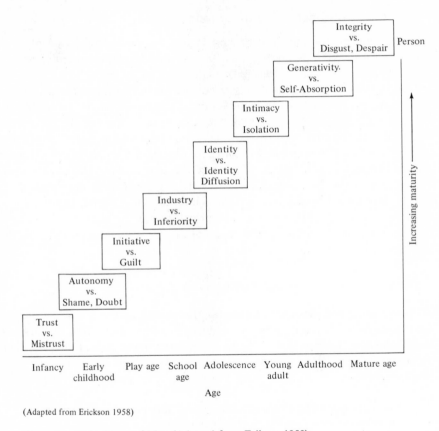

(Adapted from Erickson 1958)

Figure 5   Eight Stages of Man (Adapted from Erikson 1958)

Erikson's theory places the burden of development through these stages upon internal growth factors. Failure to grow, or arrestation, occurs because of a generally unsatisfactory environment, not a specifically mismatched environment.

A. S. Neill, the director of *Summerhill* (1960), represents an educational approach that subscribes to the internal conception of development, as the following quotation indicates:

> My view is that a child is innately wise and realistic. If left to himself
> without adult suggestion of any kind he will develop as far as he is capable
> of developing. Logically, Summerhill is a place in which people who have
> innate ability and wish to be scholars will be scholars; while those who are
> only fit to sweep the streets, will sweep the streets. (p. 4)

Based on this philosophy, Neill does not provide new methods of instruction
at Summerhill because he believes that if a child wants to learn a subject he
will learn it by any method. Summerhill, therefore, is really an inflexible
educational environment—unstructured, but inflexibly unstructured—so that,
as would be expected, its effectiveness varies with different kinds of students.
Bernstein (1968) reported that gregarious, aggressive students seem to profit
from the Summerhill environment, while withdrawn, quiet students do not,
indicating that even Summerhill is susceptible to differential effects.

Theorists and practitioners who accept the "organic growth" model view
the environment on a single dimension varying from "good" (enriched, free,
accepting) to "bad" (impoverished, restricted, rejecting). Just as they take a
firm stance on the ideal person (embodied in the highest stage of development),
they assume that there is one single best environment for everyone. Perhaps
this is why internal conceptions of development are so appealing to teachers:
one general good environment is prescribed for all students. An example of the
differential effectiveness of Rogers's educational approach is given in Chapter 5.

EXTERNAL CONCEPTS OF DEVELOPMENT

Developmental theories emphasizing the environment as the source of change
have been described in terms of the metaphors of "molding clay" (Scheffler
1960) or the "mechanical mirror" (Langer 1969). Behavioristic accounts of
socialization (for example, Bandura and Walters 1963; Whiting and Child
1963) as well as the learning theories of Skinner and Thorndike illustrate these
conceptions. Internal characteristics of the person are underplayed (the empty
organism) and only reflexes and certain emotional responses are acknowledged.

Variation in adult dependence-independence are seen as almost entirely due
to environmental (parental) gratification or frustration in early childhood. If
the environment has reinforced dependent behavior, then the adult becomes
a dependent-type person; if independent behavior has been reinforced, the
adult becomes an independent-type person. There is no development from
dependence to independence acknowledged, since the environment operates
directly on behavior dispositions. The external concept is diagrammatically

represented in Figure 6. Note that there is no concept of change over time.

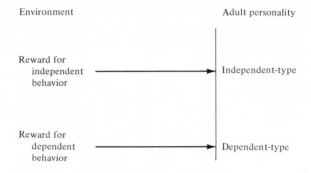

Figure 6   External Conception of Development

Although Skinner does not believe in a developmental hierarchy, Chapter 7 describes how the Skinnerian external view might be made more valuable with the incorporation of such a hierarchy. External theorists tend to emphasize short-term effects, such as changing behavior, and have less concern for changing the person in an enduring way. In terms of a distinction elaborated in the following chapter, external theories are more likely to emphasize achievement behavior than process.

INTERACTIVE CONCEPTS OF DEVELOPMENT

Most interactive concepts are stage theories that specify different environments to facilitate development, depending on the person's present stage of development (Ausubel and Sullivan 1970; D. E. Hunt 1971; Kohlberg 1966). A comprehensive theory of development should specify the sequence of the stages of development as well as the transition rules (that is, stage-specific environmental prescriptions) producing developmental growth (Kessen 1962). As discussed in Chapter 6, Piaget's theory is a weak interactive theory because the transition rules are not specifically described. Just as person-environment combinations may be considered matched for certain behavioral purposes, the relation between person and environment may also be considered matched or mismatched for purposes of developmental progression, or as Joyce and Weil (1972a) put it:

> In other words, if the growth of the individual is a product of his environment, then teaching becomes a process of matching environments to individuals. (p. 164)

As described in Chapter 8, Ausubel and Sullivan (1970) have analyzed the developmental match in terms of the relation between satellization (Person) and intrinsic acceptance (Environment). Kohlberg (1964) considered the developmental match in terms of the level of moral development (Person) and the level of concepts encountered (Environment). As described in Chapter 9, D. E. Hunt (1971) considered the issue in terms of coordinating conceptual level (Person) with degree of structure (Environment). It is important to note that only an interactive theory specifies the environment necessary to developmental progression.

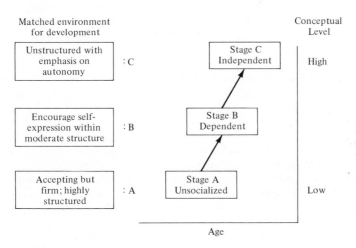

Figure 7   Conceptual Level Model, Developmental Version

Figure 7 is an interactive version of Figure 2 and specifically exemplifies Hunt's differential developmental model.

If there are few interactive concepts in psychology, there are even fewer in education. The most articulate example of an interactive concept is Montessori's postulation (1939) of "sensitive periods" in the development of the child that call for certain forms of specific stimulation from the educational environment.

> Children pass through definite periods in which they reveal psychic aptitudes and possibilities which afterwards disappear. That is why, at a particular epoch of their life, they reveal an intense and extraordinary interest in certain objects and exercises, which one might look for in vain at a later age. During such a period the child is endowed with a special sensibility which urges him to focus his attention on certain aspects of the environment to the exclusion of others. (p. 252)

Montessori postulated sensitive periods for language, order, refinement of the senses, and so on. These periods bear some relation to the concepts of critical periods proposed by the ethologists. It is not entirely clear from Montessori's description whether the child's failure to receive adequate, specific stimulation during a sensitive period merely limits the child's behavioral repertory or places irreversible restrictions on subsequent development.

As John Dewey (1902) put it:

> Other activities are signs of a culminating power and interest; to them applies the maxim of striking while the iron is hot. Selected, utilized, emphasized, they may mark a turning-point for good in the child's whole career; neglected, an opportunity goes, never to be recalled. (p. 14)

He also urges the coordination and synchrony of internal with external determinants in education, much as Lewin and Cronbach have argued in psychology. Dewey wrote:

> There are those who see no alternative between forcing the child from without, or leaving him entirely alone. Seeing no alternative, some chose one mode, some another. Both fall into the same fundamental error. Both fail to see that development is a definite process, having its own law which can be fulfilled only when adequate and normal conditions are provided. (p. 17)

The most obvious way to apply knowledge about developmental differences is to group students according to their developmental stage (Sullivan 1972) by stage-grading, a procedure discussed in Chapters 6, 9, and 11. Stage-grading does not necessarily imply homogeneous classroom grouping by stage.

Individual Differences: Fixed or Modifiable?

The most important point about individual differences is that we do not know how much, or under what conditions, they can change. Much confusion exists about the possibility of producing change in disadvantaged children, especially adolescents, primarily because of a failure to distinguish between what change *can* be accomplished and whether or not efforts to produce change should be attempted. For example, in reviewing Bloom's book *Stability and Change in Human Characteristics* (1964), Bettelheim (1964) stated:

> How much can man change and at what age is it too late to hope for very
> much change? Now, thanks to Professor Bloom's study . . . we know.
> (p. 1)

Holt's reply (1964) to this assertion was a vigorous disclaimer:

> No. We do not know. Professor Bloom's tables only show us what is
> happening. They do not and can not show us what, under other conditions,
> might or could happen. They show that, *in schools as they are,* the I.Q.'s
> and academic achievement of most children are stable. This is important
> evidence, but the conclusions that our character and intelligence are
> largely and unchangeably determined in our first four or five years does
> not necessarily follow from it. . . . Meanwhile it seems worth repeating that
> even the best statistics can only tell us what is, not what might be. When
> we are trying to find out what is possible, it is the exceptional case that
> counts. (p. 23)

In deriving specific goals for a person based on his present stage, we therefore need to know his developmental position and also how likely he is to
change. As stated earlier, we believe it is important to remain open to the
possibility of change until many more different forms of environmental intervention have been attempted. The case of the disadvantaged adolescent illustrates the kind of person whom we may disregard by stating that he cannot
be changed (which means change would be difficult to produce) when, in fact,
what is taken for his low potential for change or nonmalleability is a result of
our lack of knowledge about how to intervene—to "unfreeze" him, open him
to stimulation, and intervene with more appropriate procedures.

If an educational system has only universal goals and a limited variety of
educational approaches, it is not surprising that the results for many students
will end in failure. This is because these students did not fit the system. It is
not entirely the students who are fixed and unchangeable; it is also the system.

Lesser's (1971) distinction between universal and particular goals is relevant
here:

> One distinction among educational goals is central to our discussion of
> matching the aims and methods of instruction to individual differences
> among children: "universal" as distinguished from "particular" goals. We
> now accept in principle certain universal goals—for example, literacy—
> that we expect each child to achieve. We do not expect, however, each

child to play the violin or to become an architect or a poet; these are particular goals defined by the child's aptitudes and interests and the social forces at work in his particular environment.

When we speak of universal goals of education, the implication of recognizing individual differences is that different instructional strategies must be found which will optimally promote each child's achievement of basic, universal skills. When we speak of particular goals of education, recognition of individual differences demands that we find the directions and aims best fitted to each child's aptitudes and motivations as well as the most appropriate instructional methods for him.

Thus, the concept of individual differences generates at least two implications: Teachers must both develop different instructional strategies for the optimal achievement of certain universal goals, and select the particular goals best matched to a child's individual characteristics. (p. 533).

Omar Moore's (1966) work with the Edison Responsive Environment, or "talking typewriter," for example, has raised serious questions about what had previously been accepted as the limits of maturational capacity at a specific age. His work simply reminds us that any statement of maturational "capacity" is limited to that environment which the child has experienced and, thus, tells us nothing about the child's potential to profit from new forms of educational influence.

It is vital that the educator apply the analysis suggested by Holt to any formulation, no matter how mathematically elaborate, that pretends to specify the precise contribution of environmental influence to development. Any statement about "irreversible" arrestation in development is necessarily restricted to a limited variety of environmental interventions.

Taking a Contemporaneous Perspective

Figure 4 represents a contemporaneous perspective toward individual differences which may be described as follows:

There are individual differences that may be educationally relevant which may fall within a particular age or stage of development. . . . For example, concrete operational children may differ on other contemporaneous dimensions, such as anxiety, cognitive style, and authoritarianism. These differences may require further modifications in the types of teaching programs or strategies. (Sullivan 1972, p. 184)

Kessen (1962) sums up the contemporaneous view as follows:

> The psychologists may study *states* of the organism, in a sense catching
> the bird at the moment in flight and saying, "At this moment the organism
> has such and such characteristics." (p. 63)

The clearest representation of contemporaneous individual differences as they interact with environmental factors is the model proposed by Cronbach (1957) and shown in Figure 8.

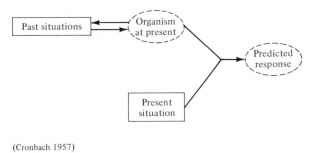

(Cronbach 1957)

Figure 8   Theoretical Network to Be Developed by a United Discipline (Cronbach 1957)

Figure 8 demonstrates that while for contemporaneous predictive purposes the person must be considered at the present time, the person has developed over time. Speaking about the significance of person-environment interactions for practical decisions, Cronbach (1957) states:

> We require a measure of aptitude which predicts who will learn better
> from one curriculum than from the other; but this aptitude remains to be
> discovered. Ultimately, we should *design* treatments, not to fit the average
> person, but to fit groups of persons with particular aptitude patterns.
> Conversely, we should seek out the aptitudes which correspond to (in-
> teract with) modifiable aspects of the treatment. (p. 681)

CONTEMPORANEOUS MATCHING

Shifting from a developmental to a contemporaneous perspective involves a change in objective. We have said that if the person is viewed in stage terms, the goal is likely to be change in the person, or growth, while if the person is viewed in terms of a type, the goal is more likely to be change in behavior (Figure 8). Therefore, contemporaneous matching will involve an attempt to produce a specified behavioral effect through coordination of a particular environment with a particular type of person. Several examples of contemporaneous matching will be described, but, first, we will consider how a contemporaneous concept, whether type, aptitude, or whatever, is most likely to be compatible with the specification of optimal environments.

If persons are viewed in terms of their "accessibility channels" to different forms of environmental influence (D. E. Hunt 1971), then such descriptions should be translatable into differential educational approaches. More simply, if a teacher has information about a student's channels of accessibility, such information can be immediately related to different ways of teaching.

> Taking account of accessibility channels is almost unavoidable when working with a physically handicapped student. Though its need is less apparent for normal students, it seems equally important to consider them in terms of channels of accessibility so that the form of educational approach can be most appropriately tuned in to each student. The CL matching model gives an example of how the accessibility channel, learner's cognitive orientation, can be used to tune in, by modulating the structure of the presentation. (D. E. Hunt 1971, p. 47)

Table 2 summarizes the relationship between person (accessibility channel) and environment (form of presentation).

Table 2.   Relation Between Accessibility Channels and
Optimal Environment

Accessibility channel (Person)	Form of presentation (Environment)
Cognitive orientation Low Conceptual Level High Conceptual Level	*Degree of structure* High Low or intermediate
Motivational orientation High social approval High intrinsic motivation	*Form of feedback and reward* Extrinsic reward and/or normative feedback Intrinsic reward and/or self-defined feedback
Value orientation	*Value context of presentation* Within "latitude of acceptance"
Sensory orientation	*Modality of presentation* Adapted to primary sensory "channel," i.e., visual, auditory.

(D. E. Hunt 1971, p. 75)

As Table 2 indicates, contemporaneous individual differences expressed in terms of accessibility channels vary not only in how much information they provide about optimal environments, or their environmental relevance, but also in the nature of such environmental prescriptions. Table 2 is a specific guide for contemporaneous matching. For example, if the student is low in conceptual level, he is more likely to function effectively in a highly structured environment (Chapter 9). Note that Table 2 prescribes an optimal environment for present functioning (contemporaneous), not necessarily for developmental growth.

Describing a student in accessibility terms is nothing more than an attempt to specify the needs of the child in terms that have some meaning for a teacher and make it more likely that the teacher will reach, get in touch, or tune in with the student. Although the concept of accessibility channels is discussed in contemporaneous terms, for example, tuning in to the student, such contemporaneous coordination of person and environment can set the stage for encouraging developmental growth.

Note in Table 2, on the right-hand side, that one could devise such a coordinated system by starting with environmental variations a teacher can provide. In most cases, teachers can vary the structure of presentation, form of feedback and reward, value context, and modality. However, there may be other variations and, if so, analysis by accessibility channels can help coordinate the use of such approaches.

An example of the relation between motivational orientation and form of feedback is illustrated in a study by French (1958), who investigated the environmental relevance of both need for affiliation and need for achievement. She found that persons high in affiliation motivation solved problems more effectively under conditions of feeling-oriented feedback, while persons high in achievement motivation solved problems more effectively under conditions of task-oriented feedback. These results are shown in the following diagram:

Optimal Form of Feedback Based on Person's Motivational Orientation

Behavior	Person (Motivational Orientation)	Environment (Optimal Feedback)
Problem-solving effectiveness	High need affiliation	Feeling-oriented feedback
	High need achievement	Task-oriented feedback

Shaver and Oliver (1968) studied several student characteristics to determine the differential effectiveness of a Socratic and a recitation approach to teaching students to think critically about social issues. They found that persons high in authoritarianism profited more from a recitation presentation, while persons low in authoritarianism profited more from a Socratic presentation, as indicated in the following diagram:

Optimal Teaching Mode Based on Person's Authoritarianism Score

Behavior	Person (Authoritarianism)	Environment (Optimal Instruction Mode)
Ability to think critically	Low authoritarianism	Socratic
	High authoritarianism	Recitation

Other examples of contemporaneous matching will be given later (and many are described in Lesser 1971), but these examples should give credence to the hypothetical educational/school psychologist of the future who assesses a student and provides an accessibility profile of the student's cognitive, motivational, value, and sensory orientations. Such an action-relevant description would be less likely to be ignored and also would provide a basis for following Cronbach's (1967) suggestion:

> Until the present time, the differential psychologist has let the institution tell him the treatments for which he is predicting success, and he has designed tests or batteries to make that prediction. I suggest that we now let the institution specify only the criterion—not the treatment—and that the psychologist select an aptitude variable and design treatment expected to interact with it. (pp. 32–33)

We conclude this section by repeating an earlier caution about types, this time with accessibility characteristics, namely, that they may themselves be the objects of change. As Cronbach and Snow (1969) observed in relation to aptitudes:

> Work on personality will have continually to contend with the technical and philosophical problems that arise from the fact that "aptitude" may

be a predictor, an intervening variable arising from the treatment, or a significant, "final" outcome. (p. 192)

Do Individual Differences Predict Behavior?

Contemporaneous individual differences have typically been evaluated by their stability and by how well they predict behavior, for example, intelligence test score as a predictor of academic achievement. Behavioral prediction is certainly desirable, but such prediction needs to take into account the nature of the behavior and the environmental setting in which it occurred.

Consider the classic example: the prediction of academic achievement indexed by an objective examination administered in the environment of a conventional classroom. Tests of fixed intelligence and verbal ability have traditionally served this purpose. Measures of fixed intelligence (P) typically correlate with academic achievement (B) about .50 or .60. However, this P–B relation is usually based on the criterion of a student's performance on objective achievement tests (B) in fairly standardized classroom procedures (E), and will not necessarily hold under other conditions. IQ will not predict achievement as well if the educational environment is adapted to the individual student or if achievement is indexed by higher level skills than those required in an objective test. For example, Claunch (1964) investigated the effect of student conceptual level or integrative complexity (Schroder, Driver, and Streufert 1967) on academic achievement as indexed by both an objective multiple-choice examination and an essay examination requiring analysis and synthesis. A group of students high on conceptual level (CL) was matched on intelligence with a group of low CL students and their academic achievements compared. The two groups did not differ on an objective examination, but the high CL group performed significantly better than the low CL group on an essay examination.

The relation between fixed intelligence and academic achievement usually assumes a fixed environment (that is, a standard classroom). This point is exemplified in a study by Hutt (1947) which investigated the effect of different testing procedures for administering the Stanford-Binet test. Hutt used two testing procedures with each of the alternate Binet forms: (1) the standard, by-the-book Binet procedure and (2) an adaptive procedure. The adaptive procedure did not change the scoring criteria but modulated the sequence of questions for each student, to minimize the occurrence of successive failure trials, and allowed the examiner to provide considerable verbal reinforcement. Hutt found in comparing a normal group with a maladjusted group that the normal group performed equally well (mean=110) under the two procedures,

while the maladjusted group performed much better under the adaptive procedure (mean=103) than under the standard procedure (mean=92). These results are shown in Table 3.

Table 3.   IQ Scores Resulting from Different Person-Environment
Combinations

Person	Environment	Behavior (IQ Score)
Normal	Standard	110
	Adaptive	110
Maladjusted	Standard	92
	Adaptive	103

(Hutt, 1947)

Which IQ score is the most valid index for the maladjusted group? Obviously, if one wants to predict academic performance in a standard classroom,
the score of 92 for members of the maladjusted group on the standard procedure gives a better estimate. Their score of 103 on the adaptive procedure gives
an index of their potential under more optimal environmental conditions than
those usually encountered in the classroom.

It is reasonable, yet regrettable, that predicting to a fixed criterion in a fixed
environment has been the most successful as well as the most widely accepted
procedure for measuring individual differences since it fits the "psychology-as-
science" model. It is reasonable because the analytic task is relatively simple.
It is regrettable because it represents another case in which psychologists have
implicitly provided the basis for continuing the practice in education of forcing
the individual to adapt to fixed environments rather than focusing efforts on
adapting the environment to the individual or equipping the individual to
adapt to a changing environment.

TEACHERS' CONCEPTS OF STUDENTS

If psychologists are to communicate with teachers about student differences,
they need to know how teachers perceive their students. Although such information is easy to come by, there is surprisingly little available. Results from
written descriptions by teachers, supervisors, and principals of the various
types of students they found in their high-school classrooms (Thelen 1967)
indicated that the students described fell into four major types: the good, the
bad, the indifferent, and the lost. The following are the "good" types:

1. Natural leaders.
2. Autonomous and self-directive.
3. Interdependent, high achievers.
4. Interdependent, low achievers.
5. Nonconforming but work-oriented.
6. Nonconforming, creative.
7. Conforming and dependent.
8. Submissive. (pp. 65–66)

The following are the "indifferent" students:

9. Happy-go-lucky.
10. Beauty queen.
11. Gone on athletics.
12. Duck-tail haircut.
13. Prig.
14. I-don't-need-an-education. (pp. 66–67)

The following are the "bad" students:

15. Teacher impressers.
16. Short-cutters.
17. Clowns and attention seekers.
18. Misdirected superior.
19. Social climbers.
20. Monopolizers.
21. Hero worshippers and blind followers.
22. Antisocial and destructive. (pp. 67–68)

Finally, the "lost souls":

23. The rejected.
24. The dreamers.
25. The sufferers.
26. The passive. (p. 68)

Fox and Lippitt (1964) have used a straightforward method to obtain information about teacher perceptions.

> For example, she was asked to sort a set of cards, on which the names of
> the pupils in her class had been placed, into as many different piles as
> might occur to her. For each sorting, she was asked to record the main
> organizing idea around which the piles were sorted, the names of the
> students in each pile, and the descriptive titles that might be given to each

of the piles. (She used such categories as "school achievement," "social maturity," "popularity," "sex," and "economic level.") This experience was called "categorizing pupils." Furthermore, she was asked to describe the relevance of each of these pupil categories for teaching practice. (p. 276)

As this example illustrates, psychologists may learn about teacher concepts of student types through methods used in person perception or in the Role Concept Repertory Test (Kelly 1955). Schroder, Karlins, and Phares (1972) have suggested a specific procedure that poses a problem of a student with the following characteristics:

(1) his grades are borderline failure,
(2) he seems to spend his time reading and building models of motors,
(3) he actively organizes his peers to join him in the pursuit of his interests. (p. 60)

Teachers are asked to use this information to help the student with his school problems. The method elicits information more about how a teacher *organizes* student characteristics than about types of students, but this capacity in teachers is very important.

STUDENT SELF-ASSESSMENT: DO STUDENTS KNOW WHAT THEY NEED?

If it is important that psychologists take account of how teachers perceive student characteristics, it is even more important for them to know how well students can assess their own characteristics. With the increased tendency toward student-determined options and courses, the problems of student self-assessment and self-matching become critical. Psychologists will need to develop ways to provide matching information to students in a constructive, nonthreatening manner so that they can arrive at effective decisions themselves.

Summary

Elaboration of the B–P–E model began with description of the person. A child may be described in developmental terms (by stage) or in contemporaneous terms (by type). Dewey's essay on "The Child and the Curriculum" was used as the basis for considering the importance of taking a developmental perspective. Understanding a child in developmental terms requires an awareness of his present developmental stage in relation to a sequence of stages and an understanding of environmental experiences required for growth. In B–P–E terms, developmental growth (B) is determined by the child's present stage (P) and the environment (E) he encounters. Developmental theories that emphasize the person (internal concepts), the environment (external concepts), and interaction (stage-environment interaction) were described and discussed.

Viewing a child in developmental-interaction terms is necessary to avoid underestimating his potential for growth when given certain forms of environmental experience. The B–P–E model was used to criticize several assertions about students' lack of modifiability after a given age. Such assertions do not take into account the possibility of growth produced by unique educational environments that may not have been experienced by students earlier.

Taking a contemporaneous perspective of the person in B–P–E terms leads to describing the person in terms of "accessibility channels," which differ from more fixed traits in that they are linked to the most appropriate form of environment. Describing students in accessibility terms was discussed as a specific attempt to define the "needs of the student" in terms that could potentially be met through providing the most appropriate form of teaching or presentation. Although both developmental and contemporaneous views were discussed, the importance of using both at various times was noted, especially since accessibility channels apply to developmental growth as well as to contemporaneous functioning.

SUGGESTED READINGS

Allport, G. W. "What Units Shall We Employ?" In *Assessment of Human Motives,* edited by G. Lindzey, pp. 239–262. New York: Holt, Rinehart & Winston, 1958.

Dewey, J. *The Child and the Curriculum.* Chicago: University of Chicago Press, 1902.

Glaser, R. "Individuals and Learning: The New Aptitudes." *Educational Researcher,* vol. 1, no. 6 (1972), pp. 6–13.

Kessen, W. H. "Stage and Structure in the Study of Children." *Monographs of the Society for Research in Child Development 27* (1962): 65–82.

Sullivan, E. V. "Developmental and Contemporaneous Individual Differences and Their Role in Curriculum Decision Making and Teacher Training." In *Perspectives for Reform in Teacher Education,* edited by B. R. Joyce and M. Weil, pp. 164–203. Englewood Cliffs, N.J.: Prentice-Hall, 1972.

chapter 3

CONCEPTS OF BEHAVIOR:

Process and Content Objectives

Of the three B-P-E components, behavior would seem to be the simplest to understand. Persons vary almost infinitely, environments seem very difficult to define, but with behavior, at least you can *see* what you're talking about. Or so it would seem. Behavior is observable and can be objectively measured. Many psychologists have therefore proposed that student behavior, such as making a correct response on a test or raising one's hand, be the basis for measuring educational outcomes, communicating with teachers, and making recommendations to them.

Because behavior is observable, measurable, and objective, it has been made disproportionately important both in psychological theory (behaviorism) and in educational practice (specification of behavioral objectives). It is not that behavior is unimportant, but that behavior can be used in different ways. Although behavior seems simple and self-evident, concepts of behavior and behavior change vary as much as concepts of persons and environments. How

56

do you define behavior? Are you concerned with immediate responses, such as the answer on a test, or with long-term change in behavior (change in the person)? Gordon Allport (1958) posed the question, "What units shall we employ?" in relation to persons, and it is an appropriate question in relation to behavior. If this seems a trivial issue, consider how you would feel if all educational efforts were directed toward producing *only* prespecified behavior, such as checking the right answer.

These questions illustrate how one's view of behavior is closely associated with how he defines psychology or education. If, as discussed in Chapter 1, psychology is defined as the prediction and control of behavior, then behavior is likely to be viewed only in contemporaneous terms, as in Figure 8. If the "psychology-as-understanding" definition is accepted, then behavior is more likely to be considered in a more complex way to provide referents for change in the person. Similarly, the conception of behavior for an educator who defines education as the learning of specified content will differ from that of the educator who defines education in terms of socialization for a position in society.

Behaviorists, such as Skinner (Chapter 7), and those who advocate specifying educational objectives in behavioral terms are apt to be impatient when considering different concepts of behavior. They argue that one must deal with behavior because that is what can be seen. The only issue is how precisely the behavior can be specified. A behaviorist approaches an educational problem by specifying the behavioral objective or asking the teacher to do so. He believes it is necessary to state in advance precisely what behavior is desired. The following are some examples of specific behavioral objectives (Kibler, Barker, and Miles 1970):

> Students will be able to state orally the correct time for any clock setting. (p. 86)
> Students will be able to draw proportionally accurate drawings of one-celled organisms from observing them in a microscope. (p. 81)
> Students will name the major painters of the nineteenth century and describe their principal works. (p. 91)

We cite these examples to illustrate the characteristics of behavioral objectives: specific, operational, observable, and measurable. We will return to a more detailed discussion of them later, but it is necessary to consider such objectives immediately in discussing behavior because of the inordinately influential role they occupy in educational planning. Once the behavioral objectives have been stated precisely, then the planning of instruction, or what a teacher does, is determined entirely by these objectives. It is easy to see why this approach has such an appeal to psychologists, educators, and especially the taxpayers. Education becomes industrial; schools become factories; educational goals become products. When the product has been specified, for example, naming the painters and their works, then the quality of the product can be measured for each student, each teacher, each school, and each district. Quality of the teacher's work on the production line then is referred to as accountability. Like the production-line worker whose performance is judged only by the quality of the product, the teacher's adequacy is based entirely on the quality of the product, that is, how well his students meet the performance criteria in the behavioral objectives. If all the students in his class know the painters and their works, he has done well, and like the factory worker he can be rewarded by merit pay. If the teacher does not deliver the product, then other steps are called for.

Small wonder that industry has moved into schools to deliver these specified products. Industrial organizations offer schools a business arrangement in which they will contract to deliver a product, that is, a specified level of student performance after a particular time. Such performance contracting is the clearest example of using only specific behavior as the educational objective and of the consequences of this practice. It is significant that the activities of educational business organizations are called only performance contracting and are evaluated as such. They emphasize behavior so much that there is never any reference to *how* such behavior is produced. Incredible as it may seem, such arrangements rarely refer to the instructional procedures that will be used to produce the specified behavior.

Performance contracting, teacher merit pay based on student performance, "accountability," and the voucher plans (in which parents can "purchase educational products" with vouchers) are current examples of the extreme behavioristic approach in education, or what may be called educational behaviorism. It is true that educational behaviorism has occurred largely because of the real, or felt, defects in educational practice and the increasing cost of such practices. There is no denying that there is much inefficiency, ineffectiveness, and waste in educational practice, and that some systematic analysis is needed.

However, the difficulty with educational behaviorism is that it becomes the *only* concern in education. In Chapter 1, we showed that when psychology is defined as the "prediction and control of behavior," psychologists study only behavior that can be operationally defined, predicted, and controlled. More complex aspects of human experience, such as problem solving, self-adequacy, fantasy, and so on, are therefore more likely to be disregarded because they cannot be objectively defined and measured. Similarly, in educational behaviorism, those objectives that are more difficult to specify precisely, such as learning to think, developing feelings of adequacy and competence, or developing new ideas, are less likely to be dealt with. If teachers are told that the only basis on which they will be judged (and paid) is how well their students perform on certain tests, it is unlikely that many teachers will encourage, or even permit, activities in any other areas.

The term educational behaviorism is used to describe an approach that considers *only* prespecified behavior objectives. It is not that it is wrong, but that, like most conceptions, it is useful for certain purposes with certain students. Therefore, we believe it is important to discuss alternative concepts of behavior or change.

The Problem of Criterion Measures

A major appeal of educational behaviorism is its objective statement of criterion measures. It is much more difficult to specify criterion measures for developmental growth than for the immediate acquisition of specific, correct responses. Not only is it difficult to specify criteria for developmental change, but teachers rarely work with a student long enough to observe a significant change in development.

Developmental change is difficult to detect, especially in age-graded classes. With the exception of some nongraded schools, few schools are organized to highlight developmental change (as mentioned earlier, stage-grading would be ideal for this purpose). As we saw in the last chapter, taking a developmental perspective is a way of thinking that does not have an associated system of measurement. One does not measure a child's developmental stage every day, but one uses this way of thinking as a background feature for viewing the child's day-to-day behavior.

Psychologists have offered few satisfactory criterion measures to assess educational change. Psychologists frequently use *rate of learning* as the index of educational change (Cronbach and Snow 1969). During the 1960s, learning rate was used extensively as a criterion for the assessment of programmed instruction, and it has generally been accepted without criticism. Recently, Cronbach and Snow (1969) have criticized the use of learning rate as a criterion from a strictly psychometric perspective. From the point of view of the educator, its widespread use is rather restrictive. As Cronbach (1966) points out:

> Although in general writing we preach that education has many outcomes, this view is not much honored in planning research on educational learning. Only gradually are we moving away from the experimental paradigm

in which amount or rate of learning is the sole dependent variable and into a timid attempt to appraise educational development multidimensionally. (p. 88)

Global Formulation of Educational Aims

To consider multidimensional criteria in educationally relevant terms is a complex problem, partly because these criteria usually reflect the ideologies current in the society, though the ideal may be far from reality. Looking at a specific society, one might discover conflicting ideologies that issue conflicting educational mandates. The pluralism in North American culture generates conflict, such as that described in Chapter 1. In Dewey's terms, the goal of the growth of the individual conflicts with the goal of fitting the person to cope with his environment (that is, life adjustment).

The goals of education change as a society evolves; therefore, it is difficult for a society in a rapid state of change, as are most nations today, to articulate a coherent, stable set of educational goals. Table 4 illustrates some of the globally stated educational goals taken from Stake's (1970) classification. At the global level, educational goals do not come into conflict, but when they are made more specific, the conflict becomes apparent. For instance, respect for the law may come into conflict with respect for humanity when laws condoning segregation are seen as denying persons or groups their claim to *human* consideration. Indeed, it is questionable whether there is any use in stating aims as global as those in Table 4. They seem more like contradictory propaganda statements than like guides for educational practice. Because many disputes about the aims of education are really disputes about principles of procedure, one can see some value in the question, "Must an educator have an aim?" (Peters 1965).

There also seems to be no clear-cut regard for individual differences in the specification of general aims or goals. For instance, should *homemaking* be an equally important objective for boys and girls?[1] Just what is the role of individual differences in shaping and planning educational goals? From the B-P-E perspective, we should keep the person in mind when determining which educational goals are important for some children and not for others. This distinction is similar to one made by Lesser (1971) between universalistic goals, or those goals that society thinks all children should achieve, for example, literacy and civic responsibility, and particularistic goals, or goals that some students should achieve because of special personal characteristics. Thus,

---

[1]We recognize that this may be a hotly debated issue in the future, and already the "Bachelor Survival" course is increasing in popularity.

Table 4.   Dimensions of the Task of Public Education:
A Conceptual Framework

A. Intellectual Dimensions
1. Possession of Knowledge: A fund of information, concepts.
2. Communication of Knowledge: Skill to acquire and transmit.
3. Creation of Knowledge: Discrimination and imagination, a habit.
4. Desire for Knowledge: A love for learning.
B. Social Dimensions
5. Man to Man: Cooperation in day-to-day relations.
6. Man to State: Civic rights and duties.
7. Man to Country: Loyalty to one's own country.
8. Man to World: Inter-relationships of peoples.
C. Personal Dimensions
9. Physical: Bodily health and development.
10. Emotional: Mental health and stability.
11. Ethical: Moral integrity.
12. Aesthetic: Cultural and leisure pursuits.
D. Productive Dimensions
13. Vocation-Selective: Information and guidance.
14. Vocation-Preparative: Training and placement.
15. Home and Family: Housekeeping, do-it-yourself family.
16. Consumer: Personal buying, selling, and investment.

(Stake 1970, p. 184)

a particularistic goal for a child with musical talent might be a more intensive study of music while the goal for other children might be the development of their painting or mechanical skills. A person-environment perspective is appropriate for both universalistic and particularistic goals because, even when a single goal or set of goals is adopted for all students, different instructional strategies may be appropriate for different students if these objectives are to be achieved (Lesser 1971).

SPECIFICATION OF EDUCATIONAL OBJECTIVES

Educational objectives have been defined as the statements of desired changes in thoughts, actions, or feelings of students that a particular course or educational program should bring about (Bloom 1963). Educational objectives have been distinguished from statements of more general goals, for example, Table 4, by their specificity and explicitness. If we consider the general goal of fostering civic rights and duties, it is apparent that the statement gives neither direction in the choice of appropriate learning experiences nor specifications for evaluation of outcomes. A more concrete educational objective related to this general aim would be "the ability to relate certain principles of a democratic constitution to current events."

The term educational objective represents a complex and multifaceted concept (Traub 1969) that varies in level of generality, type (cognitive versus affective, content versus process), and duration (long term versus short term) (Traub 1969). As indicated in Chapter 2, behavioral objectives are ultimately changes in the person along some specified dimension. Thus, our discussion of behavior, or objectives, will derive from our conception of the person, since it is the person who generates the behavior that we are observing.

The Taxonomies

The question that faces a theorist attempting to specify educational objectives is how comprehensive and exhaustive his specification must be to have practical educational significance. For example, if "ability to protect the home from fire" is a stated objective, should the ability to protect the home from flood, vandalism, tornadoes, or hurricanes also be included (Kliebard 1968)? If one attempts to be exhaustive in stating objectives, he could generate an endless list. In the 1920s, Bobbitt made the first major attempt to delineate the important issues in specifying educational objectives (Kliebard 1968). Strongly influenced by the writings of Thorndike, Bobbitt designated ten major areas of human activity and specified them as educational objectives. Bobbitt attempted to streamline the list by obtaining an arbitrary consensus from twenty-seven hundred well-trained, experienced adults on the inclusion or exclusion of the objectives (Kliebard 1968).

Bobbitt initiated an area of educational activity that has continued into the present. The most recent attempt to specify educational objectives is the *Taxonomy of Educational Objectives,* first developed in the cognitive domain in 1956 by Bloom et al. Subsequently, a classification system was developed in the affective domain by Krathwohl, Bloom, and Masia (1964). Tables 5 and 6 give summary versions of the cognitive and affective taxonomies, respectively.

These taxonomies were devised with three organizational principles in mind: (1) they should be educational-logical-psychological classification systems; (2) they should be logical classifications in that every effort should be made to define terms as precisely as possible and to use them consistently; and (3) they should be consistent with relevant and accepted psychological principles and theories (Bloom et al. 1956). Using a procedure similar to Bobbitt's, the cognitive taxonomy was sent to a large group of college and secondary-school teachers, administrators, curriculum directors, and educational-research specialists for criticisms and suggestions.

Table 5. Taxonomy in the Cognitive Domain

1.00 Knowledge
    1.10 Knowledge of specifics
    1.20 Knowledge of ways and means of dealing with specifics
    1.30 Knowledge of the universals and abstractions in a field

2.00 Comprehension
    2.10 Translation
    2.20 Interpretation
    2.30 Extrapolation

3.00 Application
    The educational implications of objectives in the application category
    Testing for Application, and illustrative test items

4.00 Analysis
    4.10 Analysis of elements
    4.20 Analysis of relationships
    4.30 Analysis of organizational principles

5.00 Synthesis
    Educational significance of Synthesis objectives
    5.10 Production of a unique communication
    5.20 Production of a plan, or proposed set of operations
    5.30 Derivation of a set of abstract relations

6.00 Evaluation
    6.10 Judgments in terms of internal evidence
    6.20 Judgments in terms of external criteria

(Bloom et al. 1956)

The taxonomy in the cognitive domain proceeds on the assumption that knowledge is ordered hierarchically, and it is assumed that the six main classes are sequential, moving from knowledge to evaluation (see Table 5). A concrete ability in the category "1.10 Knowledge of specifics" could be assessed by a simple, factual, multiple-choice item. For example: "About what proportion of the population of the United States is living on farms?

1. 10%
2. 20%
3. 35%
4. 50%
5. 60%"

At the higher levels, more complex abilities are assessed. The highest level, "6.00 Evaluation," might be assessed by the ability to evaluate a poem critically. For example, "Write an essay from 250 to 500 words, describing the poem assigned. In your description, you should use terms that will reveal your recognition of formal characteristics of the poem. Your principles of evaluation should be made clear, although they should not be elaborately described or defended." As can easily be seen, this evaluation item is tapping more complex abilities than the multiple-choice item.

Table 6.   The Taxonomy in the Affective Domain

1.0   Receiving (Attending)
 	
  1.1   Awareness
  1.2   Willingness to Receive
  1.3   Controlled or Selected Attention
 	
2.0   Responding
 	
  2.1   Acquiescence in Responding
  2.2   Willingness to Respond
  2.3   Satisfaction in Response
 	
3.0   Valuing
 	
  3.1   Acceptance of a Value
  3.1   Testing for Acceptance of a Value
  3.2   Preference for a Value
  3.3   Commitment
 	
4.0   Organization
 	
  4.1   Conceptualization of a Value
  4.2   Organization of a Value System
 	
5.0   Characterization by a Value or Value Complex
 	
  5.1   Generalized Set
  5.2   Characterization

(Krathwohl et al. 1964)

GENERAL ISSUES RELATED TO THE SPECIFICATION OF EDUCATIONAL OBJECTIVES

Developers of the taxonomies have stated that, in their work, they sought to be "value neutral" (Bloom et al. 1956). It is misleading, however, to give the impression that educational objectives can be formulated in a value-free setting. Educational goals are certainly value statements. Even when the goals are guided by, and in agreement with, psychological theory, as these taxonomies purport to be, they are based on the implicit value assumptions of a particular psychological theory. Furthermore, Polanyi (1962) has remarked that the choice of a psychological perspective itself involves a personal commitment on the part of the theorist that guides him in selecting certain aspects of reality while omitting others.

Since it is impossible to observe *all* aspects of behavior, there is merit in sketching out some of the principles that determine our selection of observations (Kessen 1960). One source of values influencing the choice of educational objectives is the "tacit dimensions" of the psychological theories on which the educational objectives are based. For example, it was pointed out in Chapter 1 that Thorndike and Dewey had quite different views about desirable educational outcomes. Not only did they differ on empirical questions but also their work was based on disparate value assumptions and theoretical views about what constitutes human growth. Dewey's "gestalt" and Thorndike's "behavioristic connections" (McDonald 1964) led them to dwell on different educational outcomes. The value differences between theorists are reflected in their selection of different criterion measures. As we will discuss in Chapters 6 and 7, Piagetians do not measure frequency of response, while behaviorists do not look at conservation responses. The tacit dimensions of the theoretical commitment obviously guide the individual to select some criterion behaviors rather than others.

Although Bloom and his colleagues tried to limit the influence of value, the objectives in Tables 5 and 6 indicate that the taxonomies were not developed in a value-free context. As the term educational behaviorism suggests, the specification of educational objectives in behavioral terms has attracted individuals with a distinctly behavioristic perspective, for example, Bobbitt who was strongly influenced by Thorndike. The present taxonomies were developed by individuals whose orientation was psychometric, or who might be called educational technologists, in that they seem to assume that knowledge follows a logical, hierarchical path and that affective development is an increasingly internalized state of affairs. Psychologists with different assumptions would no doubt have developed different taxonomies.

A major distinction in behavioral objectives, as viewed in the two taxonomies, is the relative emphasis placed on process or on content which represents the relative value of these two classes of behavior.

EDUCATIONAL ISSUES RELATED TO THE TAXONOMIES

Those who advocate the statement of educational objectives in behavioral terms have been criticized for assuming that behavioral outcomes are a result of the type of curriculum employed (Broudy 1969; Kliebard 1968). This criticism might be applied to other methods of evaluation, and it is a specific case of the general reservation about inferring causation from a single effect. For example, how would an increase in attendance at symphony concerts be explained? Is it the result of a discount rate given to students? Have music appreciation courses at an adult-education center created a wider audience? Have critics been more generous with the orchestra than formerly? Has the conductor decided to include more popular selections in the programs? It becomes obvious that the use of an extrinsic criterion measure of a single effect makes erroneous inference a possibility, but such a risk may be limited by employing multiple criterion measures.

Subject-matter content may also be a determining factor in the specification of educational outcomes. Eisner (1967) has criticized the theorists who demand specification of educational outcomes in behavioral terms for their failure to recognize the constraints that various kinds of subject matter place on possible specification. Mathematics and science are more amenable to taxonomic specification than are music and art. Also, the advance specification of behavioral outcomes may contradict the goals of a particular program of study. For example, if one of the aims of art study is the production of novel and creative forms, it seems contradictory to predict in advance what those novel forms will be. This criticism does not mean that there should be no evaluation of a curriculum program but, rather, questions advance prediction of certain outcomes and the general applicability of specific behavioral objectives.

Some critics have pointed to the lack of specificity in the design and organization of curriculum content (Eisner 1967). It has also been pointed out that, even in the classroom, good teachers often are not specific about their educational objectives nor do they deem specification important for their work (Jackson 1968). To discuss conceptions of behavior in educational terms, we will stress some positive aspects of the specification process, notwithstanding many of its shortcomings.

One does not have to agree with all the assumptions of behavioral specification to see some of its advantages. Put another way, every conception of educational objectives relies on behavioral observation; concepts differ in how such observations are interpreted and what meaning is attributed to the behavior. Those critics who dismiss attempts at specification of educational objectives on the basis that education is an "art" which defies specification are extreme in their advocacy of vagueness. At the same time, it seems foolish to say that all educational outcomes *must* be specified in behavioral terms, since in many instances this task is quite impossible. The fact that it is sometimes impossible does not mean that attempts at specification should be abandoned completely. As one critic in support of specification points out:

It would seem to this writer that it is virtually impossible to engage in an educational enterprise of any duration without having some specifications to guide one—whether one is a student, teacher, administrator, curriculum maker, educational technologist, evaluator, or guidance worker. What may be different from worker to worker is the explicitness of the specifications, the forms in which they are cast, the sources from which they are derived, and the extent to which they are used for various decisions. (Bloom 1969, p. 28).

As would be expected, researchers and teachers sometimes differ in their evaluation of specific educational objectives. However, Popham (1968) maintains that the specification of objectives has equal importance for teacher and researcher. In contrast, Jackson (1968) sees specification as tangential to good teaching. Stake's position (1970) lies between these two and is perhaps most constructive:

Goal stating succeeds to whatever extent it succeeds because people are tolerant of omissions: particularly omitted superordinate goals and omitted statements of conditions. With any statement of objectives there are assumptions about more basic needs being met. In the classroom it is assumed that certain essential educational skills—sentence making and reading comprehension and shutting up and refraining from bodily threat to the teacher, for example—will be mentioned. When these student skills falter, the teacher is likely to abandon stated objectives to attend to the "essentials." Also, there are unstated but expected conditions for the instruction. As conditions change, objectives are modified. In other words, no set of stated objectives is a fixed and final list of what the teacher will or should attend to. The list does reveal what its authors judged to be worth special attention. (p. 182–183)

When compared with the teacher's requirements, the specification of objectives for the educational researcher has a different focal point because it involves clarification of the dependent variable in research or evaluation. There are good scientific reasons for being as explicit as possible since this aids in the communication of findings between researchers. One does not have to be a radical behaviorist to espouse explicitness in one's theory and research since, in addition to clarity, specification aids the educational researcher in the comparison of different findings. However, as noted in the discussion in Chapter 1 on "psychology-as-science," educational evaluators should avoid stating educational objectives in specific terms just because such definitions permit measurement.

CONCEPTION OF THE PERSON IN GENERATING OBJECTIVES

It was pointed out in Chapter 2 that educational goals and environments that facilitate their attainment may be derived from the concept of how a person develops. Examples which characterized the person interacting with an environment (P-E) to produce an educational outcome (B) were discussed.

The theory influences the concept of behavior. For example, because behaviorists, like Skinner and Thorndike, view the organism as a creature of habits or associations that have been learned in the past, their criterion behaviors for growth of these habits are frequency or amplitude of response, that is, how often and with what intensity the organism responds. By contrast, the Gestalt psychologists who maintain that organismic development occurs as a complex, holistic response that cannot be reduced to simple associations use more complex problem-solving activities as criterion measures. Lewin (1951) gave an excellent example of this contrast between theories and its implications for selection of criterion behaviors in his discussion of "achievement concepts." In learning a complex skill, such as typing, Lewin pointed out, the learning curve first rises quite steeply and then levels off. In time, a more or less jumplike transition from that level to a higher level takes place, and so forth. The achievement concept, in this case typewriting, lumps all these processes together, as if they were a single action.

> . . . however, a trained typist's work is not actually the same process as that of a beginner; it differs not merely in quantity of training, but in its fundamental psychological character. The typing of the beginner is essentially a search for single letters. The implied process of orientation (on the keyboard) can be practiced and people can become efficient in this search. But it would be a mistake to describe the work of a trained typist as a well-practiced search of this sort: she knows her machine so that she need not search. . . . The entire process is no more a search than is the beginner's typing or lifting of fingers. (Lewin 1951, p. 90)

It is clear then that the criterion behaviors selected to index behavioral objectives are not simply a matter of taste but are strongly influenced by the explicit or implicit theory.

The behavioristic emphasis on content will be elaborated in Chapter 7, while the Gestalt emphasis on process, which is similar to Piaget's, will be discussed in Chapter 6. We now turn to a more explicit consideration of content and process in defining behavioral objectives.

Content versus Process Learning

Should education consist of learning particular subject matter or acquiring process skills that will aid in the learning of specific subject matter? Content refers to what the person learns; process refers to how and why the person learns. The issue is especially important in contemporary education because rapid social change and technological advances quickly make specific knowledge in certain subjects obsolete. The argument against emphasizing subject matter stems from the belief that much of the content will be of no use to a student at maturity. Many educators stress the acquisition of content-free skills that will help the student process educational content. In this sense, one might say that education is not the acquisition of content but, rather the development of processing skills to deal with specific types of subject matter. In terms of measurement and evaluation, it may be said that:

> The question of the relation between accomplishment and the underlying mental processes is one of the most significant problems of genetic psychology, as well as of the theory and the practice of education. It is doubtless of great value to analyze the genesis of human mentality in terms of a gradual increase of accomplishment. Measuring development by means of achievements has proved to be a successful approach, and has provided valuable insight into the laws of mental growth. Nevertheless, this method of understanding must be supplemented by an analysis of the mental processes which underlie the achievements themselves. (Werner 1937, p. 353)

Schroder, Karlins, and Phares (1973) take a similar viewpoint. Although they stress the need for process learning, they do not completely reject a content-oriented approach. They nevertheless criticize education for its heavy emphasis on content learning with its achievement orientation. The ideal process learner is the child learning to put things together. Their accent is on his learning to generate concepts. In other words, the learner practices the kind of thinking required to create concepts by combining information in response to the challenges and demands of a given learning situation.

It is empirically impossible to separate content and process completely because some content is always involved. Or as Bruner (1960) put it, "the objective of education is not the production of self-confident fools" (p. 65). The issue becomes important when content learning indicates an underlying process skill. As noted, one's concept of the person determines whether he will stress content or process skills. Skinner and Thorndike emphasize content; Dewey and Piaget emphasize process.

Thorndike viewed learning as the development of stimulus-response connections and knowledge as the accumulation of these connections. For him, education consisted of learning specific responses to stimuli with little transfer or generalization of learning from one instance to the next, except through identical elements in the stimuli. His emphasis on lack of transfer led to the recommendation of teaching for specific behavioral outcomes. Because Thorndike believed learning to be an accumulation of specific content acquired or eliminated by reward or punishment, he stressed the acquisition of specific subject-matter content as the educational objective, and he evaluated the success of instructional programs accordingly.

By contrast, Dewey's concept of the person was more dynamic and led to a quite different set of objectives, as implied in Chapter 2. Rather than viewing knowledge as the acquisition of specific responses, Dewey held that any particular content learned was acquired as the result of some underlying process skills. He was therefore more likely to look at a student's behavior as a sign of his developmental stage or processing capacity rather than as an end in itself. Therefore, while Thorndike considered behavior as behavior, Dewey viewed it as representing underlying processing skills. Dewey stated educational objectives within the framework of long-term developmental goals rather than immediate goals of specific achievements. Viewed contemporaneously, Dewey was concerned with the development and transformation of information processing skills rather than with the content of the specific information being acquired. All knowledge is limited to a specific time. Any particular educational goal implies an orderly and ordered activity which involves the completion of a process. All educational goals or outcomes must be seen within a temporal, or developmental, dimension because what is involved in the development of knowledge is the cumulative growth of the processing skills (Dewey 1916).

The distinction between content and process is related to the distinction between developmental goals and contemporaneous, or short-term, goals. It is not so much that one or the other be chosen, but that both are required. Developmental change cannot be observed on a day-to-day basis, so the teacher who ignores short-term or content goals will be continually frustrated. However, the day-to-day changes should be viewed within a developmental perspective. In the evaluation of educational progress, the two views—developmental and contemporaneous—complement each other.

As noted in educational behaviorism, some approaches emphasize specific, rapid achievement. Partly because of cultural emphasis on achievement, the correct answer may assume more importance than a clear understanding of the problem or the concepts involved. In contrast, Piaget's clinical method is not to test for achievement but to ask questions aimed at revealing some underlying process of thought. For Piaget, a child's "wrong" answer from an adult's point of view is at least as important as a "correct" one because it indicates the process of the child's thinking. Since Piaget was concerned with the organization of thought and the process of thinking, he studied children of different ages to observe the changes in cognitive process which occur at different phases of development.

Interest in a process dimension in educational evaluation is not restricted to theorists who subscribe to a cognitive-developmental view. Within the psychometric tradition, Cronbach (1966) has been one of the most articulate advocates of more multidimensional assessment. He has encouraged data collection on such process dimensions as theoretical understanding, heuristics, valuation, creative urge, and epistemology. More recently, Messick (1971) has suggested general personality dimensions, such as cognitive style (field independence-dependence, reflectivity-impulsivity) and affective reactions (tolerance for incongruous or unrealistic experience), as criteria for evaluation. Recognizing that the distinction between content and process is a way of interpreting evaluation criteria, Messick pointed out that a dimension, such as cognitive style, is not necessarily independent of content but that it tends to function across a variety of areas as a process variable.

Although it is true that contemporary theorists tend to emphasize content, a contemporary approach may also deal with process as Messick (1971) observed:

> Cognitive styles, by embracing both perceptual and intellectual domains and by their frequent implication in personality and social functioning, promise to provide a more complete and effective characterization of the student than could be obtained from intellectual tests alone. These stylistic dimensions offer us new types of process variables to appraise that extend the assessment of mental performance beyond the crystallized notion of achievement levels to a concern with patterns of cognitive functioning. These stylistic characteristics should have relevance, although direct evidence is admittedly scanty, not only for the course of individual learning in various subject matter areas, but also for the nature of teacher-pupil interactions and of social behavior in the classroom. (p. 18)

Kohlberg's stage theory of moral development (1958) is another example of emphasis on process. The key element in Kohlberg's theory is the level of moral maturity that underlies the decisions a person makes, and it clearly illustrates the distinction between *content* and *process* orientation. Kohlberg's stage theory is based on an empirical study of seventy-two boys, aged ten, thirteen, and sixteen years. The boys were given ten dilemma situations that

each involved a particular kind of value conflict, for example, a conflict between legal-social rules. Kohlberg, following the Piagetian tradition, asked the
children to judge the morality of conduct described in the stories. The following example illustrates the conflict stories presented for evaluation:

> In Europe a woman was near death from a special kind of cancer. There
> was one drug that the doctors thought might save her. It was a form of
> radium that a druggist in the same town had recently discovered. The drug
> was expensive to make, but the druggist was charging ten times what the
> drug cost him to make. He paid $200 for the radium and charged $2,000
> for a small dose of the drug. The sick woman's husband, Heinz, went to
> everyone he knew to borrow the money but he could only get together
> about $1,000 which is half of what it cost. He told the druggist that his
> wife was dying, and asked him to sell it cheaper or let him pay later. But
> the druggist said, "No. I discovered the drug and I'm going to make
> money from it." So Heinz got desperate and broke into the man's store
> to steal the drug for his wife. Should the husband have done that? Why?

On the basis of responses to these dilemma situations, Kohlberg (1958)
suggested that the child's development of moral judgment falls into six stages,
which can be grouped into three moral levels. These are:

Level 1. Premoral
   Value resides in external quasi-physical happenings, in bad acts, or in quasi-
   physical needs rather than in persons and standards.
   Stage 1: Obedience and punishment orientation. Egocentric deference to
            superior power or prestige, or a trouble-avoiding set. Objective
            responsibility.
   Stage 2: Naively egoistic orientation. Right action is that instrumentally
            satisfying the self's needs and occasionally others'. Awareness of
            relativism of value of each actor's needs and perspective. Naive
            egalitarianism and orientation to exchange and reciprocity.
Level 2. Conventional Rule
   Moral value resides in performing good or right roles, in maintaining the
   conventional order and the expectancies of others.
   Stage 3: Good boy orientation. Orientation to approval and to pleasing and
            helping others. Conformity to stereotypical images of majority or
            natural role behavior, and judgment by intentions.
   Stage 4: Authority and social order maintenance orientation. Orientation
            to "doing duty" and to showing respect for authority and main-
            taining the given social order for its own sake. Regard for earned
            expectations of others.

Level 3. Autonomous Principled Morality

Moral value resides in conformity by the self to shared shareable standards, rights, or duties.

Stage 5: Contractual legalistic orientation. Recognition of an arbitrary element or starting point in rules or expectations for the sake of agreement. Duty defined in terms of contract, general avoidance of violation of the will or rights of others, and majority will and welfare.

Stage 6: Conscience or principle orientation. Orientation not only to actually ordained social rules but to principles of choice involving appeal to logical universality and consistency. Orientation to conscience as a directing agent and to mutual respect and trust.

Each of Kohlberg's stages is defined by certain basic aspects of moral values. One aspect that we will focus on for purposes of illustration is that of the "value of human life." This aspect is defined for each of the six stages in the following examples relating to the Heinz dilemma.

Stage 1: The value of a human life is confused with the value of physical objects and is based on the social status or physical attributes of its possessor. Tommy, age ten: (Why should the druggist give the drug to the dying woman when her husband couldn't pay for it?) "If someone important is in a plane and is allergic to heights and the stewardess won't give him medicine because she's only got enough for one and she's got a sick one, a friend, in back, they'd probably put the stewardess in a lady's jail because she didn't help the important one." (Is it better to save the life of one important person or a lot of unimportant people?) "All the people that aren't important because one man just has one house, maybe a lot of furniture, but a whole bunch of people have an awful lot of furniture and some of these poor people might have a lot of money and it doesn't look it."

Stage 2: The value of a human life is seen as instrumental to the satisfaction of the needs of its possessor or of other persons. Tommy, age 13: (Should the doctor "mercy kill" a fatally ill woman requesting death because of her pain?) "Maybe it would be good to put her out of her pain, she'd be better off that way. But the husband wouldn't want it, it's not like an animal. If a pet dies you can get along without it—it isn't something you really need. Well, you can get a new wife, but it's not really the same."

Stage 3: The value of a human life is based on the empathy and affection of family members and others toward its possessor. Andy, age sixteen: (Should the doctor "mercy kill" a fatally ill woman requesting death because of her pain?) "No, he shouldn't. The husband loves her and wants to see her. He wouldn't want her to die sooner, he loves her too much."

Stage 4: Life is conceived as sacred in terms of its place in a categorical moral or religious order of rights and duties. John, age sixteen: (Should the doctor "mercy kill" the woman?) "The doctor wouldn't have the right to take a life, no human has the right. He can't create life, he shouldn't destroy it."

Stage 5: Life is valued both in terms of its relation to community welfare and in terms of life being a universal human right.

Stage 6: Belief in the sacredness of human life as representing a universal human value of respect for the individual. Steve, age sixteen: (Should the husband steal the expensive drug to save his wife?) "By the law of society he was wrong but by the law of nature or of God the druggist was wrong and the husband was justified. Human life is above financial gain. Regardless of who was dying, if it was a total stranger, man has a duty to save him from dying."

According to Kohlberg, this stage sequence is age-related and forms an unchanging sequence in the process of development of moral judgment. Thus, each stage is a necessary antecedent for the development of a subsequent stage, and it is expected that younger children will generally be at lower stages than older children. The stage is a process referent, and the content of the dilemma is only important insofar as it illustrates the underlying process. Two boys may state similar content solutions to what Heinz should do, but their reasoning processes may be quite different if one is at Stage 2 and the other at Stage 6. The Stage 6 reasoning process for stealing the drug is quite different from the processes employed by the Stage 2 child, although both may advocate the same behavioral choice.

Whether one wishes to measure immediate achievement aims or long-term developmental goals will determine the method of evaluation. For example, in devising a curriculum related to contemporary social issues, one might include the topic of the value of human life in a variety of contexts (war, operating room). In devising such a program, one would need to consider many questions, such as: At what ages would this topic be appropriate? How would it be evaluated? Multiple choice or essay? How often? The teacher may intuitively decide to try his social-issues program with Grade 10 students and devise topics on the value of human life which require the students to discuss them in class. (See Chapter 11 for an example.) The teacher's long-term goal is to help students appreciate the value of human life in a variety of contexts. Two controversial issues discussed are the Heinz dilemma of stealing the drug and the problem of mercy killing. The teacher considering how to evaluate whether his curriculum has changed the students' notions of the value of human life might decide to administer an attitude scale that would indicate the intensity of the students' beliefs on the issue as follows:

Stealing is right when it is done to save a human life.
I believe in the above statement:

Very strongly	Strongly	Neutral	Weakly	Very weakly
1	2	3	4	5

Let us assume that the end-of-year test results indicated a strong preference for human life over property values. Note that this test is focused on the attitude *content,* not on the reasons behind the attitude. Results from such a specific content item may suggest that all students are alike in their attitudes if they responded similarly. However, Kohlberg's Moral Judgment Scale might produce a different conclusion about the effects of the course. Suppose John and Charles have the same score on the attitude scale concerning the value of human life, but the teacher finds that this similarity is at odds with their comments in class discussion. Taking our initial item, we see John and Charles responding as follows:

Stealing is right when it is done to save a human life.
I believe in the above statement:

Very strongly	Strongly	Neutral	Weakly	Very weakly
(1)	2	3	4	5

Both boys respond positively to the importance of human life, but they may be doing it for different reasons, which would put them at different stages of moral development. John's response to the Heinz dilemma might be as follows:

By our society's laws, one can make a case that Heinz was wrong, but, as far as I am concerned, when a society puts property rights over human life then the law should be broken. Human life is above financial gain, when they come into conflict, financial gain goes out the window. Regardless of whether it is a person I know or a perfect stranger, I think it would be my duty to save life in the situation.

Charles's response, in contrast, might be as follows:

I think Heinz should steal the drug because he would be sad if his wife died. His wife means a lot to him so he should save her or he will be lonely. I am not sure I would save a stranger's life because I don't know the person and would probably not miss him.

Although John and Charles make the same response on the attitude scale, it is important to note the differences in their moral explanations of when, where, and why life is valuable. John's explanation is at Stage 6 on the Kohlberg moral development scale, whereas Charles's reasoning process puts him at Stage 2 on the scale. They reason at quite different levels of sophistication, even though their attitude scores are the same. This example illustrates the importance of distinguishing immediate achievement goals from long-term developmental goals. This distinction is related to the evaluation process.

If the development is conceived as being not an increasing efficiency in accomplishment, but as a transformation of mental processes from lower into higher forms, a further consequence arises. It is of equal importance to the child psychologist and the educator to bear in mind that the degree of accomplishment in a certain test does not always indicate the stage of development that has been reached by the child in a particular field. The teacher in the classroom and the diagnosing psychologist very often neglect the fact that the child who is accomplishing a task by employing functions of a lower level may ultimately be more successful than another who attempts to employ functions at a higher order. (Werner 1937, pp. 362–363)

Kohnstamm (1965) has summarized five criteria for the evaluation of a developmental change in stage. These criteria make the assessment of educational outcomes a more complex task than simple achievement assessment. Kohnstamm demands that the newly acquired behavior be (1) lasting, (2) transferable, (3) fundamentally different from the preexperimental behavior, (4) difficult to acquire (presumably on the basis that nothing that comes easy will last), and (5) resistant to extinction. Since the developmental, or process, perspective advocated by Kohlberg involves a wider view over several age spans, and immediate improvement cannot be indicated on short-term achievement tests and examinations, this approach will probably have little popularity in contemporary education where economy must frequently prevail. Jackson (1970) alludes to this problem when he comments:

> Typically, educational researchers circumvent this issue by settling on achievement test gains (or some variant of them, such as drop in error rate) as the only reasonable measure of educational outcome. Once this step is taken, it follows that the "best" method is the one associated with the largest gains in achievement per unit of instructional time. It is, of course, at once clear that the amount of educational growth (if we may properly talk of achievement test gains in that way) is not the only criterion that might be employed, even staying within the paper- and pencil-test framework. Perhaps the speed with which a given method operates will prompt us to call it best; perhaps the question of relative cost or ease of administration or apparent freedom from deleterious side effects will be a deciding factor. (p. 25)

Behavior-as-content is related to the conception of the person in terms of stimulus-response bonds and to conceptualizing development as an increase in the number of bonds. Behavior-as-process is related to a cognitive view of the person and to a conception of development in terms of structural reorganization. Behavior-as-content usually involves a short-term view, while behavior-as-process takes a longer view, as indicated in the Kohlberg (long-term) and achievement (short-term) approaches to assessing behavior in the moral domain.

The distinction between process and content does not simply divide cognitive-developmental theorists, such as Kohlberg and Piaget, from behavior theorists; it is acknowledged in other areas of psychology that have potential relevance for educational research. For example, the distinction is also made in such areas as opinion change (Kelman 1961), general personality development (Harvey, Hunt, and Schroder 1961; Loevinger 1966), and information processing (Schroder, Driver, and Streufert 1967).

Because cognitive-developmental theories are frequently used as examples for process-based theories, it should be noted that behavior-as-process does not require stage concepts. In other words, the content-process distinction does more than divide stage theories from all other theories, even though our presentation may have implied that this is the case.

THE TAXONOMIES AND THE CONTENT-PROCESS DISTINCTION

A casual study of the taxonomies in Tables 5 and 6 would seem to indicate that an evaluation of content items would be necessary at the lower levels and assessment of process skills at the higher levels. This is not always what happens, although, again, it depends on the evaluator's orientation toward his assessment procedure. In more concrete terms, illustrative definitions from the cognitive domain will be given and then elaborated in terms of the content-process distinction.

Let us consider the lowest and highest levels of the taxonomy in the cognitive domain (Bloom et al. 1956). The lowest level is concerned with knowledge items and is defined as follows:

> *Knowledge* involves the recall of specifics and universals, the recall of a pattern, structure or setting. For measurement purposes, the recall situation involves little more than bringing to mind the appropriate material ... To use an analogy, if one thinks of the mind as a file, the problem in a knowledge test situation is that of finding in the problem or task the appropriate signals, cues, and clues which will most effectively bring out whatever knowledge is filed or stored. (p. 201)
>
> *Evaluation* is the sixth and highest level of the cognitive taxonomy and is defined as ... judgments about the value of material and methods for given purposes. Quantitative and qualitative judgments about the extent to which materials and methods satisfy criteria. The criteria may be those determined by students or those which are given him. (p. 201)

The "knowledge" level embraces the specific content of subject matter. Assessment would elicit the recall of information previously given to the child: primary-assessment procedures would be objective examinations of the true-false and multiple-choice type or direct corrective feedback of a teaching machine, and so on. As we pointed out earlier, *content* learning has its place in the curriculum, and many theorists of a cognitive *(process)* bent can see its merits under certain circumstances (Ausubel 1968; Piaget 1971). Switching briefly from outcome (B) to teaching method orientation (E), it is interesting to see what Piaget (essentially of a *process* orientation, see Chapter 6) has to say of Skinner's use of the teaching machine (Piaget 1969).

> As for the intrinsic value of such a teaching method, that naturally depends upon the aims that are assigned to it in any particular field. In cases where it is a matter of acquiring a set body of learning, as in the teaching of languages, the machine does seem to be accepted as of undeniable service, especially as a means of saving time. In cases where the ideal is to reinvent a sequence of reasoning, however, as in mathematics, though the machine does not exclude either comprehension or reasoning itself on the student's part, it does channel them in an unfortunate way and excludes the possibility of initiative ... at the Woods Hole conference mentioned earlier, at which mathematicians and physicists were seeking for

means of recasting the teaching of the sciences, Skinner's propositions were received with no more than limited enthusiasm, since the particular problem facing the conference was less one of finding the means to achieve accurate comprehension than that of encouraging the development of inventive and inquisitive minds. (p. 78)

As can be seen from this quote, even Piaget can see a place for content learning at the "knowledge" level of taxonomy as we have described it. Turning to the highest level of evaluation, it seems that the more complex type of learning will demand more complex assessment. Our examples of changes in the person on either a developmental or a contemporaneous characteristic seem appropriate here. Since most of our examples thus far have been stage-developmental, we would like to present an example given by Schroder, Driver, and Streufert (1967) on the evaluation of an essay. It may be recalled that at the "evaluation" level of the taxonomy, essays are suggested as an important vehicle to give insight into process. In caution, we would like to point out that the use of essays does not mean that a process orientation governs their scoring. Essay evaluation can be just as content specific as more objective types of examinations. Schroder, Driver, and Streufert (1967) consider the following essay question:

It has been said that a democratic form of government is more satisfying to the people than an autocratic form, but the latter is more efficient in making decisions. Compare these two group structures taking small group research into account. (p. 201)

The resulting essay can be evaluated in terms of content or process, and the evaluation depends on the purpose of the evaluator. If the evaluator is interested in content, he might give high scores to students who answer the question with material identical to that in a book or lecture; thus, the scoring would be content specific and just as dependent on recall as are many objective tests. The process evaluation of this type of essay would be quite different as is outlined in Table 7.

The scoring system in Table 7 is an attempt to quantify the scoring of essays along structural or process dimensions. The system, although not ignoring the content of the essay, places much greater emphasis on the structural relationships of the content.[2] In this context, Schroder, Karlins, and Phares (1973) put forth the notion of a "process grade." The process grade is an evaluation of the student's work based on the breadth, relevance, and usage of hypotheses generated.

[2]In addition, it also shows that a process emphasis is not necessarily synonymous with a stage theory.

Table 7. Scale Points Used for Assessing the Conceptual Level Involved
in Essay Writing

Scale Point	Description
1	Presents only one side of a problem. Ignores differences, similarities, and gradations.
2	One side of the problem presented and supported much more fully than the other. Opposing views perceived as compartmentalized or negative. No interrelationships considered.
3	Two or more views clearly differentiated. Similarities and differences implied or presented. One view can be opposed, but it is understood.
4	Includes all involved under scale point 3 but begins to "consider" the similarities and differences between views. At this level, consideration is expressed . . . as qualifications of each . . . (for example, "similar, but . . . "). That is, the simultaneous effects of alternate views become apparent in the writer's thinking.
5	Considers alternate and conflicting reasons for perceived similarities and differences between views in producing the essay.
6	Begins to consider relationships, not only among direct similarities and differences between sides of the problem, but also relationships between alternate reasons as to why the differences and similarities occur.
7	The consideration of notions which include relational linkages between alternate views. Such notions are open to all conflicting components and express attempts to see these as parts of a more inclusive "construction" of the problem.

(Schroder, Driver, and Streufert 1967, p. 201)

While considering the content-process distinction in assessment, note that what applies to the cognitive taxonomy applies equally to the affective taxonomy. Although higher levels of the affective taxonomy, such as organization and characterization by a value or value complex, probably lend themselves to process interpretation, there is no guarantee or necessity that this must be the case. As with the cognitive taxonomy, one could use items from the highest levels of the affective domain and interpret them in either content or process terms.

Unintended Effects: The Problem of Unspecified Educational Outcomes

There are educational outcomes that are not initially intended but are by-products of a particular educational experience. The taxonomies deal only with educational outcomes that have been specified in advance of the learning sequence. It is clear, however, that students unsportingly learn far more than can be specified in advance (Bloom 1969; Kibler, Barker, and Miles 1970). Unspecified or unintended outcomes may be either desirable or undesirable, but it is a good idea to keep them in mind because they may be more important than the educational objectives that have been specified. Bloom (1969) makes the following observation on looking at possible unintended effects:

> The point of all this is that there are undoubtedly many outcomes of instruction and curriculum that cannot be specified in advance. Such outcomes should be investigated by clinical and other techniques in the hope that the desirable outcomes can be strengthened and the undesirable outcomes can be corrected or eliminated. One need not limit evaluation to only the desired and specified outcomes of instruction if there is some reason to believe that certain additional outcomes are likely to take place. While the medical analogy is not entirely appropriate, it does suggest the importance of searching for side effects of the particular treatment. All too frequently, the side effects of medical treatment are as important as the desired main effects. (p. 40)

It may seem contradictory to speak of unintended positive effects because presumably the intention should be to produce as many positive effects as possible. What is usually meant is that the effect was unanticipated or had not been measured before. For example, a student studying the system for cataloging books in the library *might* acquire new skill in his search strategy. Such improvement is not really unintended but rather unanticipated.

Unanticipated negative effects are, however, also unintended and usually involve "side effects" caused by an overemphasis on one kind of effect. Excessively long drill, for example, may produce immediate acquisition of correct responses (intended positive cognitive outcome) but an intense dislike for the subject (unintended negative affective outcome).

If the educational psychologist is simply interested in short-term content outcomes, he may blind himself to certain negative effects that could be measured by long-term process indicators. For example, Wallach (1967) has criticized programmed instruction because the excessive emphasis on accuracy produces a side effect of decreasing the student's tolerance for error, and its associated originality of thinking.

The word evaluation keeps reappearing in this chapter because it is inextricably tied up with educational goals, or the B in our B-P-E model. The term evaluation implies a valuing procedure. For the teacher or educational researcher, it is a means to assess whether a certain goal or goals are achieved. The problem of unintended outcomes as presented in Bloom's quote is clearly not restricted to the taxonomy. Our stress on the distinction between *process* and *content* runs the same risks of unintended hazards or gains. These unintended effects can occur for many reasons, and we will discuss some of these issues in Chapter 11.

We would like to allude briefly to some of these unintended effects, especially the possible negative consequences. First of all, a negative consequence may occur when the educational psychologist gives the teacher information about certain person characteristics. Let us assume the information is transmitted for developmental goals, such as a change in stage of moral development. The question the educational psychologist might ask is whether the psychological characteristic as it is described will have prejudicial effects on a teacher's attitude and impede his goals. For example, by telling a teacher that one child is at an "instrumental hedonist" stage, while another is at the "good boy, nice girl" stage, does the psychologist run the risk of having the teacher negatively evaluate one stage over another, instead of taking a developmental view as was propounded in Chapter 2? The effect is well illustrated by the studies in teacher expectancy (Rosenthal 1971).

Second, we can look at this negative consequence from the student's point of view. Let us say that the students know about the stages and their own stage. "Oh, we are the hedonists who are to be turned into nice guys" or "God, it really breaks me up to think I am so selfish." If the evaluation design consists of a pretest to a student's standing before an educational intervention, this procedure may unintentionally affect the results by sensitizing the student to the purpose of the program. This effect, referred to as pretest sensitization (Bracht and Glass 1968), may result from the student's interpreting the content of the evaluation procedure as an initial organizer. Unanticipated or unintended effects may also arise from the evaluation after the program (posttest sensitization) because the procedure itself creates an artificial effect that is not part of the program. Perhaps, the information conveyed has to be changed into more "unobtrusive measures" (see Webb et al. 1966) so that the learning situation will not be adversely affected.

Summary

Behavior, in the B-P-E model, may refer either to immediate observable behavior or to long-term changes in the person similar to those described in Chapter 2. Immediate, observable behavior lends itself to objective quantification. This has led to an overemphasis on behavior that can be immediately measured as the behavior that is important in both psychological theory (behaviorism) and educational practice (specification of behavioral objectives). Such exaggerated emphasis, illustrated in performance contracting, teacher merit pay based on student achievement, accountability, and voucher plans, was referred to as educational behaviorism.

The two taxonomies of educational objectives—cognitive and affective—served as the basis for considering educational objectives in B-P-E terms. The necessity of considering several levels of both taxonomies in measuring educational outcomes or in planning educational programs was emphasized because of the differential effects reflected by different criteria.

The distinction between content and process was considered in its implication for defining educational objectives. Content goals were discussed as short-term goals more likely to be represented on the lower levels of the taxonomy (and similar to a contemporaneous view of the person), while process goals are long-term goals similar to higher levels of the taxonomies (and more similar to the developmental view of the person).

When considering educational outcomes, the importance of noting possible unintended effects as well as desired, expected outcomes was discussed.

SUGGESTED READINGS

Eisner, E. W. "Educational Objectives: Help or Hindrance?" *School Review* 75 (1967):250–266.
Kohlberg, L. "Moral Education in the Schools." *School Review* 74 (1966):1–30.
Schroder, H. M. "Conceptual Complexity and Personality Organization." In *Personality Theory and Information Processing,* edited by H. M. Schroder and P. Suedfeld, pp. 240–274. New York: Ronald Press Co., 1971.
Werner, H. "Process and Achievement: A Basic Problem of Education and Developmental Psychology." *Harvard Educational Review* 7 (1937):353–368.

chapter 4

CONCEPTS OF EDUCATIONAL ENVIRONMENTS

> Social scientists are dramatically impotent in their ability to characterize environments. Generally, they do not even try. It should by now be a truism to point out that neither individuals nor groups can be adequately described without reference to some setting. . . . The language of education and the behavioral science is in great need of a set of terms for describing environments that is as articulated, specific and functional as those already posed for characterizing individuals. (Shulman 1970, p. 374)

Teachers and educational decision-makers probably find this statement an ivory tower issue because, regardless of how much is known, the teacher must create an environment, or teaching method, and the educational decision-maker must select among environments, or educational approaches. They can ill afford the luxury of critical reflection but must continue to act, guided mainly by their intuitive judgment. Their actions—in teaching and in selecting educational programs—are important factors in determining educational environments. As the above quotation suggests, the characterization of educational environments is enormously complex.

However, since the educational environment consists of the school climate as well as the teacher's approach to teaching, it is imperative that psychologists develop some ways of describing such educational environments. Whether psychologists like it or not, educational administrators must make decisions among educational approaches, and teachers must do their best, using whatever teaching method seems best. To communicate with them, the psychologist must talk in terms related to these activities. We consider such activities as teaching methods and instructional programs as well as school climate to be features of the educational environment, and it seems likely that psychologists' failure to describe educational environments in communicable, comprehensive terms is the major reason for the slow pace of psychology's contribution to educational practice.

If we state the B-P-E formula from the teacher's standpoint, it becomes E:P $\longrightarrow$ B (or an Environment radiated toward a Person produces a Behavior). The E:P $\longrightarrow$ B formulation emphasizes the central nature of the environment. Since the environment is the major component over which the teacher has some control, a language for describing the environment would provide a basis for describing what it is that a teacher does.

In this chapter, we discuss ways of thinking about educational environments with an emphasis upon those environmental elements provided by the teachers, such as teaching style, instructional variation, and models of teaching. Many readers, familiar with the much-publicized effects of pollution on the physical environment, may wonder if we plan to deal with the physical aspects of educational environments. While not denying the importance of the physical environment, we emphasize those elements in the immediately present interpersonal environment that seem most likely to be educationally relevant.

Why Psychologists Have Difficulty Conceptualizing Environment

The best way to discover why it is difficult to conceptualize environment is to try it for yourself. Try describing the interpersonal environments you encounter during a day or, better still, try describing the environment that another person is experiencing. If you seriously attempt such description, you will quickly discover some of the main problems in characterizing environment: How much of the environment to describe? What units to employ? Whose interpretation to use?

The answers to these questions depend on the purpose for which the environment is being described. A major reason for psychologists' difficulty in describing environments is their failure to accept the necessity for any description being relative. Three psychologists viewing a classroom teacher using behavior-modification procedures might disagree completely in their descriptions: one might refer to the ratio of reinforcement schedule, a second might describe the environment as "authoritarian," while a third might describe it as a specific model of teaching. Still another psychologist (or perhaps sociologist) might be uninterested in the classroom environment because of his belief that the school climate is the important environment to describe.

Which one is right? Which is the *real* environment? It is impossible to say without indicating the purpose. Psychologists may describe environments for many different purposes: to communicate with teachers about teaching methods; to determine what are the most important factors affecting a person's development and immediate behavior; to decide on what level of environmental influence to introduce a new educational practice; to characterize the difference in educational approaches. Descriptions of different educational environments for teacher trainees will differ from those used in educational research to determine specific effects. For example, the best-known system of describing teacher behavior, the Flanders system of interaction analysis, requires that teacher behavior be classified every three seconds. Such apparent precision may be useful for research purposes, but it is certainly questionable whether it is an appropriate system for communicating with teachers or teacher trainees about their behavior, even though it is often used for this purpose. If you have ever taught, you will realize the impossibility of thinking in three-second units.

This example also illustrates what may be called the "climate vs. weather" issue in describing environments. The climate of an educational environment usually refers to a larger spatial unit, such as school climate, or to a larger temporal unit, such as the preholiday class climate. The "weather" in an educational environment refers to the specific minute-by-minute events that occur. Whether to describe an educational environment in terms of climate or weather also depends on the purpose.

Disagreement among social scientists about what elements of the environment are most important is nowhere better illustrated than in the theories of educational innovation. Some educational innovators believe, for example, that "Only classroom by classroom, teacher by teacher, can schooling get better" (Featherstone 1971). Others believe that efforts to innovate educational environments must begin at the administrative level. Certainly both are important, and nothing is gained by arguing about which one is absolutely more important.

In the face of such difficulties in describing environments, many psychologists have studied tiny, often trivial, pieces of the environment in their experiments. For example, the environmental unit (independent variable) in an experiment might consist of the number of nonsense syllables in a list to be learned. The results from such work might serve as the basis for a study of more realistic, "ecologically valid" environmental units, such as different lengths of time in discussion or different amounts of textbook material. Though some psychological researchers do investigate more relevant units, others continue to investigate the effect of "list length" as if it were really of interest when, in fact, it is quite trivial.

The term "ecological validity" (Brunswik 1956) means the degree to which the conditions of an experiment represent the real world, and thus refers to what we mentioned in Chapter 1 as the relevance dimension of the independent variable in an experiment. Psychologists concerned with education need to become more familiar with how children learn and what goes on in classrooms. This is not to say that all of their research should investigate classroom learning, but that their work be translatable at some point into educational practice.

As we will discuss, the psychologist must have ways of describing the environment to conduct investigations designed to understand person-environment interaction. Characterization of the environment is essential if he is to conduct investigations that will lead to a better understanding of persons as well as produce educationally relevant statements. If psychologists are to become effective in implementing their ideas in educational practice, they must have ways of describing the environment. However, as Shulman (1970) observes, " 'Aptitude-Treatment-Interaction' will likely remain an empty phrase as long as aptitudes are measured by micrometers and environments by divining rods" (p. 374).

Why Educators Have Difficulty Conceptualizing Educational Environments

To a teacher, the very idea of characterizing or describing an educational environment is likely to seem at best an academic exercise. If the question is made more specific by asking the teacher to describe his own "way of teaching" in a particular class, he may understand the question but will have difficulty answering it. Because teachers must provide educational environments for five or six hours a day, they cannot ordinarily afford to be very self-reflective about their teaching. They simply do not have the time. However, if the time pressure were relieved, chances are most teachers would still have difficulty describing what they do.

We believe that the main reason for this is that teacher training almost never provides a language to describe different ways of teaching. If one looks at teacher-training programs, the most striking feature is that most of them fail completely to describe what teachers do, or should do. In most teacher-training programs, the educational environment of the classroom is considered primarily in terms of a "lesson plan" and secondarily with the trivia of the trainee's behavior, for example, how much he uses the chalkboard. Therefore, the major reason teachers have difficulty in describing the environments they create is the lack of a system for describing ways of teaching.

The educational decision-maker is in a similar dilemma. He is likely to consider a specific educational program or an organizational procedure, such as homogeneous grouping, as *the* environment. He is likely to be intuitively aware that different schools have different "climates," but he may have difficulty in describing such differences or how they come about.

It is clear that psychologists, teachers, and educational decision-makers need ways to describe educational environments, not only for their own specific purposes, but also to communicate with each other. Although the person and behavior components are important, the environment is essential because it describes what the educator does.

So much depends on educational environments, yet so little is known about how to describe them that any discussion is likely to be disappointing. A teacher, school superintendent, and an educational evaluator all need to describe the educational environment, though for different purposes. The remainder of this chapter discusses issues that each must face in characterizing educational environment. The discussion does not provide specific cookbook instructions for the teacher to describe classroom environments or for the educational evaluator to characterize educational programs to be evaluated, since many such specific guides are available, and frequently each situation is likely to require a different approach. The discussion is organized around the three questions mentioned earlier, since anyone attempting to describe educational environments must answer them: How much of the environment to describe? What units to employ? Whose interpretation of the environment to use?

HOW MUCH OF THE ENVIRONMENT TO DESCRIBE?

How large? A visit to a school is an opportunity to sample its educational environments. If you visit a school, you must decide how large a unit to sample: one group in a classroom, a classroom, several classrooms, or the entire school. Whatever you decide, you will nonetheless experience different chunks of the environment. When you first walk in, you will very likely receive some impression or "feel" about what the school in general is like. When you enter a classroom, you will necessarily be concerned with a smaller unit, even though for the teacher and the students in the classroom the entire school is still a part of their environment. There is no easy way to deal with these different levels of the educational environment, but it may help to have a general "taxonomy" so that one can at least know what features of the educational environment are omitted.

Describing an educational environment is similar to describing the home environment provided by parents, and Hoffman and Lippitt (1960) have suggested a system for considering parental environments that can serve as a model for viewing different levels of educational environments. The Hoffman-Lippitt system, summarized in Table 8, is a "causal sequence schema" in that the closer the environmental elements, the more likely the causal relation.

Table 8. A Causal Sequence Schema for Parent-Child Interaction

Environmental Unit	Size of Unit	Distance
1. Parental background 2. Current family setting 3. Family composition 4. Relation between parents 5. Personal characteristics of parents 6. Child-oriented parental attitudes 7. Parental behavior	Large Small	Remote Immediate

(After Hoffman and Lippitt 1960)

Thus, the most immediate environmental effect on a child at a given moment is the parent's present behavior, even though the family composition (intact or broken) affects the child as well. The present behavior of a teacher also can be said to be the most immediate environmental effect on the student. Table 8 can be adapted to describe the educational environment as follows (from the most remote to most immediate):

1. *Cultural setting:* includes national and community elements and values.
2. *Current school setting:* includes culture of the school, class values, rural-urban-suburban locale.
3. *School characteristics (or classroom characteristics):* includes size of school; number, age, and sex of students; number, age, and sex of teachers; physical characteristics, for example, open architecture.

4. *School organization (or classroom organization):* includes power relations, decision-making patterns, division of labor, communication patterns, relations among school staff, relations among students, peer influence, etc.
5. *Personal characteristics of teacher:* includes teacher characteristics specifically oriented toward the teaching function, such as personality structure, religious attitudes, social attitudes, philosophy of life, etc.
6. *Student-oriented teacher attitudes:* includes educational goals, concepts about the teacher role and the student role, attitudes toward teaching, acceptance or rejection of student, etc.
7. *Teacher behavior:* includes teaching practices, specific teaching techniques, response to student behaviors, changes in teaching strategies, etc.

Hoffman and Lippitt suggested that the order of these seven environmental variables *may* also indicate similarity. Thus, current school setting is more likely to be causally linked to school characteristics than to teacher behavior, which is further removed. However, this remains to be established. Meanwhile, the system provides a taxonomy of various levels of educational environments. Note that we can then consider the variables we are investigating more systematically: what is known about the relation of school characteristics (for example, school size) and teacher attitude? Such an approach seems more useful than arguing about whether school size is more important than teacher attitude as a feature of the educational environment. The most difficult issue in studying environmental effects is not to determine which is most important but, rather, how to consider environmental influences at different levels. Table 9 provides a basis for such integration (also see Getzels 1968).

Table 9.   Levels of Educational Environments

Environmental Unit	*Size of Unit*	*Distance*
1. Cultural setting 2. School setting 3. School characteristics 4. School organization 5. Teacher personality 6. Teacher attitude 7. Teacher behavior	Large Small	Remote Immediate

Table 9 expresses the relation in terms of Egon Brunswik's "lens model" that depicts environmental units ranging from distal (remote) to proximal (immediate) (see Snow 1968).

Table 9 provides (1) an analytic schema for viewing variables in the educational environment; (2) a basis for ordering the results of earlier investigations; (3) a reminder of what levels have been omitted; and, finally, (4) an indication of the level at which implementation is aimed, a topic discussed in Chapter 11. Regarding this last point, a psychological idea may be implemented at the level of the school setting, school organization, or at the level of teacher behavior.

To use the climate-weather analogy, the more "remote" elements of the educational environment (cultural setting, school setting, etc.) are the educational climate, while the immediate aspects, such as the teacher's behavior, are the educational weather. The educational weather of the classroom should be seen in the context of the school, community, and cultural climate.

How long? An even better example of the weather-climate distinction is the duration, or time period, over which the educational environment is described. Even within a classroom, the environment one day may not be typical of the more general climate. Like viewing the student's present behavior in developmental perspective, it is often important to view a specific class in relation to a longer time period, for example, unit, semester, or year.

One of the common difficulties in teacher-training programs is that instruction centers entirely on short-range specific teaching procedures while the evaluation of teaching methods or programs takes a long-range view. Teachers need descriptive terms that can apply to both short-range and long-range aspects of educational environments. The length of time in the environmental unit, that is, the weather-climate distinction, is similar to the contemporaneous-developmental distinction in Chapter 2 and the content (short-term) vs. process (long-term) distinction in Chapter 3.

WHAT UNITS SHALL WE EMPLOY?

Let's try to describe the educational environment of one classroom during one period. The descriptive language will probably apply to larger and smaller units and to longer and shorter time intervals, but initially the problem is more manageable if seen in relation to a specific case. This description is considered from the viewpoint of an observer; later, we consider how the same environment is seen by a teacher and by students.

An observer, attempting to characterize the environment of a specific classroom so as to distinguish it from other classrooms and from the same classroom at other times, must decide what dimensions he will use and what terms will adequately express those dimensions. Some of the terms that have been used to describe parental environments seem applicable to classroom environments. Investigators have been studying parental training practices for some time and recently have begun to approach tentative agreement about the most important dimensions of the parental environment. In summarizing this work,

Becker (1964) concluded that two dimensions of the parental environment had been identified by most investigators as important. These were the *degree of acceptance* (whether the child was accepted or rejected) and the *degree of control* (how much the parent was responsible for determining what went on). These two dimensions can be understood by considering Figure 9, which depicts the two dimensions and gives examples of different combinations of them (Schaefer 1959).

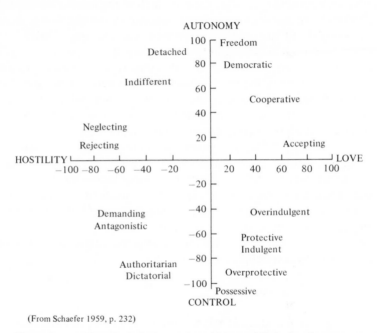

(From Schaefer 1959, p. 232)

Figure 9   A Hypothetical Circumplex of Maternal Behavior Concepts (Schaefer 1959, p. 232)

If the Figure 9 model were applied to educational environments, the observer would place the classroom environment in one of the four quadrants: autonomous-accepting, autonomous-rejecting, controlling-accepting, and controlling-rejecting. He could make such a classification by using a single judgment or by rating the classroom separately on each dimension—acceptance and control—and then combining the ratings into a pattern. Figure 9 may seem too general, but it illustrates a specific method for describing environments.

The language of Figure 9 also illustrates a problem in describing environments that was discussed in relation to descriptions of persons, that of avoiding value judgments. Within a differential framework, it does not make sense to think about one environment being absolutely better than another. Therefore, descriptive terms that minimize preconceptions about which environment is better should be used. As Cronbach (1969) observed:

> Environments cannot be arranged from good to bad, rich to poor. The highly stimulating environment that most of us think of as "rich" promotes optimal growth for some persons and may not be suitable for others. Environments can be varied along many dimensions, and the optimal with respect to each dimension depends on the person's phenotype at a given time. (p. 339)

Referring to the autonomy-control dimension in Figure 9, there is a tendency to think of autonomy as good and control as bad. However, as the Cronbach quotation illustrates, their value depends on the person and the purpose (described behavior). Harvey, Hunt, and Schroder (1961) proposed that environments be considered on a continuum ranging from unilateral to interdependent. A unilateral environment is one in which the person needs to adjust to externally defined criteria, while an interdependent environment is one in which the person himself helps define the structure. The unilateral-interdependent dimension is similar to that of degree of structure discussed in Chapter 9, and it may be slightly less value-laden.

Trying to use value-free language in any attempt to describe environments is difficult, but it is probably most difficult when describing the educational approaches that are being used in the schools. For example, if low structure is favored, it is described as "democratic" or "free" as opposed to the autocratic, "authoritarian" high structure. If one values high structure, it is described as organized and disciplined rather than "super-free" and overly permissive, as low structure might be described. Little progress is likely as long as variations in structure are confused with authoritarianism or apathetic permissiveness. Using two dimensions, as in Figure 9, may help, but it is always necessary to work at selecting terms with a minimum of value connotation.

Cronbach and Snow's comment (1969) is instructive:

> The effort to conceptualize treatment dimension is almost entirely new, and it is not astonishing that thinking is still at the level of gross concepts such as "difficulty," "degree of structure," and "degree of self-direction." There is reason enough to consider variables of this sort important, despite the ambiguity and need for sharper conceptualization which can only come from empirical research. (p. 194)

Rosenshine and Furst (1971) have reviewed the results of empirical research to identify dimensions of teaching behavior that have been found to be related to student achievement. Typically, the studies reviewed considered average class achievement gains in relation to various dimensions of teaching behavior for several classrooms. Imagine twenty Grade 6 self-contained classrooms, each with a single teacher. By calculating the gain scores on achievement tests administered before and after the school year for each class, an investigator can then consider these gains in relation to various dimensions of teacher behavior, for example, warmth, to determine whether the dimensions of teacher behavior are positively related to achievement gain. Dimensions found to be positively correlated with achievement cannot be said to cause the achievement, but such dimensions could be a promising source of variables for more systematic study. Five dimensions were found to be positively related to improvement in student achievement: clarity, variability, enthusiasm, task-orientation, and student opportunity to learn material. It is of interest that teacher warmth, a dimension similar to one of the two central parental dimensions summarized in Figure 9, was not found to be significantly related to achievement. It should be noted that these correlations are only for student achievement in general, and they do not take into account differential effects of either different achievement criteria or different kinds of students, topics we will consider in the next chapter.

Rosenshine and Furst concluded their review by suggesting that these five dimensions were promising areas for more precise investigations of the specific behaviors that comprise a dimension, for example, what are the specific teacher behaviors involved in spontaneity? These authors distinguish between dimensions and the specific behaviors from which such dimensions are inferred by noting that rating a teacher on a dimension requires a considerable amount of inference, while checking the occurrence of a specific behavior does not. They refer to dimensions and categories of teacher behavior, therefore, as high inference and low inference, respectively:

> Category systems are classified as *low-inference* measures because the items focus upon specific, denotable relatively objective behaviors (e.g., asks evaluative question), and because such events are recorded as frequency counts. Rating systems are classified as *high-inference* measures because the items on rating instruments (e.g., clarity, warmth, task-orientation, class cohesiveness) require that an observer infer constructs from a series of events. (p. 42)

High-inference measures, such as the dimensional ratings just described, must eventually be specified in behavioral (low-inference) terms to be communicated specifically in teacher training. A teacher trainee cannot become more spontaneous without some idea of the behavior associated with spontaneity. However, dimensional ratings (or concepts involving dimensions) are much more useful for analytic purposes than are low-inference measures.

Whether the same teacher behavior—saying "very good"—is counted as one occurrence of teacher approval (low inference) or taken as one of several behaviors used to infer warmth (high inference) will depend upon the purpose of the investigation and amount of information already known.

No discussion of methods for characterizing educational environments can ignore the general methods of interaction analysis that have become well known in recent years. Methods of interaction analysis differ (Simon and Boyer 1968), but most of them employ a low-inference classification system for categorizing each unit of teacher behavior for research or for feedback to the teacher. Interaction analysis systems have certainly brought teaching behavior into the open in the way Carl Rogers brought psychotherapy into the open by filming psychotherapy sessions (Chapter 10), and such objectification has been valuable. These systems also made possible the systematic analysis of teaching behavior by compiling profiles or sequential patterns to characterize the teaching environment, and the categorized profile has been used as an objective source of feedback to modify teacher behavior, especially in teacher training. The requirements of a language used to describe environments for analytic purposes are quite different from the requirements of a language used to help teacher trainees modify their behavior. The former requires a sensitive system that detects nuances and the latter requires a comprehensible system that is congruent with the way teachers think about how they teach. This problem cannot be solved by using only low-inference descriptions, and different measures may be required for each purpose.

One approach that seems potentially appropriate to both the researcher and the teacher is the "model of teaching," which Joyce and Weil (1972b) define as "a pattern or plan, which can be used to shape a curriculum or course, to select instructional materials, and to guide a teacher's actions" (p. 3). Joyce and Weil regard the approaches of Piaget (Chapter 6) and Skinner (Chapter 7) as specific models of teaching. In addition to these two classes of models—information processing and behavior modification—they recognize two other families of models, those oriented toward social relations, for example, Thelen, and those oriented toward personal growth, for example, Rogers. These models of teaching are especially appropriate for the training of teachers, but they are also appropriate for analysis of the teaching process.

Models of teaching are high-inference units in that they refer to general processes. However, a model of teaching may be stated in specific, low-inference terms through interaction analysis (Joyce and Weil 1972b). For example, a trainee learning the Bruner concept attainment model would first read about the model to understand its contextual meaning and value orientation. Next, the trainee would learn the specific moves and strategies associated with the Bruner model. Finally, the trainee would attempt to use the model in the classroom or in a microteaching situation. These authors have created a system for interaction analysis of teacher behavior for each model so that one can view a sample of teaching and compare it with the ideal model. Therefore, after attempting to teach by a specific model, a trainee can consider his attempt in terms of how closely he approximated the ideal model. He sees the disparity in his teaching performance by comparing the objective rating of his teaching behavior with the ideal model. Such objective information contrasts with the qualitative, often nonspecific criticisms of a supervisor. Thus, models of teaching are a valuable rapprochement between representations at a general level that make sense and at a specific level that describe what to do.

Put another way, a teaching model is a pattern of lower-level units and has the advantage of being both comprehensive and operationally defined. The model gives coherence and meaning to what might otherwise be an incomprehensible set of specific teaching behaviors. Of course, many educational environments may not fall into a specific model category, and other means of representation will be necessary. Nonetheless, models of teaching offer an attractive means for coordinating how a teacher views the environment and how an observer might view it.

WHOSE INTERPRETATION OF THE ENVIRONMENT?

When considering what units to employ in characterizing environments, it becomes increasingly apparent that any description depends upon whose interpretation is used. A teacher, a student, and an observer may view the same environmental event in different ways. Each one may apply different dimensions to the event, or if instructed to rate the event on a specific dimension, may rate it differently. In the last section, we noted that, although most systems for describing educational environments have been developed for use by psychological observers, systems are also needed that can be used by teachers. In teacher training, if the trainer (observer) and trainee are to communicate, they need a descriptive system they both can use. Similarly, the student's perception must be considered, and it will not always agree with either the teacher's or the observer's interpretation.

Because most systems to describe the environment are developed by researchers, they are biased in favor of observers, for example, some systems of interaction analysis require a classification of teacher behavior every three seconds, a time unit which is quite inappropriate for teachers. There is a general need for a descriptive system that will permit comparisons between the interpretations of teachers, students, and observers along the same dimensions and that will help them detect disagreements and perhaps work toward greater agreement.

In this section, we consider how teachers, students, and observers are likely to interpret environments, with some attention to how their perceptions might be compared. As in the previous section, we do not argue that one interpretation is the "right" one. Rather, we believe that some interpretations may be more valuable for certain purposes, and that more than one interpretation should be considered, whenever possible. Since the teacher is responsible for providing the classroom environment, it could be argued that his interpretation is most important. However, learning occurs in the student's head, so one could view the student's interpretation as most important. Or it could be argued that the observer, because of his objectivity, is the best interpreter. All three arguments can be rejected in favor of a more balanced construction of what an environment "really" is. Rather than argue about whose viewpoint is most important, different viewpoints for characterizing educational environments are considered. An ideal characterization would take account of all three interpretations, their similarities and differences. This would be possible only if we had a descriptive method for recording the viewpoints of the teacher, student, and observer in comparable terms.

To understand the complexity of educational environments, imagine that you have just entered a classroom and are attempting to understand what is going on. One of the students *might* be experiencing the voice of the teacher, the brightness of the sun in his eyes, the movement of the second hand on the wall clock, the color of the book cover on his desk, and so on. How does the environment look from the teacher's eyes? The teacher probably feels that he is providing some educational environment through his words and actions. He *may* feel that at the moment he is making a statement that will clarify the topic and/or he is being warm and accepting. As the observer, you may have an altogether different view of the educational environment. You may count the number of questions that the teacher asks or note the number of times the teacher says "good" or "right." What is important for the observer is to be aware of these other perspectives and to realize that the student and teacher can usually express their interpretations if asked.

Taking a more specific example, assume the teacher has just said, "An understanding of history requires that we learn something about how historians come to their conclusions." Consider how this specific statement might be interpreted by the teacher, student, and observer. From the teacher's viewpoint, he might see this particular statement as the organizer for material to follow. The student may decide that it is incomprehensible. The observer codes it as a lecture statement.

Differences between the student's perception and the observer's perception are referred to as the subjective-objective distinction, respectively. Whether to define the environment in terms of the subjective experience of the person (student) or in terms of an objective report (observer) is a recurrent issue on which a psychologist, if he is to characterize environments, must make some decision. Many early psychologists, such as J. R. Kantor, observed that persons reacted only to that portion of the stimulus that was apprehended, that is, "the stimulus function." More recently Kagan (1967) has suggested that "man reacts less to the objective qualities of external stimuli than he does to categorization of those stimuli" (p. 132).

The subjective-objective issue is further complicated because the teacher's perception of the environment may be at odds with both the subjective and objective interpretations. However, the teacher's interpretation must also be considered, since the environment is that element over which he has at least some control. This is not to say that the physical presence of a teacher is required to define an educational environment—if a student is the object of some form of programmed instruction, then only the subjective and objective views are relevant. It might be noted in passing that more information is needed about the differential effects of environments that include or do not include a human being.

There are as many examples of the disparity between teacher-student interpretations as there are between observer-student interpretations, for example, a teacher might compliment a student and feel himself to be accepting, while the student might understand the remark as an attempt to flatter or to control through flattery. It is obviously impossible to analyze classroom situations by assessing the interpretations of every student, but the practical impossibility of taking account of all interpretations does not make each of them less important.

Distinguishing between different interpretations of the environment is necessary, particularly if it is assumed that teaching is more effective when the perceptions of the environment held by teacher and student are similar. Congruence between student and teacher perception of the environment might indicate how well the teacher is "tuning in" to the student's frame of reference.

How teachers view environments. There is little systematic information about teachers' perceptions of environments. Many teachers have been taught to think of the educational environment as the curriculum and teaching in terms of "covering" the curriculum at a certain speed. Teaching seen as rate of presentation is closely related to the conception of the students rate of learning: slow learners require slower presentation, while fast learners require a more rapid presentation. The idea may seem overly simple, yet this notion is probably the cornerstone of whatever adaptation to individual differences occurs. It derives not only from thinking of students on a slow-fast dimension, but also from a conception of learning as being equal to a certain specified amount of information. This view, often referred to as the "mug and jug theory," in which the teacher pours from the jug into the mug, or student's head, leads to an emphasis on how fast the jug is poured.

A second way in which teachers learn to think about educational environments is in terms of techniques or methods. Thus, a teacher may consider variations in specific techniques—film, case study, debate, field trip, role playing—or variations of methods, such as lecture or discussion.

General dimensions such as "degree of structure" are not especially meaningful for teachers unless they can be translated into specific procedures along the dimension. To communicate with teachers, psychologists must spend more time learning about how the teacher sees the environment and how much variation the teacher thinks possible. It is only within this interpretive framework that the teacher is likely to modify his teaching behavior.

How students view environments. If little is known about how teachers view environments, even less is known about how students interpret educational environments. Students probably emphasize those dimensions central to characterizing parental environments: degree of acceptance and degree of control. Thus, students view teachers in terms of acceptance-rejection and are sensitive to the degree of control as expressed in terms of a teacher's strictness. Secondary students are especially aware of the pattern of teacher-student responsibility in the educational environment. They are particularly aware of how much independence and autonomy they are given and how responsive the teacher is to their interests.

Students also tend to view environments in general evaluative terms related to their positive or negative feelings. A particular environment may be described as interesting or boring, and since students have recently become much more vocal about insisting that environments be interesting, or at least not boring, if one takes account of a student's eye view, it is impossible to ignore this feature.

If we are concerned with assessing a student's interpretation of the environment, we can obtain measures of his subjective perceptions of the educational experience, for example, a student's perception of teachers. The Program Climate Questionnaire (Hunt and Hardt 1967) and the College Characteristics Index (Stern 1970) are instruments for measuring a student's subjective interpretation of the environment. For example, the students are asked to respond to a statement, such as "The teachers are very strict," or to rate a teacher as follows:

Your teacher

1 2 3	4 5 6	7 8 9
Makes you do what	Makes you do what	Lets you make
he wants to do	he wants to do some-	your own decisions
most of the time	times	most of the time

(From Tuckman, 1968)

How psychological observers view environments. We have already indicated that psychologists tend to look at educational environments through the grids of rating scales or classification systems. It may also be instructive to consider more generally how psychologists view environments and, specifically, their experimental manipulation of environments, called independent variables.

A psychological analysis usually considers the environment in terms of "stimulus factors" that can be varied in experiments. Psychologists have used such units as stress, amount of reward, or status of a speaker to define the psychological environment. Unfortunately, the emphasis has been on those elements that could be varied systematically rather than on their correspondence to the actual environment that persons experience. The "environment" of the psychological experiment is likely to be perceived quite differently by the experimenter and by the subject. Psychologists have recently acknowledged this variation by referring to the "task demand" of the experiment, or that part of the experiment that gives the subject his own interpretation of what the experimenter expects him to do.

For a nonpsychologist to make any sense out of the ways psychologists conceptualize and represent environments, it is important to realize that one of the guiding principles is the description of the environment as it is seen during what learning theorists call the "trial." Most of the "learning curves" reproduced in educational psychology texts are based on definition of the environment in terms of trials. That the unit of a trial does not translate into classroom practice is probably one of the most fundamental reasons for the nonrelevance of studies in learning to learning itself. Once the psychologist has established his basic temporal unit, he gives it conceptual significance by speaking of a "rewarded" trial, a "nonrewarded" trial, or a series of trials with a mixed pattern of reinforcement. Such generalizations, however, are educationally useless unless they are accompanied by a definition of what constitutes a trial in the classroom. Even the notion of a dimension may be somewhat arbitrary.

ALTERNATIVE EDUCATIONAL ENVIRONMENTS

One way to adapt to differences among students is to provide alternative educational environments, a procedure that sounds reasonable but is difficult to implement. Educational alternatives are difficult to initiate primarily because an alternative educational environment must be comprehensible to teachers, students, parents, and observers alike, who rarely agree in their description of a specific educational environment.

Consider an example in which two high schools are to provide alternative environments (D. E. Hunt 1972). The two schools are to differ primarily in their degree of structure: School A being more structured and School B less structured. One reason for selecting variation in structure to define the alternatives is its relation to variation in student learning style (Chapter 9). However, for present purposes, this project illustrates the problem of communicating a specific characteristic—degree of structure—to students, parents, teachers, school officials, and educational researchers.

The term degree of structure is, of course, general and therefore open to differences in interpretation, but it has the potential value of being understood by all parties. Since students were given the option of which school to attend, it was important that they and their parents knew how the two schools differed. First, the idea of difference in structure was described by use of a dimension:

High Structure	Low Structure

with a number of examples. Next, the two schools were described as providing a variety of experiences, that is, School A was not all high structure and School B was not all low structure, as follows:

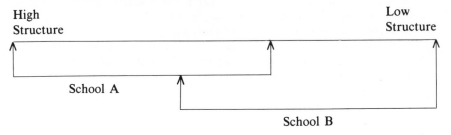

The following specific description of School A as given to the student illustrates how this school was defined:

SCHOOL A "THE EDUCATIONAL CLIMATE"

To the student:

What will distinguish School A from other schools is what we have called the "educational climate" of the school. Most of you will know that the word climate refers to the overall condition of the environment in which you live. At School A, you will be living and working in a climate which will be controlled in a number of very important ways.

What kind of climate can you expect to find at School A? As you will see from the description of courses, School A will offer you a wide variety of academic, commercial, and technical subjects which will be designed for students of differing abilities. Some of these subjects are compulsory as we believe that they are essential to the general development of every student, whatever his abilities may be. Regardless of your abilities, however, the school expects that only your best efforts are worthy of you in both the subjects you study and in your contribution to the school community through your participation in the program of activities in the school.

It is the intention of the school that the courses of study will help you to develop both mental and physical agility and to realize the value of knowledge for its own sake, in addition to its "usefulness." Subjects will be studied in a logical and orderly fashion in courses carefully designed by your teachers to develop both your knowledge of the subject and the different kinds of thinking involved in each subject.

You will be expected to meet realistic class standards set by your teachers. If you find that the class standard is not high enough for you, we expect that you will set your personal standards higher than those of the class. If you feel that your abilities are not as strong as those of others in a course, you will have to set your personal sights somewhat lower for that course. But you must remember that nothing but your best is good enough, either for you or for School A.

Recently, a great deal has been said about the importance of the development of the individual. School A will offer you every opportunity to develop your individual abilities to their fullest potential. We believe, however, that you will reach your full personal growth only when you understand that you are part of a community, a community which will grow and develop along with you as you contribute to it. Consequently, you will be expected to respect the dignity of others and to be aware that all members of the School A community deserve the same rights and privileges that you expect for yourself. We hope that you will come to realize the value and importance of service to society by accepting the responsibility of assisting others and by working for the improvement of your school community. We regard this as one of the most important aspects of the School A climate.

When you are considering if School A is the school for you, ask yourself these questions and try to answer them as honestly as you can. If your answer is yes to any of the questions, School A may be the type of school in which you will learn best. It is important for you to realize that your decision about whether School A is your kind of school will depend primarily on your own honest evaluation of yourself and the guidance of your parents and teachers.

1. Has it been your experience that you are happier in an atmosphere where the academic requirements *and* the requirements of behavior are very clear to you and your teachers?
2. Has it been your experience that you learn better in a program which is presented in a logical and orderly fashion?
3. Are you the kind of student who can find real satisfaction in your growth as an individual by contributing your best to your school community while developing your own personal aims?
4. Are you the kind of student who finds that success means more to you when you face and overcome difficulties rather than avoiding them?

Note that the climate of School A is described *both* in terms of school organization—attendance, discipline, etc.—and classroom climate and structure.

Because School A was new, a new teaching staff was selected, and the following description is the version of School A characteristics given to prospective teachers:

SCHOOL A'S EDUCATIONAL CLIMATE

It is our intention to foster a commitment to learning on the part of both students and teachers—a commitment which recognizes that only an individual's best efforts are worthy of him. This pursuit of excellence is central to the purpose of the school and gives rise to our motto: Nothing but our best is good enough

The importance of knowledge, not narrowly defined as fact, but more broadly defined as concepts, structures, and methods of discovery peculiar to the subject will be stressed. The curriculum will develop the student's mental and physical agility and help him recognize the intrinsic, as well as the more utilitarian, value of knowledge. Our approach to curriculum is one which emphasizes a structured, orderly style. The sequence of presentation of each subject will be largely determined by the inherent logic of the subject matter. Frequent references to pre-established goals for a course, coupled with specific instruction will keep the student aware of where he is heading, how he is getting there, and why.

Class standards which are realistic and compatible with the abilities of the class will be set by the teacher. It is expected that most students will want to modify the class standards slightly to match their own abilities. For example, a student may feel that the class average is not high enough for him and he would thus set his personal standards higher than the group's. Similarly, another student might recognize that his abilities in a particular subject are not as strong as those of most others in the class and, while still striving to do his very best, would set his personal standard somewhat lower than the group's. Clear, frequent evaluation and reporting will be provided as a means of giving students feedback as to how well they are measuring up to their own and the class standards.

Success in any endeavor is more meaningful to an individual if it results from a considerable effort expended by him and if there is a possibility of failure. Therefore we intend to encourage students and staff to accept the inevitable difficulties encountered in learning as a challenge to be faced and overcome rather than to reject or avoid them as an affront to individuality.

The school will offer a range of courses to suit all abilities and interests. General and Advanced phases will be available in most technical, commercial, and academic subjects with Basic, Non-phased and Enriched phases available on a more limited basis. Each student will study required subjects, selecting in each case the most appropriate phase. The student will then make a limited number of choices from the optional academic, technical, and commercial subjects.

School A recognizes the importance of good pedagogy to the educational process and to that end expects its teachers to have:

(a) a degree of excellence in, and a continuing interest in learning more about their chosen areas of study;

(b) an awareness of the interrelated nature of various aspects of knowledge and experience;

(c) the ability to co-operate with their colleagues;

(d) a conviction that the school's approach to learning is valid, and a commitment to it;

(e) a genuine liking for young people and a talent for working with them without compromising their own essential dignity and integrity.

The structure of the school was described both in terms of the entire school and instructional procedures. Similar descriptions were also made for School B.

Teaching methods may be considered in terms of their degree of structure, as the following table from Joyce and Weil (1972b) indicates:

Table 10.   Classification of Models by Amount of Structure

Name of Model	Amount of Structure
1. Inductive (Taba)	Moderate
2. Inquiry Training (Suchman)	High
3. Science Inquiry Model (Schwab)	Moderate
4. Jurisprudential Teaching (Oliver and Shaver)	High
5. Concept Attainment (Bruner)	Moderate
6. Developmental (Piaget)	Can vary from low to high (usually high)
7. Advance Organizer (Ausubel)	High
8. Group Investigation (Thelen)	Low
9. Social Inquiry (Massialas and Cox)	Moderate
10. Laboratory Method (National Training Laboratory)	The T-Group is exceedingly low structure while the exercises can be moderately structured
11. Non-Directive Teaching (Rogers)	Low
12. Classroom Meeting (Glasser)	Moderate
13. Synectics (Gordon)	Moderate
14. Awareness Training (Shutz)	Moderate to Low
15. Conceptual Systems (Hunt)	Varies from Low to High
16. Operant Conditioning (Skinner)	High

(From Joyce and Weil 1972b, p. 305)

The creation of a specific educational alternative, such as School A, therefore involves all the problems we have discussed in the chapter. For example, is it possible to provide alternatives which will not be polarized into good and bad? As noted earlier, some persons will think of School A as "authoritarian," while others will think of it as "intellectually oriented." To some, School B will seem "too permissive," while to others it may seem to be "growth-oriented."

We used this example of two alternative high schools because we believe that the most valuable descriptions of educational environments will be those that are understood by students, teachers, school officials, and psychological observers. Students need to know so they can make informed choices among environments. Teachers and school officials need to know so they can provide such environments. Psychological observers need to know so they can guide the staff in maintaining such environments.

Summary

From the teacher's viewpoint, the B-P-E formula can be restated as E:P $\longrightarrow$ B, which emphasizes the critical nature of describing the educational environment. After considering some of the reasons for difficulty in describing educational environments, the most important being the need to decide what to omit, three major issues in describing educational environments were considered: (1) how much of the environment to describe? (2) what units to employ? and (3) whose interpretation of the environment to employ? Dealing with these three questions makes it clear that any description of an educational environment is necessarily incomplete, and rather than argue about the relative merits of various incomplete descriptions, it seems more productive to clarify one's purpose and identify the persons with whom one wishes to communicate in deciding how to describe an educational environment.

Educational environments may be described in terms of the level or size of unit (varying from the culture to the specific teacher behavior) as well as length of time. Viewing environmental descriptions in terms of time was considered on a short term–long term or "weather-climate" dimension, which is similar to the contemporaneous-developmental dimension in describing the person and the content-process dimension in describing behavior. The dimensions of autonomy-control and acceptance-rejection and the model of teaching illustrated some of the units to employ. The same educational environment may be viewed differently by the student and by an observer (the subjective-objective distinction), and the teacher's view may also differ, which underlines the necessity for obtaining descriptions from more than one viewpoint.

Finally, an example of educational environments in which students select between two alternative high schools that vary in degree of structure was used to illustrate some of the specific issues in describing educational environment.

SUGGESTED READINGS

Cronbach, L. J. "The Logic of Experiments on Discovery." In *Learning by Discovery: A Critical Appraisal,* edited by L. S. Shulman and E. R. Kaislar, pp. 76–92. Chicago: Rand McNally & Co., 1966.

Joyce, B. R., and Weil, M. *Models of Teaching.* Pp. 1–28. Englewood Cliffs, N.J.: Prentice-Hall, 1972.

Kagan, J. "On the Need for Relativism." *American Psychologist* 22 (1967):131–142.

Rosenshine, B., and Furst, N. "Research on Teacher Performance Criteria." In *Research in Teacher Education,* edited by B. O. Smith, pp. 37–72. Englewood Cliffs, N.J.: Prentice-Hall, 1971.

Shulman, L. S. "Reconstruction of Educational Research." *Review of Educational Research* 40 (1970):371–396.

Solomon, D.; Rosenberg, L.; and Bezdek, W. E. "Teacher Behavior and Student Learning." *Journal of Educational Psychology* 55 (1969):23–30.

chapter 5

CONCEPTS OF INTERACTION

This chapter deals with B-P-E interactions, specifically the differential effects of environment on behavior and person-environment interactions. As stated in Chapter 1, a differential, interactive approach is necessary both to understand the complexities of the educational process and to coordinate psychology and education. To understand the interaction between components first requires a knowledge of each separate component. The descriptions of different concepts of persons, behavior, and environment in the preceding chapters should be borne in mind when considering interaction among the components. This chapter will describe how to look at psychological research and educational practice from a B-P-E, or interaction, viewpoint. Like earlier chapters, it is intended to help the reader try this way of thinking for himself. It is not intended to provide interactive solutions. The next five chapters describe how specific psychological theories provide more specifically useful information when viewed in B-P-E terms.

The first step in planning an educational program is often to pose such questions as, "What is the best educational procedure?" or "What is the best way to teach?" Although seemingly reasonable in their simplicity, questions in this form are unanswerable because they do not consider the kind of effect (B) or the kind of student (P). This tendency to look for answers to oversimplified questions is not limited to education. In psychotherapy, questions are also often posed in simple (unanswerable) terms, "Which form of treatment is better?"

The B-P-E way of thinking provides an analytic framework for posing such complex questions in a way that can be understood and answered. To repeat, the B-P-E model is *not* a theory in itself but a metatheory, or a way of thinking about theories. Posing questions in general terms, such as "Which single approach is generally best?" is also a way of thinking, but one that is unlikely to produce useful answers. Assuming that useful answers are more likely to come from answerable questions, we propose that the B-P-E paradigm provides a way of thinking about what might otherwise be an overwhelmingly complex problem.

Further, one need not use the symbols B, P, E; one can use S-O-R (Stimulus-Organism-Response) or indeed X, Y, Z, if these are more compatible. The point is that clearly defined categories are required to designate these components. If one rejects a differential approach, then he must either accept the general effects model (Which way is generally better?) or find another alternative for taking account of differential effects.

The B-P-E way of thinking should be as valuable for the teacher as for the psychologist. The teacher can benefit from viewing his work as directing an educational approach (E) toward his students (P) to produce a desired effect (B). Viewing what happens in a classroom in E:P $\longrightarrow$ B terms emphasizes the need for a teacher's having workable conceptions of environments, persons, and behaviors. Of course, no teacher can be aware of a minute-by-minute analysis of his way of teaching (E) and its effects (B). However, the descriptions suggested in the last three chapters should help in making such a E:P $\longrightarrow$ B analysis. Thus, a teacher may consider how different ways of teaching which vary, for example, in student responsibility, such as lecture or group discussion (E), produce different effects, such as recall or comprehension (B), in different types of students, such as conforming or independent (P). Although person-environment interaction (how different educational approaches are more beneficial for some students than others) has been emphasized, differential environment-behavior effects (how different ways of teaching produce different effects) are also important, and, of course, a comprehensive understanding requires all three.

Similarly, the psychologist can think of his research investigation as a treatment (E) given to an experimental subject (P) to observe the effects (B). In addition to its value for each separate discipline, the B-P-E paradigm may be used to estimate the potential educational relevance of psychological ideas. This chapter discusses E-B effects, P-E effects, and E-P-B interaction with a consideration of how one can best discover such interactions. Practical applications of interaction and differential effects (Should the teacher use homogeneous grouping?) are discussed in Chapter 11.

Differential Effects of Environment on Behavior (E-B)

Following the process-content distinction in Chapter 3, some educational environments are more likely to produce process behavioral outcomes, while others are more likely to produce content changes. Most teachers know that different ways of teaching produce different results, though they may not have verbalized this knowledge. For example, a lecture may lead to greater recall of facts, while a discussion may give the students greater opportunity to question and form hypotheses, as follows:

Environment	Behavior
Lecture	Recall of facts
Discussion	Questions and Hypothesis-Formation

The more clearly the teacher is able to distinquish different behavioral outcomes, the more likely he is to observe the different kinds of environment that produce them. A study by Solomon, Rosenberg, and Bezdek (1964) investigated the different kinds of learning (B) produced by different teacher characteristics (E). They found that the behavioral outcome, factual gain, was primarily a function of the teacher's clarity. However, teacher clarity did not affect the student's gain in comprehension, which was affected by the teacher's energy and flamboyance. These results may be diagrammatically represented as follows:

Environment (Dimension of teaching)	Behavior (Achievement outcome)
Clarity	Factual gain
Energy, flamboyance	Comprehension gain

When designing experiments, psychologists should attempt to distinguish the nature of behavioral outcomes. For example, answering the question, "Which is the better way to change a person's attitude—to give only one side of the argument or to give both sides?" depends upon not only the kind of person (P) but also the kind of attitude change desired (B). Psychological experiments frequently deal with a single behavioral effect and are used to draw general conclusions that ignore multiple effects, For example, a summary statement that "repetition facilitiates learning," without any indication of what kind of learning, is not very useful. Many laboratory studies of learning are designed to investigate only the acquisition of a specific correct response. Therefore, conclusions from such studies neglect the effect on other more complex behavioral outcomes, such as problem solving skill and attitude toward the material. The E-B formulation is a reminder of what may have been omitted.

A good example of a study in which multiple effects are considered is that of Worthen (1969). He investigated the question, "Which method of instruction is better, expository or discovery?" by including separate behavioral effects: initial learning and retention and transfer. He found that when a criterion of initial concept learning was used, the expository approach was superior. However, when the criterion of retention or transfer was used, the discovery approach was superior. These results may be considered in diagrammatic form as follows:

Environment (Instructional mode)	Behavior (Learning criterion)
Expository	Initial learning
Discovery	Retention or transfer

Worthen's results show that no answer to the question of the relative superiority of a discovery approach can be obtained without reference to the criterion measure for indexing achievement (B). The effects of a discovery approach also depend upon the kind of student (P-E) to which that approach is directed, as will be described in Chapter 9.

Cognitive and affective outcomes also may be differentially influenced by environment. Some approaches may produce satisfaction and poor performance, while others may produce dissatisfaction and good performance. It may seem reasonable to think that people learn better when they are happy, but much more information is required to establish the validity of the assumption. Differential analysis should facilitate such work and it may be that "Happy in what way?" is the real question.

Person-Environment Interactions

The teacher's view of differential effects is nicely described by Torrance (1965):

> I suppose teachers have always been intuitively aware of the fact that, when they change their method of teaching, certain children who have appeared to be slow learners or even non-learners became outstanding achievers and some of their former star learners became slow learners. They have also learned that when they change the nature of the test used for assessing achievement, such as from a multiple-choice test to one requiring creative application of knowledge and decision making, the star learners may change position in class ranking markedly. (p. 253)

Torrance refers both to E-B and P-E effects and to their interaction.

As we note in greater detail in Chapter 10, when Carl Rogers translated his theory of nondirective or client-centered counseling into educational implications in his book *Freedom to Learn* (1969), he advocated use of the student-directed approach for all students. However, a passage in Chapter 1 of his book describes differential (P-E) effects that demonstrate a student-directed approach does not work with all students. A Grade 6 teacher has tried a nondirective or student-centered approach with her class, and the following comments show its differential effects.

> Some children continued to be frustrated and felt insecure without teacher direction. Discipline also continued to be a problem with some, and I began to realize that although the children involved may need the program more than the others, I was expecting too much from them, too soon— they were not ready to assume self-direction *yet*. Perhaps a gradual weaning from the spoon-fed procedures was necessary.
> I regrouped the class—creating two groups. The largest group is the non-directed group. The smallest is teacher-directed, made up of children who wanted to return to the former teacher-directed method, and those who, for varied reasons, were unable to function in the self-directed situation.
> I would like to have waited longer to see what would have happened, but the situation for some disintegrated a little more each day—penalizing the whole class. The disrupting factor kept everyone upset and limited those who wanted to study and work. So it seemed to me best for the group as a whole as well as the program to modify the plan. (C. R. Rogers 1969, p. 15)

Operating from a general-effects model, the teacher was understandably but unnecessarily frustrated because some students could not profit from a nondirective approach *yet*. A differential approach that takes into account different student needs and different instructional requirements would alleviate this unnecessary frustration. The example may be seen as follows:

Person (Type of student)	Environment (Optimal approach)
Self-directed	Nondirected
Nonself-directed	Teacher-directed

The point of this B-P-E analysis is that a teacher can work more effectively if he makes such distinctions. In a frequently quoted observation, Cronbach (1967) noted that some teachers may overdifferentiate in terms of individual differences, and this may be true for a few teachers. However, such teachers would also be more open to revising their adaptations in an appropriate direction and would thus be more susceptible to training than would teachers who treat all students alike. Teachers may have difficulty describing exactly what they think is the best approach works for a particular student, but, as the Torrance quotation indicated, most good teachers are quite aware of P-E interactions. A psychologist may help a teacher clarify his ideas about the match between alternative ways of teaching and individual students, but the psychologist must first understand the teacher's implicit theory of matching or P-E interaction. Chapter 11 describes an example of psychologists and teachers working together to meet the student's needs by coordinating teaching methods with learning styles.

Person-environment interactions may be considered in terms of matched combinations and mismatched combinations (D. E. Hunt 1971), and the rationale of the B-P-E diagrams may be thought of in matching terms. Although we later describe how ideas of person-environment interaction are implemented, the term matching is not necessarily used as a prescription, or, as stated elsewhere:

> It is important to understand that matching is used here primarily as a description of the interactive effects of person and environment, and is a holding term to describe likely outcomes of certain interactions. It is not used in the active sense, "to match", although matching statements can be prescriptions. (D. E. Hunt 1971, p. v.)

As indicated in the previous section on environment-behavior interactions, any matching statement about person-environment interaction must specify the behavioral effects to which it applies. Person-environment combinations may be matched for one outcome but not for another. A matching statement must indicate whether it refers to satisfaction (affective) or performance (cognitive) outcomes. For example, group discussion (E) may be very satisfying (B) to some students (P) but not facilitate their performance (B). Although the term P-E interaction is used for convenience, the B is always necessary to complete the statement.

In contrast to earlier studies that investigated the general effects of praise and criticism, a study by Grace (1948) included different kinds of students as a variable under different incentive conditions. She found that when students were given tasks under three different incentive conditions—positive, negative, and neutral—some students performed best under positive, some under negative, and others under neutral conditions. When the analysis was extended to consider the specific characteristics of those students performing best under each of the three conditions, she found that those students who performed best under positive or neutral conditions were relatively well adjusted, while those who performed best under negative incentive conditions were poorly adjusted. This pattern is shown in the following diagram:

Person (Type of student)	Environment (Most effective incentive)	Behavior
Well-adjusted	Positive or neutral	Performance on form board problem
Poorly adjusted	Negative	

In a more systematic investigation, Mandler and Sarason (1952) found that persons high in test anxiety performed best when nothing was said to them (neutral), and less well when praised or criticized. Neither study is intended to prescribe the use of a particular positive or negative incentive, that is the results of the Grace study do not mean that poorly adjusted children should be criticized. Rather, the results serve as reminders of the limited generality of conclusions based only on the general effectiveness of incentives.

In the area of attitude change, the findings of McClintock (1958) are relevant:

> Our findings would seem to indicate that the understanding of the operation of certain personality syndromes is essential for the derivation of effective manipulations for producing changes in certain attitudes. On a

more applied level, the findings of this research indicate that a given influence may have little effect in moving the *total* population in the direction of that influence. What may occur is that certain types of people move predominantly in the direction of the influence, others remain relatively unaffected, and the remainder move in an opposing direction. The results of the ethnocentric influence dramatically demonstrate this. For the total population subjected to this influence, half move in the direction of the influence and half against it. When we discriminate between low and high ego-defenders within the total population, we find that within the low group twice as many people move against the induction as with it, whereas within the high ego-defensive group, twice as many people move with the induction as against it. Thus, knowing the personality structure of the individual seems necessary for the theoretical understanding of the functioning of certain attitudes, and for the devising of appropriate and effective methods for changing attitudes. (pp. 492–493.)

The McClintock results may be represented diagrammatically as follows:

Person (Personality characteristic)	Environment (Most effective communication)	Behavior
Other-directed	Informational approach	Attitude change
Moderate or low ego-defense	Insight approach	

A few studies have indicated differential P-E effects of computer-assisted instruction. Buckland found, for example, that high ability students profited more from a "block-scrambled" program than from a carefully sequenced program.

Person (Student)	Environment (Program)	Behavior
High ability	Block-Scrambled	Acquisition and transfer
Low ability	Standard sequence	

Person-Environment combinations or matching statements may be investigated without altering educational arrangements. This point is nicely illustrated in a study by Washburne and Heil (1960) entitled, "What Characteristics of Teachers Affect Children's Growth?"

The design of this study is more relevant to the present discussion than the results because it serves as a paradigm for investigating P-E interactions. The basic design was an investigation of gain in student academic achievement (B) as a function of teacher type (E) and student type (P). The design is summarized in the following chart:

Person (Student type)	Environment (Teacher type)	Behavior
Conformers Opposers Waverers Strivers	Turbulent Self-controlling Fearful	Gain in academic achievement

The teacher and student types are rather unconventional and not clearly described, but they serve, nonetheless, as illustrations. Once each of the 49 teachers and 580 students were classified, the student achievement gain was analyzed in terms of teacher type, student type, and the (P-E) interactions indicated in Table 11. The upper left-hand entry means, for example, that for the 62 "conformers" who were in a class with a "turbulent" teacher, the mean achievement gain was $+.87$. Note that these 62 students were not homogeneously grouped, that is, in each of their classes there were also "opposers," "waverers," and "strivers."

Table 11 demonstrates that it is not always necessary to alter educational arrangements to investigate P-E interactions, since all the data are based on an after-the-fact analysis in which the "matching" occurred only on paper, not in the classroom. Table 11 also illustrates that differential effects do not always occur as predicted, since the results can be described as a general effect in which self-controlling teachers produced significantly more gain than the other two teacher types ($<.01$). In terms of P-B relations, "strivers" gained more ($<.01$) than "waverers." None of the P-E interactions is significant, but there are tendencies to a match between self-controlling teachers and "conformers" and a mismatch between "turbulent" teachers and "opposers."

Table 11. Mean Gain in Achievement for One Year

Teacher type	Conformers	Opposers	Waverers	Strivers	Total
A Turbulent (12)	+ .87(62)	+ .64(40)	+ .85(28)	+ .99(36)	+ 1.01(166)
B Self-controlling (15)	+ 1.10(47)	+ 1.10(57)	+ .94(17)	+ .87(40)	+ 1.01(161)
C Fearful (22)	+ .76(94)	+ .83(72)	+ .67(30)	+ .92(57)	+ .79(253)
Total (49)	+ .88(203)	+ .88(169)	+ .76(75)	+ .96(133)	+ .89(580)

( ) = Number
(Washburne and Heil, 1960)

The discussion of person-environment interactions has emphasized the effect of the environment on the person. (E $\longrightarrow$ P). However, as Bell (1968) has pointed out, the effects of the child on the parent (Person $\longrightarrow$ Environment), and also the effects of the student on the teacher, are important. The effects of the student on the teacher may be more difficult to investigate, but it is possible, as illustrated in a study by Siegel (1966). Institutionalized retarded children of varying levels of verbal ability (P) were instructed by adults (E). Siegel's concern was the "pull" characteristics of persons of differing verbal abilities. He found systematic differences in adult vocal response (E) to the children of different verbal ability (P). Adult trainers used more redundant speech patterns with the low-level children than with the high-level children. These adults were volunteer workers, unaware of the nature of the children. Therefore, even though the training agent may be unaware of the pull characteristics of the students, he may be influenced by them, and such influence should be borne in mind in considering person-environment interactions. How much adaptation a teacher makes to a student pull also depends on the teacher's repertory of skills (D. E. Hunt 1970).

An Example of Differential Effects

A study by Noy and Hunt (1972) is a simultaneous investigation of variations in person, environment, and behavior. This investigation considered the differential effects of a student-directed instructional approach as compared with a system-directed instructional approach (E) upon students who varied in their conceptual level (P) (see Chapter 9). Effects were indexed by variations in the cognitive level (B) as summarized:

Environment (Instructional approach)	Person (Conceptual level of student)	Behavior (Cognitive level of outcome)
Student-directed	Low	Recall Comprehension
System-directed	High	Synthesis

The student-directed approach (E) was superior for knowledge acquisition, but no difference between instructional approaches was found for the higher behavioral levels of comprehension and synthesis. However, students of high conceptual level (CL) were superior to low CL students at all levels, which emphasizes the importance of considering both the characteristics of the learner and the level of behavioral objectives in evaluating instructional approaches.

These results illustrate the same point as the Washburne-Heil results (Table 11): there is no guarantee that person-environment interactions will occur in research studies that consider variations in the person and the environment. In the study by Noy and Hunt, general effects attributable to both the person and the environment were found, but there was no interaction between these effects. However, knowledge that the behavior or kind of person is relatively unaffected by variation in the environment is as important as knowledge about specific person-environment combinations.

Criteria for Person-Environment Interactions

Several B-P-E diagrams have been included in the text to familiarize the reader with a B-P-E way of thinking. These diagrams apply to psychological experiments and to what goes on in a classroom. The diagrams appear in the following general form:

Person	Environment	Behavior
A	X	
B	Y	1

The diagram is shorthand for the statement, "For Person A. Environment X is likely to produce Behavior 1, while for Person B, Environment Y is likely to produce Behavior 1." The diagram may also be translated into environmental terms to read, "Environment X is more likely to produce Behavior 1 in Person A than in Person B, while Environment Y is more likely to produce Behavior 1 in Person B than in Person A." Statements of person-environment interaction can thus be phrased in different forms for different purposes.

We need to consider how we know that Person A and Environment X and Person B and Environment Y are matched. What is the evidence for the specific person-environment combinations? Up to this point, the B-P-E diagrams have been introduced to give an idea of the interactive way of thinking, and the nature of the supporting evidence for the diagrams has been deemphasized. In most cases, specific interactions were based on empirical evidence from controlled experiments, for example, the first diagram in Chapter

1 showing the differential effects of praise and criticism on extroverts and introverts was based on the results of an experiment by Thompson and Hunnicutt (1944). Empirical evidence is important, of course, but it is not the only kind of evidence; nor is the level of statistical significance reached by such evidence the only measure of its acceptability.

To some psychologists, the idea that empirical evidence is not the only possible criterion may seem preposterous. For example, the statement "There is no evidence for an interaction of curriculum treatments and personological variables" (Wittrock and Wiley 1970, p. 210) is obviously based only on empirical criteria. However, we propose to consider other criteria in addition to empirical evidence for two reasons. First, the empirical evidence that psychological investigations provide is necessarily limited in generality and can never be completely objective. Second, educational practitioners use different criteria for evaluating P-E interactions than researchers do, and if psychological principles are to be implemented, the criteria used by practitioners must be considered (see Chapter 11). Use of multiple criteria should, therefore, provide a more comprehensive evaluation of P-E interactions.

We consider three kinds of criteria for evaluating P-E interactions: theoretical, empirical, and personal. These three criteria might apply to any domain, but here we are especially concerned with what kind of "proof" is required as evidence for a specific kind of person-environment interaction.

A *theoretical* evaluation of the Person A-Environment X and Person B-Environment Y combinations requires that the combinations be theoretically logical and consistent. Can the A-X and B-Y interactions be derived from a theory? Implicit in the theoretical criterion is the necessity for conceptualizing the process underlying the interactions—why should it be that A-X and B-Y go together? From a theoretical viewpoint, the proof for an interaction is in its logical consistency. Several examples of theoretically derived interaction are given in the next five chapters.

An *empirical* evaluation of the A-X and B-Y interactions is usually based on an experimental design as follows:

Environment

		X	Y
Person	A	#1	#2
	B	#3	#4

An *empirical* evaluation requires that both Type A and Type B persons are exposed to environments X and Y. The interaction is then evaluated statistically to find out whether the effects observed in the matched combinations, A-X (#1) and B-Y (#4), are greater than those in the two theoretically non-matched combinations (#2 and #3). The results of the study by French (1958), which are diagrammatically summarized in Chapter 2, illustrate the empirical approach. The following table of mean task scores of problem-solving effectiveness illustrates the interaction between psychological need (P) and feedback (E):

<table>
<tr><td></td><td colspan="2" align="center">Feedback Condition (E)</td></tr>
<tr><td></td><td align="center">Feeling-oriented</td><td align="center">Task-oriented</td></tr>
<tr><td>Need (P)   High affiliation</td><td align="center">38.38</td><td align="center">29.12</td></tr>
<tr><td>High achievement</td><td align="center">29.25</td><td align="center">40.50</td></tr>
</table>

Results such as these are usually treated with some form of analysis of variance. The question put to the data is: what accounts for the difference in behavior, the Environment (feedback), Person (need type), or the P-E interaction (in this case between feedback and need type)? As you can see by inspection, the upper left-hand entry, or "cell," (38.38) and the lower right-hand cell (40.50) are larger (that is, better performance) than the other two cells. In this example, neither main effect (environment or person) was statistically significant, but the interaction was highly significant (<.001). Researchers refer to this pattern of differentially matched P-E combinations where two diagonal cells are greater than the other two as a disordinal, or "crossover," interaction. It is important to realize that empirically based statements of P-E interaction derive from the results of controlled experiments that have been analyzed with a criterion of statistical significance. This is not the place for an elaborate discussion, but it should be acknowledged that criteria, such as statistical significance, although appearing precise and objective, have come under increasing criticism (for example, Bakan 1966).

The *personal* criterion involves the questions, "Does it make sense and fit in with past experience? Is it intuitively reasonable?" An example of personal criteria is the individual teacher's implicit theory of matching described in the earlier quotation by Torrance. Although both psychologists and educational practitioners apply personal criteria, the teacher is more likely to use them. The teacher may ask himself whether the A-X and B-Y combinations make sense. In answering such a question, he will resort to his own personal experience with students like these. In the French study summarized in the previous diagram one may judge in terms of one's personal criteria whether the facilitating effects of feeling-oriented feedback on high-affiliation persons and of task-

oriented feedback on high-achievement persons makes sense. To understand the personal view of P-E interaction, a teacher might simply group the students in his class according to the way of teaching that seemed better for them.

One reason why the personal criterion is more distinctive for the practitioner than for the psychologist is that the psychologist's personal criteria are likely to be inextricably interwoven with his theoretical criteria. Whether psychologists develop theories to verify their own personal beliefs or use their personal beliefs as one source of validating evidence for their theoretical arguments is unanswerable, but it seems certain that personal beliefs and attitudes influence psychologists' judgments of empirical evidence.

This inclusion of a personal criterion is in keeping with George Kelly's proposition (1955) that every person is a psychologist, in that he has his personal constructs with which he comprehends and makes sense out of his world. At a more elegant epistemological level, taking account of personal criteria is congruent with Polanyi's (1958) emphasis on tacit knowledge, or what he specifically, refers to as personal knowledge.

These three criteria are similar to what Royce (1962) described as ways of knowing. He classifies four ways of knowing and describes each one in relation to the psychological process on which it is based: rational (thinking), empirical (sensing), intuitive (feeling), which are similar to theoretical, empirical, and personal. He adds a fourth, authoritarian (believing).

AN EXAMPLE OF PERSON—ENVIRONMENT INTERACTION: DIFFERENTIAL TREATMENT OF DELINQUENTS

Although not specifically involved in education, the Community Treatment Project, or CTP (Warren and CTP staff 1966), illustrates how an idea about person-environment interaction can be evaluated by different criteria. CTP is a very sophisticated, theoretically derived differential treatment model for working with adjudicated delinquents. CTP differs from most other treatment programs in that different forms of treatment (E), especially different kinds of treatment workers, are prescribed for different kinds of delinquent youths (P). The prescriptions derive from a theory of the development of interpersonal maturity (Sullivan, Grant, and Grant 1957). Many objectives (B) of the model are complex and differ for youths at different levels of interpersonal maturity, but the immediate objective is to prevent the reoccurrence of delinquent behavior.

The heart of the CTP model is a set of prescriptions that specifies the treatment-worker characteristics most likely to be appropriate for a youth at a specific level of interpersonal maturity. A telegraphic summary of the model in B-P-E form is shown on page 123.

Person (Maturity Level)	Environment (Characteristics of treatment worker)	Behavior
Low	1. Tolerant, supportive, protective	Prevention of delinquent behavior
Medium	2. Firm, con-wise, willing to punish	
High	3. Wise, understanding, warm	

(From Grant, Warren, and Turner 1963)

We use this specific differential treatment program to consider how it might be viewed in terms of theoretical, empirical, and personal criteria.

Theoretical The theory of the development of interpersonal maturity from which the CTP model derives, considers persons at one of several hierarchically ordered stages of development. The person at the low stage primarily demands that the world take care of him. The person at the middle stage perceives the world and himself in terms of power. The person at the high stage has internalized a set of standards by which he judges his own and others' behavior. Thus, the logic of the matching model is to provide a treatment worker (environment) compatible with the person's present stage. The logic is one of contemporaneous matching and, insofar as one is persuaded by theoretical consistency, it represents supportive evidence for the model.

Empirical. Two sets of experimental results provide empirical evidence. The first study compared a group of CTP treatment youths with a comparable sample of institutionalized youths in terms of subsequent failure rate (including all revocations of parole, recommitments from the courts, and unfavorable discharge) after fifteen months of community exposure. The CTP failure rate of 28 percent was significantly lower than the 52 percent failure rate of the control group.

A second study (Palmer 1968) took advantage of the fact that it was not always possible to match the youth and the treatment worker perfectly. The CTP model may be expressed in matching terms as shown in the chart on page 124.

Each youth in the CTP program was categorized in terms of whether he had been closely matched (according to the above table) or not closely matched with his treatment worker. The failure rate for closely matched group was 19

Type of Treatment Worker

Maturity Level	Type 1	Type 2	Type 3
Low	+	0	0
Medium	0	+	0
High	0	0	+

Where + = matched
0 = mismatched

percent after fifteen months of community exposure as compared with 43 percent for the group that had not been so closely matched, and the difference was statistically significant. To the extent that one relies on the application of statistical procedures to experimental data, these findings support the interaction viewpoint.

Personal. This is a more difficult view to describe specifically because it comes from the individual's personal evaluation of the plausibility of an interaction in terms of his own past experience. It may help to think about whether it makes sense to match an immature youth who is concerned with being accepted with a treatment worker who is tolerant, supportive, and protective. How would you feel about recommending for a certain type of youth a firm, alert worker who is not afraid to punish?

Some social workers, for example, find this latter match unreasonable, and no amount of statistically significant "evidence" is likely to alter their personally based belief.

Perhaps application of the criteria to the CTP model has given some idea of the potential value of these multiple standards. We conclude this chapter by considering the sources of ideas about person-environment interaction. Many psychologists accept the logic of person-environment interactions, but, as noted earlier, do not adopt the approach because specific strategies for studying such interactions have not been made clear. In the next section, we turn to this question.

Identifying Person-Environment Interactions

The three criteria just described—theoretical, empirical, and personal—provide a basis for considering sources of information for person-environment combinations. Cronbach and Snow (1968) have made a similar proposal in suggesting the following three sources of ATI hypotheses:

(1) derived from review of literature, (2) derived from aptitude variables of particular importance for theories of cognitive and personality development, and (3) comparisons of controversial instructional methods. (p. 9)

THEORETICAL

Person-environment combinations fit or do not fit for a reason, and the better we understand this reason, the better we can derive matched combinations from theories. Why do dependent learners require more structure? Why do middle-maturity delinquents require firm treatment workers? Answering such questions requires our understanding of the *process* in which the interaction between the person and environment occurs.

Before discussing more specific theoretical ideas, it should be noted that the nature of person-environment interaction requires a language to describe interaction or relationship. As observed earlier, the first requirement is that the person characteristic and the environment characteristic be described in somewhat comparable terms. Once this has been done, then the P-E *relation* can be characterized, and this cannot be accomplished by using absolute terms, such as high, low, large, small, etc. Such terms as congruence (Stern 1970), match (Hunt 1971), or fit (Pervin 1968) are required.

One can speak of P-E interactions only in relation to a specific B. For example, theoretical models that aim for development change and growth are likely to define the match in terms of a specified degree of disparity between person and environment. Models that aim for immediate functional objectives are likely to define the match in terms of congruence, fit, or no disparity between person and environment. The latter approach is illustrated by Pervin (1968):

A "match" or "best-fit" of individual to environment is viewed as expressing itself in high performance, satisfaction, and little stress in the system whereas a "lack of fit" is viewed as resulting in decreased performance, dissatisfaction, and stress in the system (p. 56).

Snow (1970) has suggested two heuristic models for thinking about ATI relations. In some cases, the environment (treatment) may be viewed as compensating for the person's deficiency. This *compensatory model* is especially appropriate when the behavior sought is information processing as in the chart on page 126.

Person (Information processing capacity)	Environment (Optimal instructional treatment)	Behavior
Low	High structure	Effective information processing
High	Either low or high structure	

Since the person with low capacity is unable to perform the behavior, the instructional treatment compensates for this by offering him a highly structured environment, while the environment for the more capable person need not be as highly structured. Snow describes the instructional treatment (E) in the compensatory model as functioning like a prosthetic device for a particular aptitude group. He continues:

> A treatment that proves especially appropriate for a person deficient in some particular aptitude may be functioning as an "artificial" aptitude. It contains the information processing functions that the learner cannot provide for himself. (p. 21)

Using the compensatory model as a source of P-E interactions, therefore, would require a fairly thorough task analysis followed by an assessment of persons in terms of their present capacity on the tasks required. The compensatory model leads to P-E interactions only for those persons requiring the support it can provide. For others, this kind of environment may make no difference. (See Figure 16 in Chapter 9 for another example of the compensatory model.)

Some environments *may* make a difference to the capable person, and Snow proposes the *preferential model* as an alternative. In this model, the match depends entirely on the degree to which the person likes the environment. Following the preferential model, the investigator might vary environments systematically for persons of known characteristics to note their preferential reactions. Returning to the compensatory model diagram, the person high in information processing capacity might not perform well under structure because he found it unnecessarily restricting. (See Figure 17 in Chapter 9 for an example.) The compensatory and preferential models are not mutually exclusive, since the former emphasizes cognitive factors while the latter emphasizes affective factors.

Salomon (1971) has described two additional heuristic models for ATI investigators, the inducement model and the remedial model. Finally, Vale and Vale (1969) have suggested various forms of organism-environment interactions, and strategies for learning more about them.

EMPIRICAL

Although the theoretical approach is likely to be more productive, one may also use an empirical approach, or "go fishing" with a statistical dragnet. In a single experiment, for instance, one might use two or more instructional approaches (E) while studying a large number of personal characteristics simply to find out if any interactions occur (cf. Snow, Tiffin, and Seibert 1965). Vale and Vale refer to a similar approach suggested by J. C. Stanley:

> Another interesting possibility, in the case where no a priori basis for organismic classification is evident but where Subject x Treatment interaction exists in a repeated measures design, might be a computer sorting of subjects into subgroups within each of which no interaction is present. One would want to pursue this by determining the basis for the subgrouping, at which point the paradigm might be applied. (1969, p. 1106)

In a similar way, one can consider teacher-student matchings empirically without any intervention, as illustrated in Table 11. Finally, a review of the literature (Cronbach and Snow 1968; Bracht 1970; Sarason and Smith 1971) to locate empirically based interactions may provide valuable leads.

PERSONAL

Probably the best source of information for how different students learn from different approaches is to observe students or ask them. An answer to the question "How do you learn best?" for a specific student can be approached by asking the student himself, by asking his teacher, and by observing his reaction to different educational approaches. Use of options in college courses for different students (for example, Pascal and McKeachie 1970) represents one practical application of student self-matching.

Teachers' intuitive understanding of matching teaching method to student learning style should also be used more extensively. The explication of teachers' ideas about how certain students seem to learn best should not only be helpful for psychologists but also for teachers.

Summary

In this chapter, the three components—behavior, person, and environment—were combined to describe application of an interactive way of thinking to psychological ideas and educational practice. For the teacher, applying the B-P-E paradigm to classroom events involves considering what ways of teaching (E) produce what effects, for example, recall, comprehension, satisfaction (B) for what kinds of students (P). For the psychologist, it involves considering his research design in terms of the specific kinds of subjects and the specific kinds of behavior investigated.

Differential effects of environment on behavior were illustrated, for example, a lecture approach produces better initial learning but a discovery approach produces better retention and transfer. Differential effects of environment on different kinds of persons were discussed, using the concept of matching to describe person-environment combinations that were well coordinated for a particular purpose. Most teachers are aware of such differential effects but may not always have stated them explicitly. Matched person-environment combinations must always refer to a specific behavioral effect, thus a full B-P-E statement is required.

Matching statements, such as "This person is more likely to learn by experiencing this educational approach," can be evaluated through theoretical, empirical, and personal criteria. Although psychologists have emphasized the empirical basis for evaluating interactions, the importance of such statements' meeting criteria of intuitive reasonableness used by educational practitioners was emphasized. New ideas for person-environment combinations may come from theories, and experiments, but the most overlooked sources are the statements of teachers and students themselves and direct observation of how different students learn from different approaches.

SUGGESTED READINGS

Bracht, G. H. "Experimental Factors Related to Aptitude-Treatment Interactions." *Review of Educational Research* 40 (1970):627–646.

Cronbach, L. J. "How Can Instruction Be Adapted to Individual Differences?" In *Learning and Individual Differences,* edited by R. M. Gagné, pp. 23–44. New York: Macmillan Co., 1967.

Hunt, D. E. *Matching Models in Education.* Chapter 1. Toronto: Ontario Institute for Studies in Education, 1971.

Jackson, P. W. "Is There a Best Way of Teaching Harold Bateman?" *Midway,* vol. 10, no. 4 (1970), pp. 15–28.

Lesser, G. "Postscript: Matching Instruction to Student Characteristics. In *Psychology and educational practice,* edited by G. Lesser, pp. 530–550. Glenview, Illinois: Scott, Foresman & Co., 1971.

Pervin, L. A. "Performance and Satisfaction as a Function of Individual-Environment Fit." *Psychological Bulletin* 69 (1968):56–68.

Snow, R. E. "Research on Media and Attitude." *Bulletin of the School of Education-Indiana University,* vol. 46, no. 5 (1970), pp. 63–89.

Sullivan, E. V. "The Issue of Readiness in the Design and Organization of the Curriculum: A Historical Perspective." In *Curriculum Design in a changing Society,* R. N. Burns and G. Brooks, pp. 103–132, 1970.

chapter 6

COGNITIVE-DEVELOPMENTAL APPROACH:

Piaget, Bruner, Gagné, Vygotsky

As the cognitive-developmental theories of Jean Piaget have become more familiar to psychologists in the past two decades, the implications of his work for education have received increased attention. Therefore, we will consider his theories and their relevance for education within the B-P-E paradigm. Other theorists (Bruner, Gagné, Vygotsky) will be discussed as they relate to Piaget's theory. Classification of Piaget as a cognitive-developmental theorist (see Baldwin 1967; Kohlberg 1969) involves four basic assumptions. (1) Development involves basic transformations of cognitive *structure* that cannot be understood in terms of associative (S-R) bonds but must be explained in terms of organizational wholes or systems of internal relations. (However, as will be noted, Piaget's stage conception is quite different from structural concepts of other stage theories.) (2) The development of cognitive structure is a result of *interaction* between the structure of the organism and the structure of the environment; it is not the direct result of maturation or of learning. Piaget does not always specify the structure of the environment required for development, although he acknowledges the interactive nature of the environment, a point to be discussed later in more detail. (3) The cognitive structures develop through the *action* of the person on the environment. In Piaget's theory, the cognitive activities move from the sensorimotor mode through the symbolic to the verbal propositional modes, but the organization of each mode requires the action of persons on objects. Thus, cognitive-developmental theories give a primary role to the person construct in their conceptions of development. (4) The direction of development in person-environment interaction is toward higher levels of equilibrium, greater balance, adaptation at more complex levels, or reciprocity of the person with his environment.

Cognitive-developmental theories, or those meeting these four criteria, can be found in such areas as morality, ego, psychosocial, and general information processing development (Kohlberg 1969). Many cognitive-developmental theories are *stage* theories, but this is not necessarily the case. Piaget's theory is both a stage theory and a cognitive-developmental theory. His theory will first be described and then considered in relation to the B-P-E paradigm.

Theory of Intellectual Development

Piaget's theory of intellectual development will be summarized partly because of its explicit description of various stages. His theory in other areas, for example, perceptual and moral development, is less explicit in describing stages (Inhelder 1962; Kohlberg 1963), thus illustrating the point that cognitive-developmental theories are not identical to stage theories.

CRITERIA FOR A STAGE CONSTRUCT

Piaget, describes coherent stages in the direction and course of mental development.[1] The term stage is a structural term to account for the qualitative changes in children's behavior as they grow older. The criteria for stages in intelligence have been defined by Piaget's colleague, Inhelder (1962), as follows:

1. Each stage involves a period of formation (genesis) and a period of attainment. Attainment is characterized by the progressive organization of a composite structure of mental operations, (for example, the ensemble of concrete operations).

[1]This description will be schematic; the reader who desires a more complete presentation should consult Baldwin (1967), Flavell (1963), Ginsburg and Opper (1969), J. McV. Hunt (1961), and Piaget (1960). Primary French sources may be found in Flavell (1963).

2. Each structure constitutes, at the same time, the attainment of one stage and the starting point of the next, of a new evolutionary process. Thus, stages can be said to be in a *stable* stage and a *transitional* stage at the same time.

3. The order of the succession of stages is invariant, for example, the preoperational stage always occurs before the concrete operational stage for every person. If a stage is skipped, this constitutes negative evidence for the theory (Kessen 1962). Age of stage attainment varies as a function of such factors as motivation, exercise and cultural milieu.

4. The transition from an earlier to a later stage follows a process similar to integration. Earlier structures are subsumed and integrated into later structures. Thus, each earlier stage is necessarily present and integrated in the framework of the more advanced stages.

The most frequent misunderstanding of Piaget's theory is that it specifies an age for each stage. Featherstone states (1971), "Piaget has assigned these stages to definite chronological ages" (p. 26). This is not the case with Piaget or with any stage theorist. It is the *sequence* of stages that is critical, not the age at which a stage is attained.

PIAGET'S STAGE DESCRIPTION OF INTELLECTUAL DEVELOPMENT

The stages of intellectual development have varied slightly in Piaget's description, but the following are the most recent stages and substages (ages are approximate):

1. Sensori-motor stage (birth to two years)
2. Preoperational stage (two to seven years)
   (a) preconceptual thought (two to four years)
   (b) intuitive thought (four to seven years)
3. Operational stage (seven to sixteen years)
   (a) concrete operational thought (seven to eleven years)
   (b) formal operational thought (eleven to sixteen years)

These stages show how Piaget defines the concept of intelligence. Intelligence is seen as a *process* of adaptation and organization. Adaptation is the equilibration[2] occurring as the child interacts with his environment. Schemas are defined as essentially repeatable psychological units of intelligent action

---

[2]In a more recent article, Piaget has expressed a preference for "equilibration" over "equilibrium," which he feels has a static connotation. For purposes of consistency, we will use the word "equilibration" (Piaget 1965).

(Piaget 1960), that is, programs or strategies for interacting with the environment. Organization is a structural concept to describe the integration of schemas.

Adaptation involves the two invariant processes of assimilation and accommodation. Assimilation is the incorporation of the environment into present patterns of behavior. Accommodation is the change in the intellectual structure (schemas) a person must make to adjust to the demands of the environment.

Equilibration involves a balance between the processes of assimilation and accommodation. When imbalance occurs, the child is forced to change his schemas to adjust to the environment (through adaptation). When the child attempts to adapt to the environment with existing schemas, assimilation is occurring. In characterizing how past experiences are stored and affect present behavior, schemas may account for the child's perceiving the environment in terms of his existing organization. Disequilibration, or imbalance, exists when assimilation is unsuccessful. Accommodation is the result of disequilibration and the alteration of schemas as new schemas emerge. Cognitive development, or the emergence of new schemas, is marked by a series of equilibration-disequilibration states. Piaget's description of a particular stage in static terms applies when the schemas are in a state of relative equilibration. Development to the next stage involves a hierarchical reorganization of preceding and successive stages. Simply stated, the lower stage is coordinated with and integrated into the next higher stage. The general nature of development will now be described in relation to specific stages of intellectual development.

The *sensori-motor stage* begins with inborn reflex mechanisms (simple schemas) that become increasingly more complex and less reflexive as the child interacts with his environment. The sensori-motor period is exemplified by preverbal behaviors not mediated by signs and symbols. At birth, the child's reaction to the environment is determined by inborn reflex schemas, and he has no conception of object permanence, that is, he has no idea the object exists outside his perception of it. That the newborn child lacks object permanence indicates that he lacks *representative* symbolic capacity. During this period, the child is concerned with objects as objects present in his immediate field. When a toy is hidden from his view, he shows no searching movements because he lacks a schema for internal representation of the object. As he develops the concept of object permanence, he develops the capacity for symbolic representation that lays the base for early concepts of space, time, causality, and intentionality, concepts that were not present at birth.

The *preoperational stage* is subdivided into the substages of preconceptual thought and intuitive thought. In contrast to sensori-motor intelligence, adaptation during preconceptual thought is mediated by schemas of symbolic representation, that is, symbolic play, language. With the appearance of language, the objective world can be symbolized by a thought process that can be retained through primitive symbolic structures. Even though the preconceptual child's thoughts are mediated by signs and symbols in the form of words and images, the child nevertheless operates in a world of preconcepts because he cannot distinguish between the general and the particular, an essential feature of more mature thinking. Before attaining operational thought, the child's logic is transductive, which is quite different from inductive and deductive reasoning in adults. Transduction in preconceptual thought is a logic that moves from one particular instance to another. The transductive child demonstrates his logic in his uncertainty about whether the same object is reappearing or whether there are different objects in different times and places. For example, the child walking through the woods does not know whether he sees a succession of different snails or whether the same snail keeps reappearing, an example of what Piaget calls the *preconcept.*

Intuitive thought appears at approximately age four and marks the transition between preconceptual thought and the more advanced stage of concrete operations. Schemas at the intuitive level are illustrated as follows: The child is presented with two small glasses, A1 and A2, that are identical in height and width. The child alternately places beads one-by-one in each glass until both glasses are filled. The A2 glass is emptied into a taller but thinner glass B. The child in the preconceptual phase thinks that the number of beads has changed in the process, even though he realizes that no beads were removed or added. He says that there are more beads in glass B because it is taller than glass A1, or that there are more beads in glass A1 because it is wider than glass B. The child centers on one aspect of the situation, either "height" or "width," and since he cannot hold the centerings simultaneously, he is unable to solve the problem. The intuitive-stage child remains prelogical, but decenterings occur where previous centerings led to absurd conclusions. The child who estimates that there are more beads in the taller glass because the level has been raised centers his attention on height and ignores width. If, however, the experimenter repeatedly empties the beads into even thinner and taller glasses, there will be a time when this child replies that there are fewer beads in the taller glass because it is narrower. This is an example of a transition from a single centering (preconceptual thought) to two successive centerings (intuitive thought). When the child is able to reason simultaneously with respect to both relations, he will be capable of the logical process of "conservation." He will be able to state that the beads remain the same and only the glasses change. Such simultaneous reasoning does not occur, however, during the intuitive stage. As the example indicates, there is neither deduction nor true logical operations. The error is simply corrected, but the two relations are seen alternatively and sequentially instead of simultaneously. The child's responses are based upon an intuitive regulation and not upon the logical operational mechanism.

The difference between intuitive and operational thought is also seen in the formation of classes. These demonstrations involve the child's understanding of the cardinal $(3 = 1 + 1 + 1)$ and ordinal (first + second + third) properties of number. Cardinal properties of number involve the ability to classify objects and combine classes. Piaget (1960) placed twenty beads in a box, the child acknowledging that they were all made of wood (this constituted a class B). Seventeen beads were brown and were designated subclass A; three were white and designated subclass A1. To determine whether the child was capable of understanding such an operation as $A + A1 = B$, the following question was asked, "In this box (all of the beads are visible), which are there more of, wooden beads or brown beads (that is, B or A)?" Piaget found that until about seven years, the child invariably replied that there are more brown beads, "since there are only three white ones." Then the child was asked further, "Are all the brown ones made of wood?" The child usually responded, "Yes." Piaget questioned further, "If one takes away all the wooden beads and puts them in a second box, will there be any beads left in the first box?" Most children replied, "No, because they are all made of wood." The child was then asked the following question, "If the brown ones are taken away, will there be any beads left?" The child responds, "Yes, the white ones." After the interrogation is finished, the original question is repeated. The child, during this phase, continues to state that there are more brown beads than wooden beads. The mechanism underlying this response is that the child has no difficulty centering his attention on the whole class B or on the subclass A or A1. However, he is unable to handle both simultaneously, thus failing to grasp the logical and mathematical truth that the whole is equal to the sum of its parts.

The problems of ordination and seriation require concrete operational thought. Although the child is beginning to arrange things in series, his ability to arrange is only global during the intuitive stage. The child is able to compare two members of a set within a series when they follow one another in consecutive order. For example, the child knows that Monday comes after Sunday, that Tuesday comes after Monday. When asked whether Thursday comes after Sunday, the child becomes confused. Operational thought, involving logical relations between things and events that are arranged in a series, is not yet possible for the child in the intuitive stage.

The stage of *operational thought* commences with what Piaget called the advent of rational activity in the child. As stated earlier, before attaining operational thought, the child's logic is transductive. The capacity for deductive and inductive logic depends on schemas referred to as operations. *Opera-*

tions are defined as internalized actions that can return to their starting point and that can be integrated with other actions also possessing this feature of reversibility (Piaget 1960). Stated simply, operations are mental acts that have reversible properties.

Concrete operational thought is characterized as concrete because the starting point of the operation is always some real system of objects and relations that the child perceives in relation to these objects. The emergence of concrete operations is often sudden in the child's development. Piaget (1960) attributes the appearance of concrete operational thought to a sudden thawing out of intuitive schema that earlier had been very rigid despite their progressive articulation.

In formulating the properties of concrete operations, it is necessary to outline five specific operations:

1. *Combinativity:* an operation in which two classes may be combined into one comprehensive class that embraces them both (for example, $X + Y = Z$, or black beads + white beads = wooden beads).
2. *Reversibility:* every logical or mathematical operation is reversible in that there is an opposite operation that cancels it (for example, $4 + 3 = 7$ can be reversed to $7 - 4 = 3$). In this example, subtraction is the converse of addition. Reversibility therefore refers to subtraction as the converse of addition and to division as the converse of multiplication.
3. *Associativity:* an operation combining several classes without regard to order (for example, $[a + b] + c = a + [b + c]$).
4. *Identity:* an operation that can be nullified by combining it with its opposite (for example, $+A - A = 0$).
5. *Tautology:* an operation related to logical classifications. Here repetition of a proposition, classification, or relation leaves them unchanged.

Although these operations seem simple, the child is unable to accomplish them prior to this stage. Concrete operational schemas are analogous to particular operations that have been identified in mathematical and logical disciplines. Thus, operational thought structures are modeled after logico-mathematical operations. To understand the internal process that brings about this transition from intuitive to operational thought, it is necessary to see how concrete operational structures are brought to bear on the problems previously quoted in the discussion of the intuitive stage.

Reconsider the conservation problem (pouring the beads from one glass to another): The child in the intuitive stage is characterized by slow-moving centerings and decenterings; he sees the problem first from one point of view (height) and then from another (width). During the concrete operational stage, the child holds both centerings simultaneously and thus deduces the conservation concept. He explains his conviction by verbally pointing out that the quantity of beads in both glasses is the same, because if you poured them back into the other glass the two would be the same height again (reversibility), or that the quantity is the same now because it was the same before (identity).

Conservation is not necessarily a unitary concept; it manifests itself in different ways at different times. Conservation of discrete quantities, such as *number,* in which two groups of discrete objects in one-to-one correspondence are perceived as equivalent even when moved to a new arrangement wherein correspondence is not perceptually evident, occurs slightly before conservation of continuous quantities, such as *substance.* Conservation of *weight,* the downward force of an object, and *volume,* or the space occupied by an object, follow *quantity* in developmental order.

Evidence confirming this sequential order of conservation has varied somewhat from Piaget's original findings, but, in general, it has confirmed his age trends. Thus, the principles of conservation do not at first hold in all systems or ideas, and they emerge in some systems later than in others. Reasoning during the concrete operational stage is tied to the child's concrete experience.

This limited reasoning is further seen in the class inclusion problem (for example, the brown beads-wooden beads problem). At the concrete operational stage, the child understands class inclusion (combinatory operation) in the wooden beads experiment, yet he does not solve a verbal test involving an identical structure until the stage of formal operations.

The *formal operational stage* marks the emergence of the ability to solve problems at a level that in some ways transcends concrete experience. Formal thinking marks the completion of the child's emancipation from perception and action. In contrast to the concrete, action-oriented thought of the child, the adolescent thinker goes beyond the present and forms theories about everything. Such thought though is considered "reflective" because the adolescent reasons on the basis of purely formal assumptions. He can consider hypotheses to be either true or false and then deduce what would follow if they were true.

A good example of formal operational thought is seen in the problem of seriation between three terms presented as propositions. "Edith is fairer than Susan; Edith is darker than Lily; who is the darkest of the three?" This is a simple problem of seriation for a seven-year-old when the problem is presented in concrete form. When the problem is presented in verbal form, it is not solved until the child is about twelve years old. Most of the responses before twelve were as follows: "Edith and Susan are fair; Edith and Lily are dark; therefore, Lily is darkest" or "Susan is the fairest, and Edith is in-between." In other words, the concrete operational child cannot solve problems at the formal level that he can solve at the concrete level. The cause of this difficulty is that the premises are purely verbal postulates, and the conclusion must be drawn without recourse to concrete operations.

The formal operational adolescent can make logical experiments, not merely factual ones. Propositional logic enables the child to test the validity of statements by reference to their purely logical properties rather than by reference to their correspondence with the concrete empirical world. In other words, formal operations permit the child to deal with the *form* of a proposition rather than the content.

In contrasting formal operations with concrete operations, Piaget (1960) pointed out that concrete reasoning concerns action or the reality of first-degree groupings of operations (that is, internalized actions that are capable of combination or reversal), whereas formal reasoning consists of reflecting on operations or on their results and consequently effecting a second-degree grouping of operations (that is, operations on operations). At the stage of formal operational thought, the adolescent is able to manipulate intellectually the hypothetical and to evaluate systematically a lengthy set of alternatives. He learns to deal with the logical relationships of Identity (I), Negation (N), Reciprocity (R), and Correlation (C). This permits him to deal with problems of proportionality, probability, permutations, and combinations. These operations are often called the I.N.R.C. logical group.

In summary, Piaget's theory of intellectual development is concerned with the enormously complex unfolding abilities of the child as seen in his ontogenetic evolution from infancy to adulthood. At the stage of sensori-motor development, the child first combines perceptual experiences and later develops the concept of object permanence that is implicit in the notions of time, space, and causality. Conceptual thought follows an elaborate evolution starting with the development of imitative language, concrete imagery, and symbolic play activity. The concrete operational child begins to represent the world of empirical reality symbolically rather than through the action representation seen in the preoperational stages. The formal operational child extends the world of empirical reality by representing the world not only as it is, but also as it could be. Abstract logic and mathematics are now at the child's disposal in dealing with problems.

Conception of the Person

Piaget's conception of the person is defined strictly along developmental lines. The dimensions of *contemporaneous* individual differences are not applicable in Piaget's theory because the *developmental* dimensions are the prime focus of almost all of his theoretical and empirical work. Each person is described according to his stage, which is defined by structural characteristics, not by chronological age. The stages of intellectual development are diagrammatically represented in Figure 10. As we have already indicated, age is not an essential criterion because development depends on the interaction of stage and environment. Nevertheless, it may be said that as age increases, structures (stages) become more highly differentiated and integrated, which allows for more complex information processing and manipulation of environmental input. As stage increases, the person moves from concrete to more abstract forms of thinking.

Furth's application of Piaget's stages is to use them both as the means for specifying appropriate curriculum and as objectives. Furth's basic goal for elementary education is the development of more abstract operational stages of thought. The ultimate goal for elementary education is the student's advancement toward the formal operational stage of Piagetian thought.

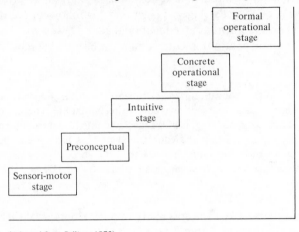

(Adapted from Sullivan 1972)

Figure 10   Piaget's Stages as Dimensions of Person (Adapted from Sullivan 1972)

Although the stages in Figure 10 appear useful in person-based curriculum planning, their potential value needs to be considered in relation to specific areas (Sullivan 1971). A Piagetian "stage" (P) is an "accessibility channel" for kinds of informational input (E) in certain subject-matter areas. This B-P-E view restricts the scope of Piagetian stages of development as "educational objectives"(B) in the curriculum, in that they need not have the ubiquity Furth attributes to them. Piaget's stages of intellectual development appear more relevant to science and mathematics than to social science. This is because of the type of concepts employed in science and mathematics and the degree of complexity of the concepts. For example, compare the intellectual thought structures (summarized in Figure 10) with the thought structures in the development of morality (Chapter 3). The development of formal operational thought in Piaget's theory of intellectual development usually begins at about age eleven, whereas the most advanced stages of moral ideology, as defined by Kohlberg (1966), appear at about age sixteen. This age differential indicates that some of the more advanced concepts in social education (for example, moral ideology) develop much later than advanced concepts in the areas of physical science and mathematics.

Conception of Behavior

Many Piaget-based curricula are committed to fostering spontaneous growth in the intelligence of the child. The educational objective is to promote development in terms of Piaget's stages. Piaget and his followers are not the first to view general development as an educational goal. Dewey was a most ardent proponent of the conception that education must be synonyomous with development.

> When it is said that education is development, everything depends on how development is conceived. Our own conclusion is that life is development, and that developing, growing, is life. Translated into its educational equivalents, that means (1) that the educational process has no end beyond itself; it is its own end; and that (2) the education process is one of continual reorganization, reconstructing, transforming. (Dewey 1916, pp. 49–50)

Dewey's proposals lacked the specificity of a developmental theory such as Piaget's. Although there are other reasons why Dewey's proposals were never really adopted, a major reason may be that he did not make his suggestions within the context of any well-explicated theory of development. The British infant-school movement illustrates that Piaget's theory is sufficiently explicit to permit implementation.

Piaget's psychological counterpart of Dewey's philosophical position on development adds a process dimension that follows generically the course of the "continual, reorganizing, reconstructing, transforming" of the structures of knowledge. For Dewey, the goals of change were to derive from the process of development. Piaget's theory makes this derivation possible. However, whether or not the specification of educational goals makes sense in the long run over all ages of students remains a question, as we have indicated.

Although the Piagetian stages are specific, it is very difficult to prescribe the environments that are apt to produce developmental change. Although this problem will be discussed in the next section, it may be noted that Piaget's concept of the source of growth and development in the person fluctuates between internal factors alone and the interaction of internal-external factors (cf. Chapter 2).

Piaget's theory clearly calls for process rather than content goals. In Furth's curriculum suggestions (1970), for example, his position is that any particular content experience is good only insofar as it stimulates the ongoing processes of development as defined in Piagetian thought structures. The "thinking games" that he devised follow no strict sequence and are simply designed to stimulate the ongoing development of operational thought structures.

To use progression in Piagetian stages as an educational objective, like any other process goal, causes measurement problems because a change in cognitive structure is unlikely to be detected by a single objective test. A Piagetian emphasis requires multiple criteria to indicate educational change. As described in Chapter 3, Kohnstamm has summarized five criteria for evaluating newly acquired behavior. Piaget had originally proposed that the newly acquired behavior should be "(1) lasting, (2) transferable, and (3) fundamentally different from the pre-experimental level of behavior" (Kohnstamm 1966, p. 4), to which Kohnstamm added (4) difficulty of acquisition (presumably on the basis that nothing that comes easily will last,), and (5) resistance to extinction.

Conception of the Environment

Can educational environments be conceptualized in Piagetian terms? Whose interpretation of the environment is used? What are the temporal units employed, if any? What kind and form of dimensions are used to characterize the environment? These questions are difficult to answer because Piaget has never explicitly stated a systematic conception of the environment. Therefore, any Piaget-based educational program must necessarily make some inferences about environments on the basis of little information. Piaget's ideas are most likely to be adopted by educators who are disposed to discovery and activity-learning approaches rather than to more didactic methods. For example, Furth (1970) contended that the focus of the elementary-school curriculum should be congruent with the child's concrete operational stage. The elementary-school program should make use of concrete events that do not emphasize concepts derived from verbal propositions to stabilize concrete thought structures. In secondary school, where students are more capable of formal operational thought, the programs based on Piaget's theories can use more verbal propositions because a fixed curriculum is not specified, but certain general guidelines are adhered to in program planning.

Duckworth (1964) maintained that the chief result of Piaget's theory of intellectual development is to provide a basis for recommending that children be allowed to do their own learning (that is, equilibration). Thus, Piaget is ideologically aligned with John Dewey, and indeed Piaget has praised Dewey as a great man (Piaget, in Hall 1970). For Piaget, good schooling provides the child with an opportunity to experiment. In a good Piaget-based school, the child manipulates things, manipulates symbols, poses questions, and seeks his own answers, reconciling what he finds at one time with what he finds at another time and comparing his findings with those of other children (Piaget, in Hall 1970).

Piaget minimizes the importance of teacher-child verbal interaction (Piaget 1964). The teacher is ideally a collaborator in the learning process and provides an environment for the child's own discovery through equilibration. The "thinking games" devised by Furth are examples of activities derived in a guided-discovery mode. Almy et al. (1966) noted that the application of the equilibration idea, or self-regulation, to education means that students should be allowed a maximum of activity on their own and should be directed by useful materials rather than by teachers. For example, children have real understanding of logico-mathematical structures only when they invent structures themselves through their own activities. Conversely, if a teacher tries to teach them too quickly, this will only prevent learning (Piaget, in Hall 1970). Piaget takes a dim view of many of the acceleration studies on the conservation concept. He feels that much time is wasted here that could be used in the development of improved methods of guided discovery (Piaget 1964). This belief rests on his general conception of knowledge:

> The development of knowledge is a spontaneous process, tied to the whole process of embryogenesis. Embryogenesis concerns the development of the nervous system, and development of mental functions. In the case of the development of knowledge in children, embryogenesis ends only in adulthood. It is a total development process which must re-situate in its general biological and psychological context. In other words, development is a process which concerns the totality of the structures of knowledge. (p. 8)

His position becomes even clearer when we examine his distinction between learning and development.

> Learning presents the opposite case. In general, learning is provoked by situations—provoked by a psychological experimenter or by a teacher, with respect to some didactic point; or, by an external situation. It is provoked, in general, as opposed to spontaneous. In addition, it is a limited process—limited to a single problem, or to a single structure. (p. 8)

Piaget views development as an explanation for learning rather than the converse. The reduction of development to a series of specific learned items constructed by a psychologist is considered insufficient. Such tasks are viewed as atomistic because Piaget believes that development is the essential process and that each element of learning occurs as a function of total development rather than acting as a cause of development.

Piaget's ideas about self-regulation are not simply restricted to the development of logico-mathematical structures. Active manipulation has two meanings—acting on material things and doing things in collaboration with a group. This social collaboration leads to a child's learning to think more critically when he must communicate with others. Peer-groups interaction is an essential factor in the child's progress from the egocentric stage to a sociocentric stage. Piaget also notes that peer solidarity and mutual respect between equals enhance the child's general social and moral development (Piaget 1932).

In summary, it appears that Piaget is in substantial agreement with Dewey concerning the type of classroom atmosphere most conducive to learning. Learning based on the child's direct activity and discovery and learning through social interaction with peers are both essential elements of a Piagetian educational environment. The teacher's role is to help or guide the child make his own discoveries rather than to instruct directly. Piaget contends that direct verbal instruction is appropriate only at the level of formal operations, which usually occurs sometimes between the ages of eleven and thirteen. Because of his emphasis on self-regulation, Piaget says little about environments, except for certain value statements about the role of the teacher.

Person-Environment Interaction

Piaget's theory of intellectual development is generally considered an interactive theory that draws on both person and environment in describing the course of development. To clarify this interaction, Piaget has stated his position on the mechanisms of transition from lower to higher stages of development (Piaget 1964). Four transition factors, taken singly or in combination, account for development.

1. *Maturation:* Piaget believes that cognitive structures are not innate, but rather that the maturation of the nervous system determines the possibilities for development at a given stage. His definition restricts the concept of maturation to the underlying growth of the nervous system.
2. *Social interaction:* Knowledge may be acquired by educative transmission or, more generally, language. Social interaction is important because it helps the child progress from egocentric, concrete modes of thought to more sociocentric, abstract modes of thought.

3. *Physical experience:* The child's experience in acting on objects enables him to obtain knowledge about an object and to abstract from this knowledge. Thus, in the sensori-motor stage, the child's repetitive interaction with the physical environment leads to the development of object-permanent schemas. Concrete operational thought develops through the manipulation of concrete objects and the internalization of these manipulations, that is, the operation of reversibility which was once a concrete action becomes internalized in thought.

4. *Equilibration:* Equilibration is a central process that serves to balance assimilation and accommodation. Equilibration, or the self-regulation of equilibrium, is fundamental because it subsumes other factors. Equilibration is defined as the progressive interior organization of knowledge in a stepwise fashion. That knowledge is progressively interiorized through assimilation and accommodation is part of a hierarchical model in which each stage is a necessary foundation for the next higher stage.

From the interactive, or person-environment, view, the stages in Figure 10 provide a basis for studying didactic processes, especially in the field of mathematics and science teaching, as well as in other fields where concepts with a clearly defined logical structure are formed (Aebli 1970). The stages may also serve as educational goals. However, Piaget does not specify an environment for a person of a given stage (for example, Furth 1970) because the child's own self-regulative processes must determine this. Piaget believes that with increasing age, the person has different intrinsic structures available that enable him to process information in new and more complex ways. Progress on this concrete-abstract dimension is attributed to these changing intrinsic structures in a manner not unlike a predeterministic theory. The person, however, is not seen as a mere *tabula rasa;* he incorporates information into the system through these intrinsic structures. Therefore, Piaget's theory lies somewhere between a completely interactionist position and an entirely predeterministic position.

Piaget assesses the child's developmental stage by questioning him about concepts that are *spontaneously* learned rather than directly taught in school. If there are developmental differences in the way children view the world, it is wise to tap these structural differences through questions that prevent children from mimicking adult responses. Use of questions to probe the child's spontaneous concepts guards against the child's giving rote-learned school information, which emphasizes content rather than process learning.

As discussed in Chapter 2, some stage theories place the locus for developmental change entirely within the person. Such predeterministic theories emphasize the orderly unfolding of the person's intellect and de-emphasize or ignore environmental effects. At most, the environment supports or inflects developmental change to some extent, but does not determine its basic form or sequence.

It is clear that Piaget's consistent reiteration of the functional invariants of assimilation and accommodation (J. McV. Hunt 1961) and his emphasis on the effects of social experience (Piaget 1964; Sigel 1968) distinguish his theory from the more predeterministic theory of Gesell, at least in emphasis. Piaget appears to be a modified predeterminist. It can be said without exaggeration that:

> Piaget tends to ignore the effects of antecedent conditions and the environmental variables in development, relegating them to a place of definitely subsidiary importance to the unfolding of internal structures. This does not mean that he advocates a strict nativist position, for he has frequently emphasized the continual interaction between external and internal forces. Nevertheless, biological orientation and interest in structure lead him to take external factors for granted and to regard the form which this interaction takes as largely predetermined from the start. The only problem, then, is that of specifying the successive stages through which the organism passes; little leeway is left for differential manifestations of external conditions. (Wohlwill 1962)

Piaget Compared with Other Contemporary Theories

BRUNER

The theories of Bruner and his colleagues (1966) are very similar to Piaget but take a different view of the relation between culture (environment) and cognitive growth of the child. Bruner places much less emphasis on Piaget's operational structures (for example, the concrete operations) and essentially renames some of Piaget's stages while retaining Piaget's observations. Bruner (1964) delineates the course of cognitive growth in three stages, or modes of information processing: enactive, iconic, and symbolic. The *enactive* mode involves representation through habitual patterns of action, learning by doing. Enactive thinking is similar to Piaget's sensori-motor intelligence. The *iconic* mode involves the representation of the environment through percepts or images. Unlike enactive thinking, iconic representation is spatial and not limited to the present. Relying on iconic representation means that the child deals with reality on the basis of a "point-at-able" correspondence that does not deal with the invariant features of the environment as seen in Piaget's concrete operational thought. Thus, it would appear that iconic representation encompasses Piaget's preconceptual and intuitive stages of thought.

The *symbolic* mode is the most advanced stage of representation. It is bound neither by the temporal, serial features of enactive representation nor by the spatial and immediate features of iconic representation. Symbolic thinking corresponds to Piaget's concrete operational stage of thought.

The value of Bruner's renaming Piaget's stages is open to question, but it is clear that Bruner wants to emphasize the role of culture and its interaction with the cognitive growth of the child. Bruner and his colleagues (Bruner et al. 1966) reported cross-cultural studies and experiments on accelerating cognitive growth to show the role of culture in cognitive growth, an area that Piaget omitted. These studies (Bruner et al. 1966) summarize the role of schooling, language, and other factors which influence the course of cognitive growth.

The developmental relation between language and thought is still a controversial and unresolved "chicken or egg" problem. Historically, two extreme views have prevailed concerning the relation between language and thought. The first viewpoint is that thinking is speaking; the thought and the words in which the thought are expressed are one and the same thing. The second viewpoint is that thought occurs independently of language; language is merely the vehicle of already accomplished thought. Bruner emphasizes the directive function of language on thought, while Piaget and his colleagues consider thought to be internalized actions. The beginnings of thought is seen by Piaget as anticipating language and existing as a "symbolic function." The child's language reflects the maturing of his thought processes, and the coordination of sensori-motor schemas built up during the first eighteen months of life is the necessary condition for language acquisition (Sinclair-de-Zwart 1967; 1969). In Piaget's theory, language is a means of sharing and communicating thoughts, but it does not facilitate thought or its development. For this reason, Piaget takes exception to the language-training experiments (by Bruner and associates, 1966) that are intended to encourage the development of "operational thought."

Bruner (1964) assigns to language a more prominent role in cognitive development. He contends that:

> Translation of experiences into symbolic form, with its attendant means of achieving remote reference, transformation, and combination, opens up realms of intellectual possibility that are orders of magnitude beyond the most powerful image forming system. ... Once the child succeeds in internalizing language as a cognitive instrument, it becomes possible for

him to represent and systematically form the regularities of experience
with greater power and flexibility. (pp. 13–14)

The prominent role of language in cognitive functioning is supported by the
effects of schooling or instruction on intellectual skills (Bruner et al. 1966). By
contrast, Piaget de-emphasizes the effect of direct educational intervention. In
fact, it is in his statements to educators that Piaget is most insistent on
distinguishing between development and learning. Development concerns the
totality of the structures of knowledge. Learning, on the other hand, is seen
as a more restricted process provoked by the situation, for example, teaching,
and limited to single problems or single structures. Piaget and his followers
(for example, Smedslund 1961) deny that a specific learning experience or
practice, particularly of a verbal nature, has any significant influence on the
emergence of stages of intellectual development. Presumably, this reservation
about the developmental value of any purely verbal training would apply to
most educational procedures.

GAGNÉ: DEVELOPMENT AND LEARNING

The development and learning distinction made by Piaget, with its emphasis
on development, has brought criticism from theorists who place a greater
emphasis on learning (Gagné 1968). Gagné discussed his conception of "readiness" by distinguishing between two general processes, learning and development, but he differs from Piaget in this distinction. *Learning* involves changes
in behavior capabilities with respect to relatively specific forms of behavior,
usually over limited periods of time, for example, hours or weeks (Gagné 1968,
p. 177). Gagné defines *development* as another major class of capabilities
observed over longer periods of time, for example, months, years. He is justifi-
ably disturbed by Piaget's underplaying the role of learning in developmental
change and offers the following alternative to the Piagetian conception of
cognitive development:

> The point of view I wish to describe here states that learning contributes
> to intellectual development of the human being because it is *cumulative*
> in its effects. The child progresses from one point to the next in his
> development, not because he acquires one or a dozen new associations, but
> because he learns an ordered set of capabilities which build upon each
> other in progressive fashion through the processes of differentiation, recall
> and transition of learning. (Gagné, 1968, p. 181)

It is clear that Gagné places a marked emphasis on learning in the course
of the organism's development. Although he postulated an interaction between

genetically determined growth, that is, maturation, and learning in the developmental progression, it is apparent that learning is paramount in his system, while maturation is taken for granted. Gagné regards the growth processes that Piaget attributed to equilibration as a result of cumulative learning.

Gagné described a hierarchy of learning processes that are increasingly complex (see chart below).

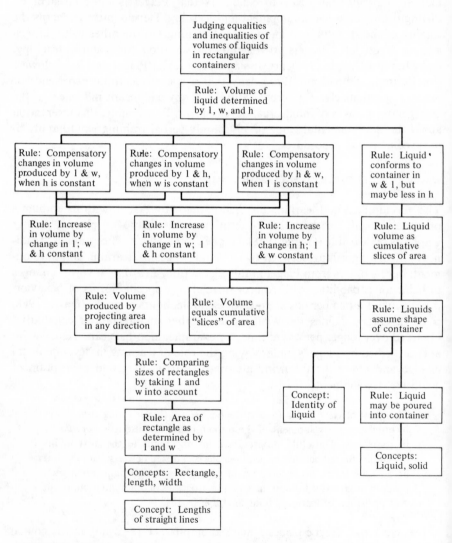

A Cumulative Learning Sequence Pertaining to the Development of Nonmetric Judgments of Liquid Volume (From Gagné 1968, p. 184)

Readiness is attributed not to maturation or equilibration but to the presence of prerequisite subordinate capabilities that form the foundation for the learning of more complex superordinate capabilities. For Gagné, the organism is ready if it has the necessary subordinate capabilities. The reason that development takes time is not that it is maturationally governed, but simply that subordinate capabilities presented in the correct logical order take time to be learned (Gagné 1968). He further observes that when development is the dominant theme, educational events are designed to wait until the child is ready to learn. When learning is the dominant theme, the years are to be systematically filled with planned events of learning, and there is virtually no waiting, except for the time required to bring about those changes.

It is unfortunate that when the polarities are dramatized, the proponents of both positions distort one another's concepts. Under these conditions one may be sympathetic to Piaget when reading Gagné and sympathetic to Gagné when reading Piaget. As Cronbach (1964) points out:

> Somewhere between the dual approaches—enrich the environment and let development occur—there would seem logically to be some optimal curriculum of experiences arranged in some predetermined sequence with intervention by the teacher systematically regulated. But we do not know nearly enough about such questions. (p. 77)

Gagné (1968) assumes that the answers to such questions lie in a logical "task analysis" of the learning situation. Although he rejects a simple associationistic conception of learning, his general positions represent an external growth metaphor approach to development. However, in some of his legitimate criticisms of Piaget, Gagné virtually denies the entire concept of development. Dewey's characterization (1956) of the early associationists can be applied with equal force to Gagné's "cumulative learning" position:

> Subdivide each topic into studies; each study into lessons; each lesson into specific facts and formulae. Let the child proceed step by step to master each one of these separate parts, and at least he will have covered the entire ground. The road which looks so long when viewed in its entirety is easily travelled, considered as a series of particular steps. Thus emphasis is put upon the logical subdivisions and consecutions of the subject-matter. Problems of instruction are problems of procuring texts giving logical parts and sequences, and of presenting these portions in class in a similar definite and graded way. Subject-matter furnishes the end, and it determines methods. The child is simply the immature being who is to be matured; he is the superficial being who is to be deepened; his is narrow experience which is

to be widened. It is his to receive, to accept. His part is fulfilled when he is ductile and docile. (Dewey 1956, p. 8)

From our framework Piaget has emphasized the (P) component whereas Gagné's task analysis emphasizes the (E) component.

VYGOTSKY

Vygotsky's comments (1965) on this rigid dichotomy appear in his discussion of Piaget's notions of spontaneous concepts (concepts that are learned from external sources):

> There are errors in Piaget's reasoning that detract from the value of his views. Although he holds that the child in forming a concept stamps it with the characteristics of his own mentality, Piaget tends to apply this thesis only to spontaneous concepts and assumes that they alone can truly enlighten us on the special qualities of child thought; he fails to see the interaction between the two kinds of concepts and the bonds that unite them into a total system of concepts in the course of the child's intellectual development. (Vygotsky 1965, p. 84)

To be educationally relevant, such a stage theory as Piaget's must somehow coordinate the evolving intrinsic structures with teaching-learning situations. This linking of educational strategy of Piaget's theory of development is complicated because research studies have intentionally underplayed environmental effects, placing emphasis on spontaneous concept formation (Vygotsky 1965). Especially in the research studies, the theory ignores the interaction between school-learned concepts and intrinsic structure (stage). Therefore, Piaget's development stages are thought to affect the learning of school concepts, but the learning of school concepts is thought not to affect Piaget's development stages.

Therefore, his present position severely limits the role of school learning in fostering intellectual development. If Piaget's views on the nature of nonspontaneous concepts were valid, then school learning would be unnecessary for development (Vygotsky 1965). Obviously, this feature of the theory limits its value for education. Another limitation is the problem Piaget's equilibration model poses for curriculum developers. Aebli (1970) has pointed out that an empirically based theory or multistep construction cannot be derived within a Piagetian framework. He noted that:

> Since disequilibrium occurs during the long unobserved periods of spontaneous activity of the child, the psychologist is not able to follow the

construction process through. In fact, Piaget has very rarely been able to show how a concept or operation, once attained, becomes disequilibrated again and then is integrated into a concept or operation of a higher order. Rather, once constructed, it merges into the confusing matrix of the child's spontaneous activity, where it is never again recovered for the study of further development. (Aebli 1970, p. 16)

Therefore, it is clear that any educational derivation from Piaget will be somewhat speculative. In the examples that follow, therefore, the person (P) and educational goals (B) are Piagetian, but the environmental (E) specifications are not. The studies discussed do not use Piaget's theory to derive the structure and sequence of the curriculum, nor do they share Piaget's assumption that spontaneous concepts can be altered only by the indirect internalized activities of the child. Rather, they share Vygotsky's assumption (1965) that nonspontaneous school-learned (scientific) concepts can alter the child's spontaneous concept formation. However, the studies illustrate the general effects of Piaget on educational practice, if not his value for specific derivations.

The first study concerns teaching kindergarten and first-grade children the concept of specific gravity (Ojemann and Pritchett 1963). In the preassessments of the children Piagetian materials on specific gravity were carefully avoided, and this approach was maintained in the "guided teaching" phase. Piaget's procedures for assessing children's concepts of specific gravity were followed only in the post-test to guard against the criticism that the children might simply parrot answers supplied by the teacher. After a pretest, the children were randomly assigned to experimental and control groups. Children in the experimental group were given a three-session learning program designed to guide the child's perceptions to relevant aspects of the specific-gravity concept. The guided experiences consisted of calling the child's attention to those aspects represented by "weight of object" and "weight of an equivalent amount of water," while ignoring other aspects, such as shape, color, and form.

The control group did not receive these experiences. The experimental group showed a significant gain over the control group on the post-test series, a gain also evident in the Piagetian assessments of specific gravity. Although the question of the comparability of the Piagetian tests with the other tests of specific gravity is unanswered, the study gives tentative evidence that Piaget's spontaneous concepts can be significantly altered by the nonspontaneous (scientific) concepts learned in school. This result, although contradictory to Piaget's assumption, is completely compatible with Vygotsky's interactive position. The use of Piaget's assessment tasks in the post-test indicates some generalization of the learning experience beyond the specific learning situation.

Note here that Piaget's conceptions are used only as assessments of educational outcome (B). If a Piagetian pretest were given, it could incorporate the person (P) and behavior (B) parameters simultaneously.

A second, similar study involved the teaching of the concept of density to children in the seventh and ninth grades (Gulpers 1968). Procedures to evaluate the effectiveness of a particular curriculum centering around the concept of density were derived from test instruments originally inspired by Piaget (Laurendeau and Pinard 1963). The scale specifically assessed the nature of the child's reasons for why objects sink or float. Children's responses are classified into four stages: (a) Stage 0, incomprehension; (b) Stage 1, precausal explanations (finalism, animism, etc.); (c) Stage 2, physical explanations tainted with illogical reasons; (d) Stage 3, physical explanations that are coherent and noncontradictory.

Pretest results indicated that the average stage for each grade was Stage 2. Students were then divided into experimental and control groups, with the experimental groups receiving a curriculum program based on a task analysis (Gagné 1968) for learning the concept of density. Gulpers (1968) found that both experimental groups improved significantly compared with control groups, in that experimental post-test scores increased to Stage 3, whereas the controls remained the same. In this study, Piagetian instruments were used to demonstrate the effect of learning experiences on the child's developmental stage. The study ignored Piaget's prescriptions for the learning-development distinction (Piaget 1964) but used Piagetian questionnaires as a person measure and as an evaluation of educational outcome (P-B). This study also demonstrated the effects of nonspontaneous learned concepts on the child's development of spontaneous concepts.

These studies give some cause for optimism concerning the effect of systematic teaching on general development. This does not necessarily mean that Piaget's stages can be markedly altered by teaching. Rather, guided discovery may enhance and elaborate a stage, helping the child structure and generalize to move content situations (Flavell and Wohlwill 1969). We agree with Aebli (1970) on the possible role of systematic teaching in the child's conceptual development:

> Systematic teaching guides the child in his search for the adequate assimilation schemata, it helps him apply them correctly to the problem situation, it repeats difficult steps of elaboration until they are consolidated, it varies the situations as well as the operations in order to render the structures mobile and transparent, it introduces adequate perceptive supports and symbolic terms that fix attained results, and it finally creates

opportunities for independent assimilation of new exemplars of the objects
and situations studied. (p. 22)

The disposition of the child toward the learning situation has frequently
been considered in terms of his "readiness" for a particular program. Readiness is important if educational practices are viewed developmentally, as Piaget did. As the studies described illustrate, there is more to these procedures
than accelerating development. The conception of the person-environment
interaction can take on a time perspective that will clarify the concept of
readiness and produce practical educational outcomes. Wohlwill (1970) makes
a pertinent observation:

> In any event, greater attention to the role of structure is clearly indicated
> for those who would provide the young child with experience calculated
> to stimulate his development, if only that we may insure that we are
> putting the child's energy to optimal use. The question is one of optimal
> balance between externally imposed programmed tasks, and instructional
> activity initiated and directed by the child himself. (p. 26)

In our terms, Wohlwill is describing the optimal match between the person (P)
and the environment (E) as presented to him through the curriculum.

Piaget in the Curriculum

Although Piaget does not consider himself an educational psychologist, his
work has been used increasingly as the basis for educational practice (Sullivan
1967; 1969). For example, curriculum developers have used Piaget's natural
stages of development as indicators of readiness for educational programs (J.
McV. Hunt 1961). Piaget's work is seen as relevant to education because of
the importance of an appropriate "match" between the circumstances that a
child encounters and his present state of conceptual development.

> The description of stages of intellectual development provided by Piaget
> is extremely helpful in the matching process as it is seen in a grosser sense.
> The periods between the various behavioral landmarks that mark Piaget's
> transitions or stages are, in a sense, critical periods for various types of
> environmental encounters. (J. McV. Hunt 1961, p. 273)

Following the matching idea, Adler (1963) used Piagetian stages in planning
curricula. He suggested that, for the young child, the world must be defined
initially in terms of action-linked concepts because the sensori-motor child
encounters knowledge only through his own actions. For children at the more

advanced stage of concrete formal operations, Adler suggested that the presentation be less concrete and more theoretical. Adler's prescription in B-P-E terms can be seen as follows:

Behavior	Person (Stage of learner)	Environment (Recommended instructional approach)
Learning of concepts	Sensori-motor stage	Action-linked experience
	Formal operational stage	More theoretical experience

Szeminska (1965) found that children studying physics who had reached the formal operational level were most successful on a written test of the acquisition of knowledge. She concluded that there is a direct relation between the possibility of assimilating school information and cognitive maturity. She maintained that learning takes place more effectively when the child's present conceptual structure is matched with the complexity of the subject matter. Szeminska's prescriptions in B-P-E terms can be seen as follows:

Behavior	Person (Stage of learner)	Environment (Recommended instructional approach)
Learning principles of physics	Formal operational stage	High in complexity
	Concrete operational stage	Low in complexity

More recently, Furth (1970) has proposed that the entire elementary-school curriculum could be based on the development of Piagetian thought structures. Furth recommended that Piaget's sequence of stages serve as the educational aims of the elementary-school curriculum. Furth sees the task of the elementary school as strengthening the child's spontaneous thinking, which can be characterized in Piaget's stages. Thus, Furth proposed procedures related to concrete operational and formal operational stages of thought at different grade levels. Furth maintained that the curriculum, during the concrete operational stage, should be geared to activities that would stabilize concrete operational structures. The continuous use of these structures expands the child's physical and social world until the beginnings of formal operational intelligence enable him to use formal propositions.

Furth used Piaget's theory to suggest that the elementary-school curriculum should be geared to the thinking structures of a concrete operational child. He proposed that the school promote the development of operative thinking not by any fixed curriculum but by the use of exercises to encourage the development and stabilization of concrete operational thought structures. Furth gives many examples of "thinking games," which are appropriate to this end. The following is one simple example:

> Ten red marbles and ten yellow marbles are spread on a table. The teacher puts eight red marbles and one yellow marble into a bag and shakes it well. The bag is handed from one child to the other; each has to guess the color of the marble he will draw from the bag. After a marble is taken out and its color noted, it is put back into the bag. The little children were greatly surprised that the answer "red" remained the safer bet, draw after draw. The tendency to switch the prediction is very strong. On another trial the children saw that eight red and no yellow balls were put into the bag. Yet some six-year-old children, when they had their turn to pick a marble, still persisted in changing their guess to yellow! (Furth 1970, p. 107)

Furth does not prescribe a fixed sequence of exercises. He believes that the child will invariably find his own level along the continuum of difficulty. Thus, the exercises may be as appropriate for the six-year-old as for the nine-year-old. These thinking exercises should not be confined to logical thinking exercises related to objective, impersonal knowledge in the example. Furth suggested that children be guided not only to discover and apply objective invariants of logical rules and symbolic articulation but also to recognize the invariant factors underlying social responsibility.

Educational Domain of Relevance

The summary of the critical appraisal of Piaget by Sullivan (1967) is appropriate:

> The objective of the present paper has been to critically evaluate Piaget's potential contribution to the educational process. The focus of the appraisal centers on four main topic areas which the author feels to be

pertinent considerations for the educator who is interested in using Piaget's findings in an educational framework. The four areas are as follows:

1. *Piaget's Description of Development Used as an Assessment of Intellectual Capacity*

Standardization of Piaget's stage observations shows considerable promise in the area of intellectual assessment. The desirability of devising an ordinal scale of intelligence, coupled with the fact that Piagetian items appear to be more sensitive to intellectual differences at an earlier age than other infant intelligence scales, makes Piaget's contribution in this area a potentially exciting one. The necessary research is just in its germinal stage, and it is expected that systematic attempts at further standardization will be performed.

2. *Piaget Stage Theory as an Aid to the Structure and Sequencing of Subject Matter in a Curriculum*

The Piagetian contribution to the structure and sequencing of subject matter is more apparent than real. This is clearly not the fault of Piaget, but rather of his educational followers. Uncritical extrapolation of Piaget's observations and his metatheoretical considerations (e.g., logico-mathematical model) is, in the opinion of the present author, harmful to the advancement of educational knowledge. The use of Piaget's stages as indicators of "learning readiness" seems most premature and needs more careful consideration on both the research and theoretical levels.

3. *Piaget's Description of Development as an Aid in Assessing Learning Outcomes in a Curriculum*

Piaget's genius is apparent when he is probing the concepts children have of the world. The teacher who reads Piaget is struck by the amazing differences illustrated between adults and children on a variety of concepts. The ability of Piaget to explore a concept in its depths and widths, and all its implications, makes him a model to be emulated by teachers. If teachers could use some of his probing techniques to explore concepts they are trying to teach they might find that the concept they teach is quite shallow. It would seem that the Piagetian-type probing is an excellent model for evaluating the outcomes of certain teaching sequences.

4. *Piaget's Observations on Development as Suggestive of Certain Types of Learning Atmospheres*

The ability of Piaget's theory to prescribe a particular type of learning atmosphere is pure extrapolation from his "equilibration model" of development. His followers in education who frequently quote him as an authority are the proponents of the "self-discovery" and "activity" methods. In a sense, Piaget is being used to foster the "mystique" of discovery learning (Ausubel 1961). Piaget's popularity in this area stems from the fact that his "equilibration" or "auto-regulation" model of development falls into the present *zeitgeist* of the discovery mystique. The educator who quotes Piaget in this area is taking the weakest part of the theory (i.e., equilibration) to substantiate his point of view. (Sullivan 1967, pp. 33–34)

Summary

Piaget's theory of intellectual development was considered in B-P-E terms with special attention to its educational relevance. Piaget uses intellectual stages to describe persons: sensori-motor stage, preoperational stage, and operational stage. He maintains that these stages form an invariant sequence that every child must go through, but Piaget does not, as many have mistakenly believed, maintain that each stage occurs at a specific age. Each Piagetian stage describes a mode of thinking that determines how a child will experience (or fail to experience), organize, and respond to various environmental (instructional) encounters. Thus, Piagetian stages may be considered contemporaneous accessibility characteristics because they provide valuable leads to differences in children's susceptibility to different educational approaches.

Since Piaget's theory is a developmental theory, he is concerned with learning-as-process. Although some of his followers have assumed that stage progression, or developmental growth, is the logical educational objective, Piaget himself does not agree with such an explicit objective. This is because he does not specify explicitly the environmental requirements for development from one stage to another, but he does believe that developmental growth (person-environment interaction) is determined by several factors: maturation, social interaction, physical experience, and equilibration.

Although Piaget has strong reservations about how much educational experience can accelerate or actively promote cognitive development, his followers have devised educational procedures, mostly involving some form of discovery, toward this end. It was concluded that Piagetian stages are probably more useful as accessibility characteristics than as determiners of educational objectives or curriculum sequences. A discussion of Bruner, Gagné and Vygotsky's theoretical views were included to provide a more balanced discussion of cognitive-developmental theories (in this case Piaget) within our B-P-E framework.

SUGGESTED READINGS

Aebli, H. "Piaget and Beyond." *Interchange,* vol. 1, no. 1 (1970), pp. 12–24.
Joyce, B., and Weil, M. *Models of Teaching.* pp. 180–198. Englewood Cliffs, N.J.: Prentice-Hall, 1972.

Sullivan, E. V. "Piagetian Theory in the Educational Milieu: A Critical Appraisal."
   Canadian Journal of Behavioral Science 1 (1969):129–155.
Wohlwill, J. F. "The Place of Structural Experience in Early Cognitive Development."
   Interchange, vol. 1, no. 2 (1970), pp. 13–27.

chapter 7

SKINNER

Having considered Piaget's theories, it is appropriate to review next the theories and experiments of B. F. Skinner. He is not only one of the most influential contemporary psychologists with respect to educational practice, but also his theories are strikingly different from those of Piaget. In his 1964 review of "Educational Psychology," Smedslund stated that "the outlines of a Skinner-Piaget controversy are becoming clearer" (p. 268). Therefore, a comparison is in order. Skinner's behavior theory was selected for consideration because of its current importance to educational practice and because of its contrast to Piagetian theory. It is not, however, an interactive theory. Skinner has never been concerned with conceptualizing the person.

This chapter has three major purposes: (1) to give another example of how B-P-E analysis is applied to a psychological theory; (2) to illustrate how B-P-E analysis sharpens the distinctions between alternative theories, in this case,

Piaget and Skinner; and (3) to indicate how Skinner's theory might be more valuable if it were explicit in the conceptualization of the person.

No attempt is made to provide a comprehensive description of Skinner's theory because such descriptions are available elsewhere (Skinner 1938; 1968). The theory is merely summarized briefly so it can be analyzed. Again, the analysis centers on the conceptions of person, environment, and behavior and their interaction, with attention to the educational relevance of the theoretical ideas.

Summary of Skinner's Theory

Skinner's theory is the outstanding contemporary example of behaviorism, or Stimulus-Response (S-R) theory. For the behaviorist, the B-P-E formula could be stated as $S \longrightarrow R$ (or Environment $\longrightarrow$ Behavior). If forced to include the person in the equation, the behaviorist would extend the formula to $S \longrightarrow O$ (Organism) $\longrightarrow R$. However, since behaviorism has discarded the introspective research method that puts the person at the center of the theory, it has devoted little attention to the organism. Indeed, Skinner's theory has been described as an "empty organism" theory.

As noted in the discussion of E. L. Thorndike, theories focusing on observable behavior are very attractive to educational decision-makers. Much of what is said here about Skinner would apply to Thorndike in an earlier time, and the Skinner-Piaget controversy today is fairly comparable to the Thorndike-Dewey differences of half-a-century ago.

Skinner's basic approach is a functional analysis of the relationship between the observable behavior and the external variables that have preceded the behavior. His Stimulus-Response notions are intended to identify those elements of the environment associated with the occurrence of a behavior or a response.

Skinner's (1938) behaviorism is based on two kinds of learning. The first, called *Type S* because of its dependence on the Stimulus, is identical to classical conditioning as described by Pavlov. Type S learning, or conditioning, is based on an original association between a stimulus, such as food in the Pavlov example, and a response, that is, salivation by the dog. Conditioning occurs when a previously neutral stimulus, such as the ringing of a bell, is presented before the food. Through this temporal association with the food, the ringing of the bell becomes a conditioned stimulus because it produces salivation.

The second kind of learning, called *Type R* because of its dependence on the *Reinforcement* of a response, is operant conditioning, as exemplified by a rat learning in a Skinner box. When a rat depresses the bar in the box, a food pellet (reinforcement) is made available. Subsequent increase in the animal's rate of bar-pressing (change in response) is therefore seen as determined by the food (reinforcement). In contrast to classical conditioning or Type S learning, operant conditioning requires the organism to act, or operate, on the environment. In classical conditioning, the environment operates on the organism.

Although Skinner recognizes the importance of classical conditioning, he places greater emphasis on operant conditioning and its potential survival value for the organism's interaction with its environment. In addition, Skinner contends that much of our everyday behavior can be clearly analyzed in operant terms. For example, the verbal statement "give me the pencil" operates on the environment (that is, another person) to obtain a pencil. If the person receives the pencil as requested, this is considered a reinforcement; in other words, the probability increases that one will *request* a pencil from that person again should the need arise.

REINFORCEMENT

Skinner has been adamant in his rejection of mentalistic concepts, and this antipathy for mentalism can be seen in his definition of reinforcement. If the occurrence of a reponse increases or is strengthened by the subsequent presentation of a stimulus, then that stimulus is a reinforcement. In the Skinner-box example, the reinforcement stimulus is the food because it increases the rate of response. Note that Skinner's definition of reinforcement makes no mention of any state of the organism. He rejects as mentalistic any reinforcement concepts that demand an interpretation of the organism's internal state. Even Thorndike's definition of reward as a condition producing a "satisfying state of affairs" would be considered mentalistic from Skinner's point of view.

Kinds of reinforcement. For Skinner, a positive reinforcement is a stimulus, that, when added to a situation, strengthens the probability of the operant response. The food pellet received by the rat is a positive primary reinforcer contingent on the animal's response. Food and water are therefore classified as positive reinforcers. A *negative reinforcer* is a stimulus that, when *removed* from a situation, strengthens the probability of an operant response. A Skinner box may have electrically charged grids for floors. If the electric charge is stopped by an animal pressing the bar, this response is likely to increase in the presence of the aversive stimulus. Electric shock, loud noises, extreme warmth or cold are examples of negative reinforcers.

Skinner distinguishes negative reinforcers from punishment. When he speaks of positive or negative reinforcers, he is referring to stimuli that increase response probability either by their presence (positive) or absence (negative). In contrast, punishment decreases response probability. Punishment is usually applied after a response to eliminate or suppress it. Skinner disagrees with this procedure of controlling behavior because the desired response is not occurring.

Secondary reinforcement. This describes a previously neutral stimulus (which was not a reinforcer) becoming a reinforcing stimulus through repeated association with a reinforcing stimulus. In a Skinner box, for example, colored light can become a secondary reinforcement if presented with the food pellet. Most of the reinforcements in everyday life, such as money, approval, and attention, are secondary reinforcements. In educational practice, giving a student his results on an examination may be a secondary reinforcement.

Reinforcement schedules. In Chapter 4, it was noted that psychologists frequently segment the environment into units called *trials,* and this is especially true for Skinner. A trial is defined as an arbitrary time period during which a response either occurs or does not occur. Segmenting the organism's experience into trials is critical for Skinner's theory because he is concerned with the *pattern* of reinforcement. A trial may be reinforced or nonreinforced, which makes it possible to describe reinforcement *schedules* in terms of the proportion of reinforced trials, for example, 50 per cent reinforcement schedule.

Ferster and Skinner (1957) have empirically tested the effects of a large number of reinforcement schedules. Although it should be noted that many schedules have been investigated, only four patterns will be discussed here. Before discussing and defining these schedules, however, a distinction between continuous and intermittent reinforcement is needed. Continuous reinforcement is reinforcement given for each operant response that is made. Intermittent reinforcement is given at ratios or intervals that are not continuous in nature. Intermittent reinforcement can be described in terms of ratio reinforcement and interval reinforcement. These two schedules can be further subdivided into fixed or variable ratio or interval reinforcement as follows:

Fixed-interval reinforcement is given at standard intervals of time (for example every ten minutes) determined by the experimenter.

Variable-interval reinforcement is given at variable intervals gauged around an average. In the variable-response schedules, responses may be rewarded every ten minutes on the *average,* although in some cases the reinforcement may follow immediately after a previous reinforcement and at other times it may be delayed.

Fixed-ratio reinforcement is given for a fixed rate of response. Instead of delivering pellets of food at standard intervals of time, a pellet is given after a standard number of responses, for example, reinforcement occurs after ten responses.

Variable-ratio reinforcement is given around an average rate of responses, for example, reinforcement occurs after an average of sixteen responses more or less.

The absence of reinforcement. What happens to an operant response when it is not reinforced? Skinner describes this in terms of extinction. Extinction is defined as the decrease in operant strength when reinforcement is not forthcoming. Schedules of reinforcement not only affect the operant rate of response acquisition but are also related to the persistence of operants in the process of extinction. Continuous schedules of reinforcement are more susceptible to extinction of operant strength after reinforcement is removed. Intermittent reinforcement produces greater resistance to extinction. Variable-interval schedules are more resistant to extinction than fixed-interval schedules. The gambler, reinforced on a variable ratio of reinforcement, is more likely to continue to gamble.

Next, because of their different educational implications, the terms discrimination of stimuli and response differentiation used by Skinner need to be distinguished.

Discrimination of stimuli. An operant response can become a discriminated operant if it is conditioned to a particular class of stimuli. For example, in the bar-pressing experiment, if the food pellet is given in the presence of a supporting stimulus, such as a red light, and not in the presence of a nonsupporting stimulus, such as a blue light, the operant response will only be made when the red light (or discriminated) stimulus appears. When the food is delivered in the presence of the discriminated stimulus and not with other stimuli, the situation is comparable to controlled intermittent reinforcement in which bar pressing is reinforced only on certain trials. As learning occurs, the response occurs almost exclusively in response to the discriminated stimulus and not to other stimuli.

Response differentiation. In operant conditioning, reinforcement may be contingent on either (1) the stimulus attributes of the situation (that is, discrimination) or (2) on variations in the response. The second case in which the reinforcement is based on the characteristics of the response is called response differentiation, or shaping. The rat in the Skinner box is taught to press the bar with a given force and for a given duration to produce the reinforcement. Many variations in response can be shaped: rapid pressing, slow pressing, rhythmic pressing. Performing animals in circuses are trained by using response differentiation techniques in which their behavior is gradually shaped through progressive differentiation to finely patterned responses that are the marvel of onlookers. As we shall see, shaping, or response differentiation, is also used to modify certain types of classroom behavior and to construct computer-assisted programs.

Educational Relevance

Because much of Skinner's original work was conducted on subhuman subjects, one might think that his theory would have fewer practical implications than a theory based directly on human behavior. Such is not the case. His principles, most of which have been verified at the human level, are appealing to educational practitioners.

Skinnerian behaviorism is a beacon in the wilderness to educators who are seeking methods to produce specific behaviorally defined objectives. The Skinnerian approach is to elicit the desired objective from the practitioner in specific, observable behavioral terms and then to suggest the technology to produce such behavior. Skinner is the classic example of psychology defined as "the prediction and control of behavior." For those educators who feel that educational objectives are complex and may be manifest in different ways, Skinner is likely to be less appealing. The Skinnerian reaction to such complexity may be that the educator does not know what he wants if he cannot specify his goal in precise, operational terms. Therefore, the educational problems to which Skinnerian behaviorism has contributed most are those that involve explicit, observable outcomes: computer-assisted instruction, control of classroom behavior, and language learning.

Skinner (1968) agrees with William James that teaching is an art and psychology is a science. It follows that it is important to have an inventive intermediary mind to mesh the two disciplines. Skinner believes that educational technology provides such an intermediary and points out that his functional analysis of behavior has produced something approaching an art and also a technology of teaching from which one can "deduce programs and schemes and methods of instruction" (Skinner 1968, p. 59). The best-known forms of educational technology derived from the functional analysis of behavior are teaching machines, programmed instruction, and the use of behavior modification in the classroom.

TEACHING MACHINES AND PROGRAMMED LEARNING

Although Skinner (1968) credits Sidney Pressey with originating teaching machines, the popularity of these machines in schools today is due largely to Skinner's pioneering efforts to make his laboratory principles applicable in real-life educational settings. In 1958, Skinner attempted to link his principles of operant conditioning to educational technology by showing their applicability to the development of teaching machines. One aim of teaching machines was to alleviate the teacher shortage. Although Skinner's theory was not concerned with individual differences, teaching machines serve to individual-ize instruction.

Based on the principles of functional analysis, the first teaching machine was built in the early 1950s. The machine poses a question to the learner in printed form. The question appears in a small window, called a "frame," in a box in front of the learner. Close to this window is another window that exposes a plain piece of paper on which the learner can write his answer, or, in Skinner's terms, respond. Skinner (1968) noted that a good teaching-machine program should require the student to compose his own response rather than to select it from a set of alternatives. Therefore, he disapproves of teaching machines that utilize the multiple-choice format for answers.

After the student responds with a written answer, he then checks his re-sponse against the correct answer. To do this, he releases a lever that brings the desired answer to a third window, where he can read both the question and the correct answer. If the student's answer is correct, he tries the next question, following the same procedure. If his answer is incorrect, he modulates the machine to show this question after the entire sequence of questions has been tried. The learner proceeds through the teaching program, question by ques-tion, until he completes the program.

Several features of the teaching machine are similar to operant conditioning. The learner constructing his own response to Skinner's teaching machine exemplifies an operant response and is of special importance because Skinner wants the learner to recall rather than to recognize the correct response among several alternatives. Skinner's disagreement with multiple-choice format is that it contains wrong responses that may throw off the delicate balance of shaping behavior by strengthening undesirable responses.

Because the emitted response is controlled by a question, it is under the control of a discriminated stimulus, that is, the question as stimulus, and the learner is unlikely to make random responses. A good program enables the learner to make those responses that are desired under a specific stimulus situation.

Another derivative from operant conditioning is that the learner gets imme-diate corrective feedback or reinforcement. That wrong answers are not rein-forced in Skinner's program illustrates his attempt to extinguish incorrect responses by nonreinforcement rather than by punishment. Finally, the learner's working through a carefully designed sequence of steps is analogous to Skinner's process of shaping, or successive approximation of responses. Skinner (1968) contends that each step in the program should bring the learner closer to fully competent behavior. The program assures the learner that these steps will be taken in a carefully prescribed order, usually of increasing difficulty. Shaping, or successive approximation, is a step-by-step process by which the learner is led, controlled, or reinforced into more complex behavior.

Skinner views the teaching machine as one avenue for more individualized instruction (Skinner 1968). He compared the teaching machine with a private tutor as follows: First, there is a constant interchange between program and learner. In contrast to ordinary textbooks and audio-visual aids, the machine induces sustained activity that keeps the learner alert. Second, like a good tutor, the machine insists that a given point be thoroughly understood, frame by frame, before the student proceeds further. Third, the machine presents only that material for which the student is ready. The purpose of small-step sequence is to allow the learner to succeed. Fourth, like a skillful tutor, the machine helps the learner make the correct response in part by the orderly construction of the program and in part by such techniques as hinting, prompting, and suggesting. Finally, the machine reinforces the student for every correct response, using immediate feedback to *shape* his behavior efficiently and to maintain the strength of response in a manner that the layman describes as "holding the student's interest" (Skinner 1968).

The fact that Skinner's assumptions ignore an explicit person dimension leaves him open to criticisms that we think are cogent. For example, Ausubel (1967) notes that the advocates of programmed instruction (proponents of a short-frame, small step-size approach stressing the importance of reinforcement) take a neobehavioristic position. In terms of ecological validity, most programmed materials in school are meaningfully learned rather than rote learned. Ausubel's position (1967) is that programming characteristics and principles, based as they are on rote-learning theory, are neither theoretically cogent nor empirically supportable.

Programmed learning is not limited to the teaching machine and can be applied to other media, such as books or more-automated computer-assisted instruction. In fact, Skinner has devised a programmed-learning textbook that outlines his viewpoints on the functional analysis of behavior (Holland and Skinner 1961). The same principles of operant conditioning apply to the textbook as to the machine.

BEHAVIOR MODIFICATION IN THE CLASSROOM

Skinner's functional analysis of behavior has also been used to devise procedures for dealing with problems that arise in the classroom. Since the student behavior to be modified has been primarily "problem" behavior of a nonacademic variety (Hanley 1970), behavior modification in the classroom is essentially synonymous with classroom control.

Because classroom control is a major problem for many teachers and because successful instruction requires some form of control, Skinnerian procedures for controlling classroom behavior are popular. Skinner's first premise in recommending classroom-control procedures to teachers is to make the teacher aware of the reinforcing effects of his behavior on students. A study by O'Leary, Becker, Evans, and Saudargas (1969) is a good example of Skinnerian principles applied in the classroom. The general aim of this study was to examine the separate effects of classroom rules, educational structure, teacher praise, and a token reinforcement program on children's disruptive behavior. The subjects in this study were seven lower-class elementary students, all noted for their disruptive behavior. Disruptive behavior was characterized by (1) motor behaviors: wandering around the room; (2) aggressive behaviors: hitting, kicking, striking another child with an object; (3) disturbing another's property: grabbing another's book, tearing up another's paper; (4) disruptive noise: clapping, stamping feet; (5) turning around: turning to the person behind or looking to the rear of the room when the teacher was in front of the class; (6) verbalization: talking to others when not permitted by teacher, blurting out answers, name calling.

The study proceeded through the following phases: (1) *Base Period*—disruptive behavior was estimated before any control techniques were utilized. (2) *Classroom Rules*—after an initial base rate was estimated, the teacher wrote certain rules on the blackboard, such as "We sit in our seats." The teacher reviewed these rules every morning. (3) *Educational Structure*—the teacher organized her program into four thirty-minute sessions in which the whole class participated (spelling, reading, arithmetic, and science). (4) *Praise and Ignore*—in addition to structuring and reiterating the rules, the teacher praised appropriate behavior and ignored disruptive behavior as much as possible. In keeping with Skinner's philosophy about punishment, the teacher was asked to discontinue all use of threats. (5) *Token Reinforcement*—a token-reinforcement system was introduced by the teacher in combination with the conditions introduced earlier. The children were told that they would receive points or ratings that reflected how well they followed the rules. The children could exchange their points (tokens) for reinforcers, such as candy, comics, and dolls. The variety of reinforcers made it probable that one item would be specifically appealing to each child. The more tokens the student collected, the more valuable the reinforcer. (6) *Withdrawal*—to demonstrate that the tokens and reinforcers were effective over other contingencies, the token system was discontinued for a time and later reinstituted. (7) *Follow-Up* —the token system was again discontinued to see if the appropriate behavior could be maintained under normal classroom conditions.

The results of the study indicated that the procedures outlined for the Classroom Rules, Educational Structure, and Praise and Ignore had very little effect on the disruptive behavior of most of the children. One child's disruptive behavior decreased, but the others did not change. With the introduction of the Token-Reinforcement system, however, there were significant reductions in disruptive behavior for all children. Disruptive behavior increased when the token system was withdrawn and decreased again when the token system was reintroduced. The Follow-Up procedure seemed to be effective for some children but not for others.

This study was conducted in a single classroom and focused on only seven of the twenty-one students. The results point to the greater effectiveness of token-reinforcement systems over other means of classroom control. Why token systems should be more effective than teacher praise is an issue not readily understood in Skinner's theory. However, there are enough examples of the utility of behavior modification in the classroom to suggest the relevance of Skinnerian principles to educational problems. It seems that the more clearly the problem can be stated in objective, operational terms, the more relevant Skinnerian principles are likely to be in its solution.

Before turning to a B-P-E analysis of Skinner's theory, it may be useful to make one or two points about the study. Although it seems initially that there is no acknowledgement of individual differences in Skinnerian principles, the use of a variety of reinforcers that can be exchanged for tokens is a bow in that direction. Once variation in preference for (or reponse to) concrete reinforcers is acknowledged, the idea that persons are differentially susceptible to praise versus concrete reinforcers does not seem too farfetched, a point expanded in the next section.

Conception of the Person

As just noted, the application of behavior-modification principles to a specific individual requires attention to what that individual will find reinforcing. The applied Skinnerian is in a curious dilemma. The theory has no terms to describe individual differences, yet the principles will not work with a specific person unless the reinforcement is appropriate. The applied Skinnerian, therefore, must be an astute clinician who assesses the person with whom he is working to decide what reinforcer(s) will be most effective. Put another way, teachers may not be as unaware of reinforcement principles as Skinner implies. What they often need most is information about what will constitute a reinforcer for a specific student.

If persons were conceptualized in terms of their motivational orientation, such information should be useful in specifying the form of reinforcement most likely to be effective. Zigler (1970) is one of the few researchers who makes an attempt to conceptualize the person when he considers the possible role of "social-class" differences and their relation to reinforcement contingencies. Zigler is influenced by Piaget because he suggests that a person's cognitive structure may determine the most effective type of reinforcement. Zigler cited evidence that the type of verbal reinforcement most effective with lower-class seven-year-old children was personal praise, while the most effective reinforcers for middle-class children were statements indicating that their behavior was correct. This may be represented as follows:

Person	Environment	Behavior
Lower-class	Praise	Effective Performance
Middle-class	Correctness	

Zigler has considered these social-class differences in terms of both contemporaneous and developmental explanations. The contemporaneous explanation is that middle-class children are more receptive to correctness because "being right" is more highly valued in the middle class than in the lower class. In contrast to this sociogenic interpretation is a developmental explanation that argues for a developmental hierarchy of reinforcers from approval to correctness to self-reinforcement as shown in Table 12. As persons develop, they become more susceptible to reinforcers higher on the hierarchy, and many lower-class children may be developmentally slower in this progression. Choosing between the contemporaneous and developmental explanations could be approached by measuring the children's motivational orientations separately. Thus, each child might be assessed in terms of his need for approval and his need to be correct (achievement).

Conception of Behavior

While Piaget emphasizes process, Skinner is concerned with the content of behavior. The Skinnerian approach begins with a specification of the behavior to be modified, a procedure that implicitly restricts the range of problems dealt with. Complex processes, such as fantasy, problem solving, and creative production, do not readily lend themselves to behavioral specification. Therefore, they are unlikely problems for behavior modification.

Specification of the behavior to be modified as the necessary first step eliminates many complex problems. The Skinnerian response to a complex process, such as problem solving, may be that there is nothing to analyze until the behavior has been objectively and operationally defined. The effect on education of Skinner's functional analysis of behavior is an overemphasis on recall, objective tests, and lower-level skills, not because they are important but because they can be recorded objectively and operationally. In his conception of behavior, Skinner is similar to those educational researchers who emphasize the measurement of specific objectives. There is nothing wrong with such precision, but it is when the specification becomes the exclusive criterion that difficulty begins.

Because of this similarity between Skinner's theory and educational approaches requiring specification of objectives, Skinnerian principles are popular with the business-educational firms that contract with school boards to deliver a certain amount of performance increase at a specified rate. The first step in performance contracting is to specify the desired performance in operational terms, for example the student's score on a specific test. The desired performance may be specified in more comprehensive terms, but it is nonetheless true that when the educational process is "objectified," as in performance contracting or accountability, the criterion is likely to be only a single-test score. Once this first step has been taken, the Skinnerian principles are appealing as a basis for deriving procedures to increase student's test scores.

Wohlwill (1962) makes this point in discussing the values implicit in the use of teaching machines:

> From the writings of workers in the teaching-machine field, it would appear that their activities represent essentially an engineering venture, altogether neutral with respect to broader questions of the philosophy of education. Whatever the educator wishes to see taught, they assert, can be made suitable for instruction via teaching machine, provided only the particular behaviors which he wishes the student to learn are specified precisely enough. But in application such a prescription tends to impose in itself a very definite conception of the objectives of the educational process, i.e., the acquisition of *particular correct responses.* (pp. 142–143)

This is not to say that Skinnerian principles might not be applied to more complex processes, but at this point their relevance in this domain is unknown. Hanley (1970) noted that behavior-modification procedures had not been applied directly to academic behavior, but there is no reason why this could not be done.

The responses that have been modified most effectively are disruptive behavior in the classroom. The shaping of such behavior, which is more affective than cognitive, is illustrated by Hewitt's work (1964) with mentally retarded children. Hewitt used the following seven-step behavioral hierarchy to shape the children's behavior:

1. *Primary task level.* At this most primitive level the teacher provides maxi-

mum gratification and tries to establish contact with the student on his own terms, providing a basis for future interactions where more control and direction can be exercised.

2. *Acceptance task level.* At this level, the teacher attempts to move the child into a relationship with him (her) as a social object. The teacher has the student compete only with his own record, no grades are given, and academic demands are kept at a minimum.

3. *Order task level.* After acceptance seems secure enough, the teacher attempts to increase control and gradually impose structure, routine, and definite limits in the learning situation.

4. *Exploratory task level.* At this level, the teacher and child explore the environment together. The teacher moves from order to introducing a rich variety of multisensory experiences and the child is encouraged to reach out and explore the real world around him with his eyes, hands, nose, etc.

5. *Relationship task level.* The teacher attempts to increase her value as a social reinforcer by forming a genuine relationship with the child. The child is concerned with gaining the teacher's approval and recognition. Social approval and disapproval are now used as a means of motivation and control.

6. *Mastery task level.* The first five levels did not stress academic accomplishment in any way. The teacher's task at the mastery level is to help the student acquire essential information and understanding about the environment and to develop intellectual and vocational skills. Here reading, writing, and arithmetic are introduced as skills to be learned.

7. *Achievement task level.* At this highest level, the child is consistently self-motivated and eager for new learning. His activities are socially well-integrated in classroom functioning.

These tasks take into consideration the mentally retarded child's position on certain behavioral dimensions. Here, person and behavior are used interchangeably. The tasks are geared to the lowest hierarchical level the child attains on any of the behavioral dimensions. Hewitt (1964) feels that the chances that a student will be successful at a given task are greatly increased if he is adequately functioning at all lower levels. Hewitt's hierarchy might provide a basis for characterizing persons at different "need" levels, a combination that would make explicit the differential effects of behavior modification.

Conception of the Environment

Skinner's view of the role of environment is similar to the educational growth metaphor suggested by Scheffler (1960), in which the environment molds the organism (clay). One of Skinner's major contributions has been to provide a basis for an objective characterization of the environment. Just as behavior must be objective and operational, so must the environment.

Skinner views environmental effects as reinforcing or nonreinforcing. Therefore, the first step in studying an environment is to decide on a time unit or "trial." Once this has been settled, one can speak of a reinforced or a nonreinforced trial. For example, say the behavior to be modified is Bobby's leaving his seat. Behavior modification requires a unit of time to determine (1) whether the desired behavior (Bobby in his seat) was occurring or not so that (2) if the desired behavior were occurring, a reinforcer could be administered. Thus, all of the more complex characterizations of the environment require establishing the unit of a trial.

With teaching machines, of course, there is no problem involved in defining a trial. The program is constructed around built-in trials, and the occurrence of reinforcement or nonreinforcement can be clearly measured.

Reinforcement, like behavior, is defined entirely in objective terms. The relative value of the same reinforcement for different persons (subjective definition) is not considered, and it is only in the procedure that permits a person to select from among reinforcers in exchanging tokens that this is considered.

Table 12 is based on Hewitt's seven-step hierarchy, described in the last section, and includes those hierarchically specific reinforcers that a teacher should provide at each level.

Conception of Person-Environment Interaction

Table 12 gives an example of B-E interaction, but it could also serve as a guide for P-E interaction. The Zigler (1970) study discussed earlier is another example of P-E interaction. However, there are not many examples, and we suggest a hypothetical example to illustrate how behavior modification might be made more valuable with the explicit inclusion of a person conception. We use a personality dimension proposed by McDougall in the early 1900s as a developmental hierarchy of social development. The four levels are as follows:

Stage 1 Anomy—the first and lowest stage is characterized by purely instinctive behavior where conduct is modified by the experience of pleasure and pain.

Stage 2 Heteronomy—in this stage, the child is ruled by others, for example, teachers and parents, and is dominated by their imposition of rules.

Stage 3 Socionomy—in this third stage, there is increasing control of the child's conduct through the use of social praise and social opinion.

Stage 4 Autonomy—the highest stage is that in which the individual has his own internalized ideals of conduct that are no longer dependent on a form of authority or public opinion.

Table 12.   Differential Behavior–Environment Interactions for
Hewitt's Mentally Retarded Children

	Behavior	Appropriate teacher environment
I	Primary task level	Teacher provides maximum support for student
II	Acceptance task level	Teacher attempts to move into a personal relationship with student
III	Order task level	Teacher increases control and imposes structure
IV	Exploratory task level	Teacher mutually explores environment with student
V	Relationship task level	Teacher attempts to increase value of social reinforcers
VI	Mastery task level	Teacher attempts to help student acquire academic skills
VII	Achievement task level	Teacher encourages student to do more self-motivated learning

For the environment dimension of our hypothetical system of reinforcements, the following examples are given. The reinforcement varies differentially from extrinsic to intrinsic forms of reinforcement. Extrinsic rewards would be candy, gum, balloons, etc. Intrinsic rewards might be science projects and puzzles, field trips, etc. See Figure 11.

A study by Hidi (1971) indicates some differential susceptibility to reinforcement. Hidi's study investigated the effect of social approval at different levels of ego development. The person dimension of ego development devised by Loevinger (1969) postulates certain invariant stages. The stages are roughly as follows:

1. Presocial-symbiotic
2. Impulsive
3. Self-protective
4. Conformist
5. Conscientious
6. Autonomous
7. Integrated

Hidi (1971) used the social-desirability scale to test the prediction that motivation to gain social approval would increase with ego development until the conformist stage and would decrease thereafter, and this prediction was confirmed. These results provide indirect support for the interactions in Figure 11.

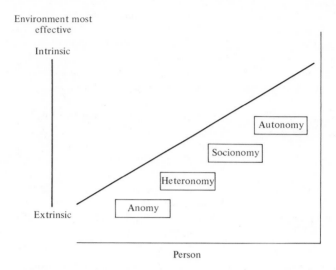

Figure 11   Hypothetical Model of Differences in Persons Related to Skinner's Theory

Summary

Skinner's behaviorism has been especially attractive to educational practitioners because it emphasizes the use of reinforcement (environment) to change behavior. His ideas are also in agreement with an emphasis on the specification of educational objectives (B).

Teaching machines and behavior modification in the classroom were discussed as two major examples of the application of Skinner's theory in educational practice, and both involve the manipulation of the environment to produce the desired behavior.

Although Skinner has explicitly ignored the person in stating his principles ("empty organism theory"), the B-P-E paradigm was used to point out how the introduction of variations in the person might make Skinner's ideas more valuable in educational practice. Although persons who apply behavior modification must make some assessment of the person, Skinner's theory provides no basis for making such a description. Several dimensions of the person were suggested as accessibility characteristics that would define the nature and form of reinforcement most likely to be effective.

SUGGESTED READINGS

Baer, D. M.; Wolf, M.; and Risley, R. "Some Current Dimensions of Applied Behavior Analysis." *Journal of Applied Analysis* 1 (1958):91–97.

Burger, H. G. "Behaviour Modification, an Operant Psychology: An Anthropological Critique. *American Educational Research Journal* 9 (1972):343–360.

Hewett, F. M. "A Hierarchy of Educational Tasks for Children with Learning Disorders." *Exceptional Children* 31 (1964):207–214.

Joyce, B., and Weil, M. *Models of Teaching.* pp. 271–292. Englewood Cliffs, N.J.: Prentice-Hall, 1972.

O'Leary, K.; Becker, W.; Evans, B.; and Saudargas, R. A. "A Token Reinforcement Program in a Public School: A Replication and Systematic Analysis." *Journal of Applied Behaviour Analysis* 2 (1969):3–13.

chapter 8

AUSUBEL

Introduction

The work of David Ausubel in educational psychology provides an interesting contrast and comparison with Piaget and Skinner. First, he defines himself specifically as an educational psychologist, and throughout all of his writings Ausubel takes an interactionist perspective in theory or in practice, or in both. Therefore, this chapter will deal primarily with the interactionist perspective without necessarily looking at all facets of his theory. Some of his work has been done with collaborators (Ausubel and Robinson 1969; Ausubel and Sullivan 1970) and, in this chapter, the use of his name refers to him and his collaborators. Ausubel addresses virtually all aspects of educational psychology with an emphasis on the cognitive domain. His main treatment of the affective domain is found in his theory of ego development discussed at the end of this chapter.

Ausubel is a cognitive theorist whose work can be understood in the tradition of Vygotsky (1965), as described in Chapter 6. Certain aspects of Ausubel's theory have yet to be validated by long-term research studies, and he acknowledges this fact (Ausubel and Robinson 1969):

> ... the products of reasoning within a comprehensive theoretical system are to be preferred as guidelines to classroom practice to extrapolations from research studies which, at best, relate tangentially to critical elements in classroom learning. (Ausubel and Robinson 1969, p.vi)

Theory of Meaningful Verbal Learning

EDUCATIONAL RELEVANCE

His specific cognitive views and his unique contributions are in an area that he designated *meaningful verbal learning* (Ausubel 1963). This position developed as a result of his conclusion that the relevance of psychological learning theories to pedagogy is highly questionable (Ausubel 1967). As he pointed out:

> Much of the disillusionment regarding the relevance and applicability of learning theory to classroom results from the tendency, among educational psychologists, to uncritically extrapolate research findings from laboratory studies of simplified learning situations to the more complex classroom environment. This practice accounts in large measure for our lack of knowledge about school learning processes, and reflects the fascination which many research workers feel for the basic science approach to research in the applied sciences, as well as the failure to appreciate the inherent limitations of this approach. (Ausubel 1967, p. 1)

According to Ausubel, the task of the school is to identify clear, stable, and organized bodies of knowledge within disciplines. The educator's task is to transmit these bodies of knowledge in such a way that they will be incorporated meaningfully by the learner into his own system and become functional for him. Meaning is a clearly articulated and precisely differentiated conscious experience that emerges when signs, symbols, concepts, or propositions are related to and incorporated within a given individual's *cognitive structure*[1] on a nonarbitrary and substantive basis. Meaning therefore requires a plausible basis for relationships and a content that does not depend on a particular wording but could be expressed in different wording without loss or change

[1]Cognitive structure refers to the total content and organization of a given individual's ideas, or the content and organization of his ideas in a particular area of knowledge.

in meaning (Ausubel 1967; 1968). Meaningful learning depends on the nature of the material to be learned (E) and the availability of relevant content in the particular learner's cognitive structure (P). The two criteria for potentially meaningful learning are *nonarbitrariness* and *substantiveness.* These two properties of relatability give the material its logical meaningfulness. To determine meaningfulness of material, therefore, one must estimate the degree to which it is nonarbitrary and substantive. To clarify these ideas, the following table of learning tasks is given to highlight our discussion.

Table 13.   Illustrative Learning Tasks

Item	Content	Nature of Item
1.	"lud"	Nonsense syllable
2.	strong-liable	Paired associates (Task is to recall second word when the first is given)
3.	Mr. Jones	Name of specific object
4.	they went out slowly together when it came with her check	4th order approximation to English[*]
5.	The cat climbed the plum tree.	Simple declarative sentence (proposition)
6.	An equilateral triangle with three equal sides	Definition of a concept
7.	The sum of the three internal angles of any plane triangle equals 180°	Generalization (proposition) which is true in plane Euclidean Geometry

[*]A 4th order approximation to English is achieved in the following manner. A number of persons contribute one word each to a chain, of which they see only the four immediately preceding words, with the additional requirement that the word which they contribute must make sense in the context of the preceding four words.

The first item in Table 13 is a nonsense syllable containing letters that are individually identifiable but taken together make no sense. A nonsense syllable would probably not be sensibly (meaningfully) related to anything that the learner might already know. To remember this item at some future time would probably demand rote-learning (that is, letter-by-letter learning).

In item 6, the "equilateral triangle" presents a completely different learning situation. It is likely that the learner who is presented with this item (assuming he has some mathematics) has probably already encountered and can recognize and define the general concept of triangle, so the item to be learned is merely a specific instance of something that he already knows. In this instance, he is able to relate the new item to his existing knowledge and therefore make sense of it. Each item in Table 13, in its turn, is roughly arranged in an order of increasing strength of relatability, the strength of the relationship depending in large measure upon the number of items in a cognitive structure to which the new material can be related.

The increasing meaningfulness, or relatability, in Table 13, is specifically indicated by substantiveness and nonarbitrariness. Substantiveness means that the relationship is not altered if a different, but equivalent, form of wording is used. For example, item 6 in the table can be useful in illustrating substantiveness because the relationship of an equilateral triangle to a general triangle is not changed in any way if one were to reword the definition of the former to read "an equilateral triangle is a triangle that has all of its sides equal" (Ausubel and Robinson 1969). By contrast, item 1, the nonsense syllable "lud," is not capable of substantive relationship with any item of existing knowledge, so that if any letters are changed, the learning requirements change completely.

Meaningful verbal learning is considered nonarbitrary because the relationship between the new item to be learned is congruent with existing ideas in a cognitive structure. For example, the relation of an "equilateral triangle" and "triangle" is the relationship of a specific instance to a general case and is clearly nonarbitrary, as is item 7. By contrast, item 2 is somewhat arbitrary, since the particular members of the given pair of adjectives are linked together in a purely arbitrary or random fashion. There seems no plausible basis for nonarbitrarily relating the learning task to the person's cognitive structure, and this applies even more to item 1. Ausubel (1967; 1968) stressed the importance of the person in this process when he states that for meaningful learning to occur:

> the cognitive structure of the particular learner must include the relevant ideational content and the requisite abilities. Since these are idiosyncratic (peculiar to an individual) the potential meaningfulness of learning materials will necessarily vary with such factors as age, I.Q., occupation, subject-matter, sophistication, social class, and cultural membership of the particular learner. (Ausubel 1967, pp. 18–19)

Ausubel's theory is interactionist in nature, and he aligns himself with Vygotsky in criticizing both Piaget for his overemphasizing the person and the behaviorists for their overemphasizing the environment (Ausubel and Sullivan 1970).

CONCEPT LEARNING

His interactionist view is illustrated by his description of concept learning, in which he distinguishes between concept formation and concept assimilation.

Concept formation. This is a process of abstracting essential common features from a class of objects or events that vary contextually, in other non-criterial respects, or along dimensions other than those being considered (Ausubel 1968; Ausubel and Sullivan 1970).

Taking a developmental perspective, Ausubel contends that at any stage in the child's development there may be a considerable discrepancy between the "criterial attributes"[2] that he has discovered (which give psychological meaning to the concept) and those criterial attributes that define the logical meaning of the concept (Ausubel and Robinson 1969). For example, young children may have a limited and imprecise concept of "triangle" which, as a result of experience and feedback, will become progressively more similar to the logical concept.

As the child grows older, possibly entering school, he learns the concept name or concept word "cube," which is indicated in Figure 12 as stage II. The learning of the concept name is a kind of representational learning because the child learns that a spoken or written symbol "cube" is to represent the concept already acquired in stage I. The concept word, or "name," will thus acquire a *denotative* meaning and will elicit a differentiated representative image comprising the criterial attributes of the concept. The child now associates the word "cube" with his existing conception of "cube-ness." The *connotative* meaning depends on the idiosyncratic, personal affective and attitudinal reactions that the term elicits in each child, according to his particular experience with the class of objects.

Concept assimilation. The formation of concepts, as described above, is typical of the learning of young children (Ausubel and Robinson 1969). However, after the preschool years, the meanings of most concept words are learned by definition or by being encountered in appropriate contexts. For example, a definition furnishes for the learner the criterial attributes expressed in already meaningful terms. Learning by definition is a form of proposition learning. Proposition learning involves the learning of a new composite idea in sentence form (for example, "Crocodiles eat children.") (Ausubel and Robinson 1969). When the learner acquires the criterial attributes of a concept through defini-

---

[2] *Criterial attributes* refer to the essential features of an object and/or idea which make it part of a class or species (for example, an orange has such essential features as roundness, color, texture, etc., which distinguish it from an apple and also make it part of a class or species).

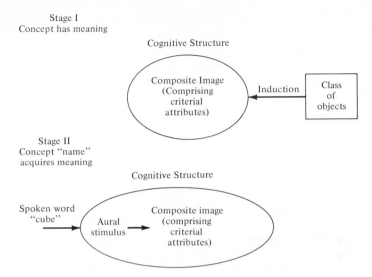

Stage I
Concept has meaning

Cognitive Structure

Composite Image (Comprising criterial attributes) ← Induction ← Class of objects

Stage II
Concept "name" acquires meaning

Cognitive Structure

Spoken word "cube" → Aural stimulus → Composite image (comprising criterial attributes)

Figure 12   Two Stages in Learning of Concept Names (Taken from Ausubel and Robinson 1969, p. 62)

tion rather than through discovery (as in concept formation), the learning involved is referred to as concept assimilation. The issue of discovery learning and its relation to didactic approaches will be discussed later in the chapter.

As the child develops, reception learning gradually becomes ascendant over discovery learning in the acquisition of concepts. Beginning with the child's entrance into school, an increasing proportion of his concepts are acquired by definition or use in context. But it is only as he approaches adolescence that such nonspontaneous concepts manifest true categorical and generalized meaning. Prior to this time (during the stage of concrete logical operations), his concepts are likely to be somewhat particularistic and intuitive because of their dependence on concrete empirical supports.

Concept assimilation gradually becomes the predominant mode of concept acquisition once the child reaches school age. By contrast, concept formation, although possible at any age level, is usually more characteristic of the preoperational or preschool stage of cognitive development. Concept assimilation characterizes the acquisition of secondary concepts; it presupposes sufficient intellectual maturity to relate to cognitive structure the abstracted criterial attributes of a new generic idea. Since this degree of maturity does not exist before school age, and exists initially in the school-age child only through the support of concrete empirical experience, the principal alternative open to the preschooler is to discover the criterial attributes of concepts by himself, using the necessary conceptualizing operations of abstraction, differentiation, hypothesis generation and testing, and generalization. In so doing, he is obviously limited to the simpler kinds of primary concepts whose referents are either perceptible and familiar or represented by known concept words. But the criterial attributes of a concept that are discovered through concept formation obviously meet the developmental conditions for relatability to cognitive structure, since they have been abstracted from and tested against particular exemplars of the concept during the process of conceptualization. Hence, there is no problem with respect to the potential meaningfulness of criterial attributes that he discovers by himself.

However, once the child can meaningfully relate to his cognitive structure the criterial attributes of a new concept without first relating them to multiple particular instances that exemplify it, he can acquire concepts much more efficiently. By the time he reaches this stage of development he has also already acquired most of the available primary concepts with familiar and perceptible referents. He would thus find it relatively difficult to discover by himself (to acquire by concept formation) the more abstract and complex concepts he attains relatively easily through concept assimilation. Hence, after discovering the body of simple everyday concepts that are available to them when they enter school, most individuals discover few concepts by themselves thereafter. Contributions to culture's store of more difficult concepts are made by its more gifted members over the course of generations and become readily available to all other adequately mature members through concept assimilation (Ausubel and Sullivan 1970).

During the elementary-school years, it thus appears that progressive development of the ability to *assimilate* concepts depends on the same three aspects of cognitive and language development that generally bring about the transition from concrete to abstract cognitive functioning: (1) gradual acquisition of an adequate working body of higher-order abstractions that provide the component properties and relational elements constituting the criterial attributes of more difficult concepts; (2) gradual acquisition of "transactional" terms (that is, of substantive words, such as "state," "condition," "basis," "property," "quality," and "relationship") and of functional terms, or terms of syntax, such as conditional conjunctions and qualifying expressions, that are necessary for bringing abstractions into relationship with each other in ways characteristic of the dictionary definition of new concepts; and (3) gradual acquisition of the cognitive capacity that makes possible the relation of abstract ideas to cognitive structure without benefit of concrete empirical support.

It is important to recognize and take into account the highly significant interaction that takes place between many assimilated concepts and their subverbal or intuitive precursors. As Vygotsky (1965) noted, the elementary-school child, in acquiring assimilated concepts, is greatly assisted by the existence in his cognitive structure of analogous spontaneous concepts at the preoperational level, which he uses nondeliberately and with relatively little cognitive awareness.[3] These provide a springboard for the acquisition of "scientific" concepts[4] and for their "downward" exemplification and everyday reference. But although these spontaneous concepts undoubtedly enhance the meaningfulness of their analogous assimilated counterparts, and probably discourage rote-reception learning, they may also, because of their primacy and vividness, interfere with the learning of more precise and categorical criterial attributes. The same kind of relationships also undoubtedly prevail between the more precise and abstract concepts acquired at the secondary-school level and their more intuitive elementary-school precursors.

It is important to note here Ausubel's developmental perspective. In teaching scientific concepts, it is essential to take into account the nature of their spontaneous precursors; that is, explicitly to contrast the two sets of criterial attributes and to indicate why the adoption of the more abstract and precise set is preferable. Within the limits imposed by developmental readiness, systematic verbal instruction in abstract concepts at the elementary-school level, combined with appropriate use of concrete empirical support, is pedagogically feasible and can greatly accelerate the acquisition of higher-order concepts. Ausubel (1968) contends it is unnecessary and educationally wasteful to wait for such concepts to evolve spontaneously from direct experience. Further, many abstract concepts (for instance, "photosynthesis," "ionization") can only be acquired verbally, since they are not susceptible to direct experience. Other, more concrete concepts ("house," "dog," "red," "hot"), on the other hand, are practically meaningless in the absence of actual experience with the objects or phenomena in question.

Both Piaget and Vygotsky agree that awareness of the cognitive operations involved in concept acquisition does not develop until the child approaches adolescence and has been exposed to considerable systematic instruction in scientific concepts.

As Vygotsky stated:

> In operating with spontaneous concepts the child is not conscious of them because his attention is always centered on the object to which the concept refers, never on the act of thought itself. . . . A concept can become subject

[3]"Work," for example, is both a spontaneous concept acquired from direct experience and a more formal, abstract concept with precise criterial attributes.

[4]Vygotsky's term for assimilated concepts in contradistinction to concepts acquired by concept formation ("spontaneous concepts").

to conscious and deliberate control only when it is part of a system. . . .
In the scientific concepts that the child acquires in school, the relationship
to an object is mediated from the start by some other concept. . . . A
superordinate concept implies the existence of a series of subordinate
concepts, and it also pre-supposes a hierarchy of concepts at different
levels of generality. . . . Thus the very notion of a scientific concept implies
a certain position in relation to other concepts. . . .
The rudiments of systematization first enter the child's mind by way of his
contact with scientific concepts and are transferred to everyday concepts,
changing their psychological structure from the top down. (Vygotsky
1962, pp. 92, 93)

Awareness of concept acquisition develops late, Vygotsky (1965) believes,
because it requires awareness of similarity. This, in turn, presupposes a more
advanced structure of generalization and conceptualization than mere awareness of difference. Nevertheless, even though a child cannot use a word like
"because" deliberately in a test situation and does not really grasp causal
relations except in a primitive and intuitive sense, he is able to use "because"
correctly in everyday conversation. The rules of syntax, too, can generally be
employed correctly by young children despite complete lack of awareness of
the nature of these rules. However, deliberate use of such words as "because"
is possible in relation to scientific concepts because the "teacher, working with
the pupil, has explained, supplied information, questioned, corrected, and
made the pupil explain" (Vygotsky 1965). Ausubel (1968) is not surprised that
concept acquisition and deliberate use of concepts arise earlier in relation to
scientific than to spontaneous concepts, and he is therefore in essential agreement with Vygotsky on this point.

Conception of the Person

Of the several dimensions Ausubel proposed to describe persons, this section
deals primarily with the concrete-abstract dimension of intellectual development. Because this dimension is similar to Piaget's stages discussed in Chapter
6, it serves as the best example of Ausubel's conception of the person.

Ausubel roughly outlines this sequence as the *preoperational stage* of
thought, the *concrete operational stage* and the *abstract logical stage.* In terms
of school learning, these stages in our own culture cover respectively the
preschool, elementary-school, and the adolescent and adult periods of development.

PREOPERATIONAL STAGE

This stage encompasses all of the characteristics of Piaget's preconceptual and
intuitive stages. For Ausubel (1963; 1968) this period is best understood in

terms of the child's concept acquisition. At the preoperational stage, the child has the capacity to acquire and utilize primary abstractions. Primary concepts are those concepts whose meanings a given individual originally learns in relation to concrete empirical experience (Ausubel and Robinson 1969). The previous example of the acquisition of the concept "cube" is appropriate in this context. Recall that the child was exposed to a series of examples of the concept and, from this experience, he was able to abstract its criterial attributes and to form a representative image (see Figure 12, Stage I), which constitutes the meaning of the concept. Even if the "cube" concept was acquired in another way (for example, direct instruction), the essential conditions for the learning of primary concepts are the availability of a series of concrete examples and the child's recognition that each of these examples contains the set of criterial attributes defining the concept. Therefore, Ausubel agrees with Piaget in the belief that the child's cognitive processes at the preoperational stage tend to be dominated by his perceptions (that is "stimulus bound").

CONCRETE OPERATIONAL STAGE

This stage corresponds to Piaget's stage of concrete operations. However, Ausubel emphasizes the type of capacity in concept acquisition, rather than stressing the operational groupings as Piaget does. The emergence of conservation as described in Chapter 6, indicates an increasing facility to manipulate images:

> This facility is also reflected in the chief characteristic of this stage, the child's ability to comprehend concepts without proceeding through the abstracting phase characteristic of the learning of primary concepts. Concepts acquired without this abstracting phase are referred to as *secondary abstractions* (concepts). Thus in the concrete operational stage the child may be given a verbal definition containing the criterial attributes of a concept, then in order to acquire the meaning of the concept, he need only be provided with concrete exemplars of one or more of the criterial attributes. (Ausubel and Robinson 1969, p. 185)

For example, the child in this stage of development would be able to comprehend the meaning of the term "rhombus" when defined as "a quadrilateral with two parallel sides," provided he was given concrete examples of "parallel" and "quadrilateral" (Ausubel and Robinson 1969). Thus, given stimulus support provided by concrete images of examples of the criterial attributes, the child is able to construct mentally a representative image embodying the meaning of the concept.

The distinguishing characteristic of the concrete operational stage (the ability to comprehend secondary abstractions) emphasizes the child's ability to assimilate concepts verbally and is in marked contrast to Piaget's ideas about the relation between stage of development and language:

> In the most general terms, we may say that the learner in the second stage does not abstract criterial attributes from a series of exemplars of the concept, but utilizes in his comprehension of the concept specific exemplars of its criterial attributes. Thus, while the concept work is being learned as a primary concept, the pre-operational child will eventually hypothesize such attributes as activity, necessary, and useful as criterial, by abstracting them from farming, fixing cars, keeping house, nursing, and so on. In this case, however, he tests each of the attributes against each of the exemplars before relating them to his cognitive structure. If the concrete operational child learns the concept of work as a secondary concept in elementary school, he is given its attributes in the form of a definition, and may use an exemplar for one or more of the attributes (for example, necessary) in relating them to his cognitive structure. These exemplars of the attributes serve as *props* in facilitating the learning of concepts at this stage. (Ausubel and Robinson 1969, pp. 185–186)

Ausubel contends that once secondary concepts are acquired, the concrete operational child is no longer dependent upon stimulus supports in understanding or usage of their meanings (Ausubel 1968). The concrete operational child is still restricted, since he cannot yet understand propositions involving secondary concepts or manipulate such propositions in problem solving, unless he is provided with a particular example for each of the abstractions involved. For example:

> . . . if the child has learned the meaning of "trapezium" as a secondary abstraction he would be able to understand the statement "a parallelogram is a trapezium in which both pairs of opposite sides are parallel," unless we provided him with a specific instance of a parallelogram and trapezium to use as concrete props for the proposition. (Ausubel and Robinson 1969, p. 186)

ABSTRACT LOGICAL STAGE

Beginning about junior-high-school age, the student becomes decreasingly dependent upon the availability of concrete empirical props to form meaningful, abstract relationships in his cognitive structure (Ausubel and Sullivan 1970). Eventually, he no longer needs such props to understand and manipulate any relation between abstractions in a meaningful way. For instance, in the example previously given on the concept "work" where concrete images are not immediately evident, the student is able to understand the dictionary definition of this term without the aid of supports (Ausubel and Robinson 1969). At this stage, the student becomes capable of understanding and manipulating relationships between abstractions without any reference whatsoever to concrete empirical reality. Instead of reasoning directly from a particular set of data, he is capable of indirect second-order logical operations for structuring the data. Instead of grouping data into classes or arranging them serially in terms of predetermined or given variable, he can formulate and test hypotheses. His concepts and generalizations, therefore, increasingly tend to be second-order constructs derived from relationships between previously established verbal abstractions that are already one step from the data. Such use of second-order concepts allows more "concept assimilation" over "concept formation," since the student is freed from dependence on nonabstract contact with empirical data in independently discovering meaningful new concepts and generalizations and is obviously liberated from this same dependence in the much less rigorous task of merely apprehending these concepts meaningfully when they are verbally presented.

The relationship between Piaget's stage of formal operations and Ausubel's abstract logical stage is obvious, but they differ in emphasis on particular points. As Ausubel and Robinson (1969) pointed out:

> ... it is sometimes said that it is only at the formal stage that the child is able to engage in "hypothetical-deductive," or "if/then" thinking. However, it seems clear that children in the concrete operational stage, and even in the pre-operational stage, are quite capable of undertaking a certain kind of "if/then" thinking. For example, the pre-operational child's ability to understand the proposition "if it rains this afternoon we will not be able to go on a picnic," can be inferred from his later deduction. "Since it is raining this afternoon, therefore we cannot go on a picnic." For the very young child, the concepts involved in the original "if/then" proposition in our example, and in the manipulation of the original proposition represented by the deduction, are all primary concepts derived from concrete empirical experience. It is somewhat misleading then, to suggest that "if/then" thinking is peculiar to the stage of formal operations. Actually what distinguishes the various stages is not so much the kind of logical process involved as the degree of abstraction involved in the data, upon which this process rests. (p. 188)

Table 14, taken from the Ausubel and Robinson (1969) text, summarizes some of the aspects of the cognitive change that occurs with age.

Ausubel also differs with Piaget on whether the ability to use "syllogistic reasoning" occurs before formal operational thought. An example of a syllo-

Table 14.   Some Aspects of Cognitive Growth

ASPECTS OF COGNITIVE CHANGE AS CHILD AGES

1. Tendency to perceive the stimulus world more in general, abstract, and categorical terms and less in tangible, time-bound, and particularized contexts.
2. Increasing ability to comprehend and manipulate abstract verbal symbols and relationships, and to employ abstract classificatory schemata.
3. Increasing ability to understand ideational relationships without the benefit of direct, tangible experience, of concrete imagery, and of empirical exposure to numerous particular instances of a given concept or proposition.
4. Tendency to infer the properties of objects more from their class membership rather than from direct experience of proximate, sensory data.
5. More disposed to use remote and abstract rather than immediate and concrete criterial attributes in classifying phenomena, and to use abstract symbols rather than concrete imagery to represent emerging concepts.
6. Acquisition of an ever-increasing repertoire of more inclusive and higher-order abstractions.
7. Cognitive field tends to widen both spatially and temporally.
8. Becoming more capable of making both broader and more subtle inferences from empirical data.
9. Cognitive products tend to become both selectively more schematic and less subjective and egocentric in nature.
10. More capable of viewing situations from a hypothetical ("as if") basis or from the standpoint of others.
11. Attention span increases markedly.

(Adapted from Ausubel and Robinson 1969, p. 181)

gism is as follows: a conclusion is drawn in the form "A is greater than C," following from the premises "A is greater than B" and "B is greater than C." Ausubel cites evidence indicating that children between the ages of six and eight can easily draw correct inferences from hypothetical premises involving abstract relationships provided they have an opportunity to utilize concrete models or exemplars in the process of such reasoning (Ausubel 1968).

Finally, Piaget's concept of formal operational thinking is derived from *problem-solving* tasks while the abstract logical stage thinking proposed by Ausubel is based on acquiring the meaning of concepts as propositions. There is an obvious gap between the ability to understand abstract concepts and the ability to solve syllogistic problems. Put in another way, Ausubel's stage of abstract logical reasoning constitutes a *necessary* but by no means *sufficient* condition for the most abstract kind of combinational thinking involved in Piaget's formulation (Ausubel and Sullivan 1970).

Conception of Behavior

The major long-term, developmental objective of classroom learning, according to Ausubel (1967), is the learner's acquisition of a clear, stable, and organized body of knowledge. Such acquisition, therefore, is the criterion (or dependent variable) to be used in evaluating the effect of various instructional approaches on meaningful learning and retention. From a contemporaneous perspective, this same body of knowledge at every stage of its acquisition is also in its own right the most significant independent variable influencing the learner's ability to acquire more new knowledge in the same field (Ausubel 1967).

In considering behavior-as-content, Ausubel maintained that each discipline has its own unique set of concepts, and that the greatest power of each discipline is reached when it is considered on its own terms rather than being integrated with other disciplines. His position is in distinct contrast to that of many followers of Piaget who propose to integrate the disciplines through Piagetian stages (Sullivan 1967). Ausubel recommended teaching the disciplines separately rather than integrating them in an interdisciplinary approach (Ausubel 1968). Chemistry, physics, and biology should therefore be taught as separate subjects, rather than integrated. His position, at odds with much present emphasis on interdisciplinary coordination, is based on the idea that as each discipline grows through research and other types of scholarship, a structure will emerge that will be unique to that discipline, and that such a unique disciplinary structure would be unlikely to emerge in an interdisciplinary approach. Ausubel's disciplinary structure is similar to the map proposed by Dewey (Chapter 2) in that the structure of the discipline becomes an intellectual map that can be used to analyze particular domains and to solve problems within those domains.

In specifying educational objectives, Ausubel distinguishes reception learning from the other forms. Reception learning is that kind of learning in which the entire content of what is to be learned is presented to the learner in more or less final form (Ausubel and Robinson 1969). Reception learning is not the only form of learning, but Ausubel stressed it because it is frequently ignored in curriculum objectives. Ausubel (1967) insists that other types of learning build on meaningful reception learning. Ausubel and Robinson (1969) discussed this relationship in detail and the outline of this may be seen in Figure 13. For Ausubel the movement from discovery learning to creativity has developmental roots in concept formation engendered through meaningful reception learning. In Figure 13, it is assumed that reception learning is involved in all the other types of learning.

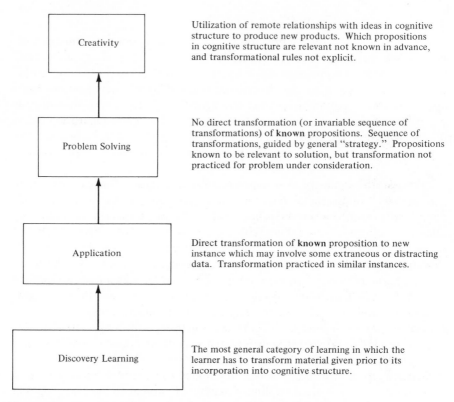

Figure 13   Relationship between Application, Problem Solving, and Creativity (From Ausubel and Robinson 1969, p. 72)

Figure 13 is helpful in relating Ausubel's views on educational objectives to Bloom's taxonomy in the cognitive domain (see Table 5). Ausubel and Robinson (1969) maintain that the knowledge level of Bloom's taxonomy depends chiefly on memory, since the majority of the tasks assigned to that level require rote learning. Rote learning is distinguished from meaningful verbal learning by its mode of acquisition. Rote learning involves the acquisition of arbitrary associations in learning situations where either the learning task cannot be meaningfully related to cognitive structure or where the learning exhibits a nonmeaningful learning set, for example, nonsense syllables in Table 13.

Meaningful verbal learning is required at the level of comprehension and above (Table 5).

Ausubel's taxonomy, as seen in Figure 13, is derived from the psychological *processes* that the learner (P) brings to the learning situation, and he introduces two additional considerations at the level of comprehension. First, the learning of propositions at the comprehension level is a more complex process than simple concept learning. Propositional learning involves the combination of concepts to form more comprehensive ideational units. Second, Ausubel and Robinson (1969) distinguish between the two processes of discovery and reception learning, a distinction with educational as well as psychological implications. Thus, Ausubel believes that it is not only important to test the content of what a student learns but to recognize the process of how the student has learned the content. In Ausubel's conception of the learning situation, the process could be reception or discovery learning.

Ausubel acknowledged that both his own system and Bloom's system present difficulties at the level of application (see Figure 13 and Table 5) in that there is no precise means to distinguish application and comprehension. Making such a distinction is not considered an issue of major importance:

> Theoretically it could be held that applying a principle (rote, algorithm, and so forth) in a context not previously encountered requires that one go beyond the minimal criterion for comprehension (that is, restating the principle in one's own words, correctly identifying variant forms of its verbal expression, or recognizing exemplars, and nonexemplars presented in concrete embodiments). While, for the sake of theoretical consistency, we adopt this position, we recognize that any given task might be thought to require "adequate" comprehension by some, and application by others. This is not in our opinion, a very important discrepancy. (Ausubel and Robinson 1969, p. 73)

The next level, as seen in Figure 13, is that of problem solving, which is distinguished from analysis in Bloom's taxonomy (Table 5) because the latter term seems to restrictive. Performance at the problem-solving level involves the transformation of existing relevant propositions to produce some required end. The transformation is not adequately described by the term analysis in the cognitive taxonomy. The difference between problem solving and analysis is illustrated by the difference between students of mathematics or science and students of the humanities. Problem solving is more likely to occur in mathematics and science, while analysis is more likely in the humanities (Ausubel and Robinson 1969). Ausubel does not rule out problem solving in the humanities, however, as seen in the following statement:

An essential query, is whether intellectual tasks that might be described as problems exist in history or English literature, to cite two examples from the humanities. Certainly, teachers in these fields do not tend to use the terms problem or problem solving. Nevertheless, granting that the content of such fields exhibits fewer formal propositions and less clearly defined transformational rules (strategies), our contention will be that is is still useful to think of problem solving tasks in these areas—tasks which fall within the general criteria we have set for problems. (Ausubel and Robinson 1969, p. 73)

Which term will eventually be most useful will depend partly on its utility for communication between psychologists and educators.

Finally, Ausubel considered his level of creativity to be quite similar to the synthesis level in the cognitive taxonomy, both involve the emergence of a product that is unique in terms of the individual's past experience. Ausubel, however, stipulates an additional requirement for creative behavior to distinguish it from problem solving: the background propositions and strategies that are brought to bear on a problem to produce a solution have not been taught as specifically relevant to the task at hand. Ausubel views creativity as a unique outcome and for him creativity is what Cronbach calls (1966) "big-D" discoveries where the mind comes to a startling reorganization of interpretation (Kepler, Einstein, etc.). Ausubel would probably agree with Cronbach that these big-D discoveries are infrequent and it is doubtful that educational psychologists can arrange for the conditions that precipitate these outcomes. Cronbach (1966) talks about little-d discoveries where the learner is discovering some simple connection or possibly a formula or inductive generalization. Ausubel would probably characterize little-d discoveries at the level of problem solving or lower.

Conception of the Environment

Ausubel (1968) has dealt with problems of classroom climate, peer-group relations, teacher variables, types of programming, etc., but for present purposes the discussion will focus on two major areas in which Ausubel has made a unique contribution, his criticism of discovery learning and his concept of advance organizers.

THE ISSUES OF MEANINGFUL VERSUS ROTE AND DIDACTIC VERSUS
DISCOVERY LEARNING

Ausubel (1963, 1967; 1968) has criticized educational theorists and practitioners who have proposed discovery learning as the only important learning process. This applies especially to followers of Piaget because of their unidimensional conception of the appropriate learning environment (Ausubel and Sullivan 1970). Ausubel (1968) makes a sharp distinction between rote/meaningful learning and reception/discovery learning. He disagrees with educational psychologists who claim that autonomous or discovery learning is a prerequisite for understanding or acquisition of knowledge.

Ausubel's criticisms are similar to those discussed in relation to Piaget (Chapter 6), although they can also be directed at other educational theorists. For Ausubel, reception learning can be meaningful if the learner employs a meaningful learning set and studies potentially meaningful material. The distinction between reception and discovery learning that Ausubel is making here needs clarification. Ausubel defines discovery learning as that in which the principal content of what is to be learned is not given but must be discovered by the learner before he can incorporate it into his cognitive structure (Ausubel and Robinson 1969). Reception learning is that in which the entire content of what is to be learned is presented to the learner in more or less final form.

Although reception learning does not involve any independent discovery on the part of the learner, it does not, of necessity, have to be entirely passive. In reception learning, the learner must (1) relate new material to relevant established ideas in his cognitive structure, (2) understand the similarity and dissimilarity to related concepts and propositions, (3) translate what is learned into a frame of reference of his own experience and vocabulary, and (4) formulate new ideas, which most probably requires a reorganization of his existing knowledge. In its more advanced forms, such as concept assimilation, reception implies a higher level of cognitive maturity because it makes possible a simpler, more efficient mode of cognitive functioning in the acquisition of knowledge.

Ausubel does not denigrate discovery learning when he emphasizes the importance of reception learning. Discovery learning (E) is necessary for the development of problem-solving abilities (B) but not indispensable for the occurrence of meaningful learning. As mentioned earlier, Ausubel (1968) contends that discovery learning may be useful during the early years of schooling when concept formation is typically acquired. Discovery learning intensifies and personalizes both the concreteness of the experience and the actual operations of abstracting and generalizing from empirical data. However, once the abstract stage is reached, verbal expository learning is more efficient because discovery learning is too time-consuming to be used as a primary teaching method. Moreover, the verbal expository type can directly induce a level of abstract understanding that is qualitatively superior to the intuitive level in terms of generality, clarity, precision, and explicitness (Ausubel and Sullivan 1970). The above conclusion is based on our previous discussion of concept assimilation versus concept formation.

Ausubel also disagrees with the two related beliefs that all reception learning is invariably rote and that all discovery learning is invariably meaningful. Rather, he views each distinction—rote/meaningful learning and discovery/reception learning—as independent dimensions of learning. Put another way, both reception and discovery learning can be either rote or meaningful depending on the conditions under which the learning took place. Meaningful learning presupposes that the learner is able to relate a new learning task nonarbitrarily and substantively to his existing cognitive structure and that the learning task itself is potentially meaningtul to him. Therefore, the learning process and the learning outcome will be rote or meaningless if (1) the learner internalizes a new task in an arbitrary or verbatim series and if (2) the learning task itself consists of purely arbitrary, verbatim associations. An example of the former would be the case where students memorize the steps necessary to solve different types of problems and cues by which to identify each type and then mechanically apply them. An example of the latter would be the memorization of nonsense syllables. In sum, Ausubel feels that discovery learning can be rote learning, while reception learning can be meaningful learning, although the converse can also be the case.

Although meaningful reception learning is paramount in Ausubel's theory, he is nevertheless aware of some of its possible disadvantages. If reception learning occurs in rote, or memorization, fashion, the learner may delude himself and others, creating the appearance of knowledge by learning through rote verbal responses without any reorganization of his cognitive structure. Ausubel proposed supplementing meaningful reception learning with a critical-thinking approach to subject matter to offset the possibility that rote learning might result in pseudo-knowledge. Critical-thinking criteria require the learner to recognize and challenge the assumptions underlying new propositions or to distinguish between facts and hypotheses. Ausubel views such critical thinking as a transitional state between discovery and expository learning, and he called it "guided discovery." To insure that the learner does not receive new material passively, guided discovery is recommended, since this method elicits the learner's active participation by requiring him to reformulate his own generalizations and integrate his knowledge in response to carefully programmed leading questions. As such, guided discovery is more structured than most discovery methods.

To learn meaningfully, the learner needs access to sets of ideas that can subsume the new material and that simultaneously provide him with ideational anchors[5] for the new material. Such anchors are the basis for the next topic, advance organizers.

[5] Anchoring ideas are those established ideas in a cognitive structure that are related to new ideas stored in the course of meaningful learning and retention.

ADVANCE ORGANIZERS

An advance organizer is introductory material (E) presented in advance of, and at a higher level of generality, inclusiveness, and abstraction than the learning task itself that is designed to provide a cognitive anchor for the learning task. An advance organizer is also intended to increase the discriminability between the new ideas and related ideas in a cognitive structure (Ausubel and Robinson 1969). Ausubel (1968) points to the importance of the organizer in his emphasis on the cognitive structure of the learner as it now exists, reflecting the outcome of all previous meaningful learning.

> In principle, deliberate manipulation of the relevant attributes of cognitive structure for pedagogic purposes should not meet with undue difficulty ... it can be accomplished: (a) *substantively,* by using for organizational purposes those unifying concepts and propositions in a given discipline that have the widest explanatory power, inclusiveness, generalizability, and relatability to the subject-matter content of that discipline; and (b) *programmatically,* by employing suitable programmatic principles of ordering the sequence of the subject matter, constructing its internal logic and organization, and arranging practice trials. Hence transfer in school learning consists primarily of so shaping the learner's cognitive structure by manipulating the content and arrangement of his antecedent learning experiences in a particular subject matter area that subsequent learning experiences are maximally facilitated. (Ausubel 1968, pp. 147–148)

The control over the accuracy, clarity, longevity in memory, and transferability of a given body of knowledge can be most effectively exercised by attempting to influence the crucial variables in cognitive structure. Ausubel's principal strategy for deliberately manipulating cognitive structure is the use of appropriately relevant and inclusive introductory materials (organizers) that are maximally clear and stable. Organizers differ from summaries and overviews, in that the latter are presented at the same level of abstraction, generality, and inclusiveness as the learning material itself. Summaries and overviews simply emphasize the salient points of the material by omitting less important information and largely achieve their effect by repetition and simplification (Ausubel 1968). This distinction will become clear when we consider the organizer in more specific detail.

Ausubel (1968) describes two types of organizers—expository and comparative—each with a specific purpose. When material to be learned is completely new and unfamiliar, an expository organizer is recommended, since it provides a unified conceptual structure to which the learner can relate the new material (that is, ideational anchorage). When material being presented is already familiar to the learner, a comparative organizer is recommended to help the learner integrate new concepts with basically similar concepts in his cognitive structure, as well as increase discriminability between new and existing ideas. Joyce and Weil (1972b) give a succinct example of both types of organizer which we quote here:

> Suppose that material to be presented to learners is a matrix of multiplication facts. This matrix might be preceded by the commutative property with respect to multiplication (that is, that $A \times B = B \times A$). In this way, the exposition of the material in the multiplication matrix can be at least partly organized by the learner in terms of commutation. He will be prepared for ideas like $3 \times 2 = 2 \times 3$, and his memory task will be considerably reduced. The organizer, the commutative property, is more abstract than the multiplication facts themselves, but they are explainable in terms of it. In fact, they could be presented in commutative pairs. Later on, when the learner is being introduced to long division, a comparative organizer might be introduced that would stress the similarity and yet differences of the division facts from the multiplication facts. For example, whereas in a multiplication fact the multiplier and multiplicand can be reversed without changing the product, that is, 3×4 can be changed to 4×3, the divisor and dividend cannot be reversed in division without affecting the quotient, that is, 6 divided by 2 is not the same as 2 divided by 6. This comparative organizer can help the learner see the relationship between multiplication and division and therefore anchor the new learning about division in the old ones about multiplication. At the same time, the comparative organizer can help him discriminate the new learnings so that he does not carry over the concept of commutability to a place where it does not belong. (pp. 173–174)

Conception of Person-Environment Interaction

READINESS

Ausubel's (1968) theoretical ideas are clearly interactive, and each dimension of the B-P-E is presented within a differential perspective. Throughout all of Ausubel's writing is a theme that indicates his sensitivity to person-environment matching and mismatching. His theoretical similarity to Vygotsky leaves him sympathetic to the criticisms that Vygotsky made of Piaget concerning his concept of readiness (Chapter 6). For Ausubel, readiness is a cumulative developmental product reflecting the influence of all prior genic effects, all prior incidental experience, and all prior learning on cognitive patterning and the growth of cognitive capacities. Thus, readiness reflects the effects of prior subject-matter learning, but only its general effects on cognitive capacities or mode of cognitive functioning, as distinguished from the acquisition of the particular learnings that constitute the basis of subject-matter readiness. In some cases, readiness may be general in that the person manifests the required level of cognitive functioning for a wide range of intellectual activities. In other cases, readiness may be limited to the highly particularized cognitive capacities necessary for the learning of a narrow segment of new subject matter, and even to the particular teaching method employed in acquiring that knowledge.

Ausubel distinguishes between cognitive and empirical readiness (Ausubel and Sullivan 1970). Cognitive readiness refers to the adequacy of existing cognitive processing equipment to cope with the demands of a specified cognitive learning task. Empirical readiness is indicated by the ability to profit from practice or learning experience. An individual manifests readiness when the outcomes of his learning activity, in terms of increased knowledge or academic achievement, are reasonably commensurate with the amount of effort and practice involved. Readiness, in the development sense of the term, is a function of general cognitive maturity, which, in turn, largely reflects age-level differences in intellectual capacity or stage of intellectual development. For any particular person, it also reflects individual differences in genic potentiality, incidental experience, intellectual stimulation, and educational background.

The particular subject matter studied determines the person's specific readiness for other particular kinds of subject-matter learnings (that is, transfers and contributes to general changes in his cognitive readiness that are partially independent of the subject matter). For example, the study of elementary-school science prepares a pupil for high-school science, and the study of elementary-school grammar prepares a pupil for high-school grammar. In addition, however, experience with each subject contributes to his general cognitive development and helps determine the general level of his cognitive functioning. Thus, in appraising cognitive readiness, Ausubel world consider all relevant age-level changes in ability to cope with different kinds and levels of subject matter to be reflective of growth in cognitive capacity or mode of cognitive functioning. Examples of such changes in cognitive capacity that influence learning, retention, and thinking processes, and hence influence developmental readiness, have already been summarized in Table 14. Some of these changes in cognitive sophistication have implications for general developmental readiness insofar as they bear on the breadth-depth issue in curriculum.

Ausubel contends that cognitive readiness always crucially influences the efficiency of the learning process and often determines whether a given intellectual skill or type of school material is possible to learn at a particular stage of development. Most educators also accept the proposition that an age of readiness exists for every kind of learning. Postponement of learning experience beyond this age of readiness wastes valuable and often unsuspected learning opportunities, thereby unnecessarily reducing the amount and complexity of subject-matter content that can be mastered in a designated period of schooling. On the other hand, when a pupil is prematurely exposed to a learning task, he not only fails to learn the task in question (or learns it with undue difficulty), but he also learns from this experience to fear, dislike, and avoid the task (Ausubel and Sullivan 1970).

Ausubel clarifies his differences with Piaget and others by distinguishing the principle of readiness from that of maturation (Ausubel and Sullivan 1970). Readiness, as expressed in the idea that his attained level of developmental capacity limits and influences an individual's ability to profit from current experience or practice, is empirically demonstrable and conceptually unambiguous. Difficulty first arises, however, when readiness is confused with maturation, a confusion that increases when maturation is equated with a process of "internal ripening." Readiness, according to Ausubel, refers to the adequacy of existing cognitive capacity or level of cognitive functioning (not knowledge) in relation to the demands of a given learning task. He does not specify how this capacity is achieved. On the other hand, maturation has a different and much more restricted meaning that includes those increments in capacity that take place in the demonstrable absence of specific practice experience, that is, those increments that are attributable to genic influences and/or incidental experience. Maturation, therefore, is not the same as readiness but is merely one of the two principal factors (the other being learning) that contribute to or determine the organism's developmental readiness for coping with new learning tasks. Readiness, therefore, does not necessarily depend on maturation alone but may result from cumulative prior learning experience. Most often, it depends on varying proportions of maturation and learning.

Since Ausubel (1968) accepts a stage concept, he disagrees with behaviorists and behavioral technologists such as Gagné (See Chapter 6). He is essentially in agreement with Vygotsky's criticism (1965) of behaviorists:

> We found that intellectual development, far from following Thorndike's atomistic mode, is not compartmentalized according to topics of instruction. Its course is much more unitary, and the different school subjects interact in contributing to it. While the processes of instruction follow their own logical order, they awaken and direct a system of processes in the child's mind which is hidden from direct observation subject to its own developmental laws. (p. 102)

Since Ausubel (1963; 1968) uses a modified version of Piagetian stages, it would seem that he would agree with Vygotsky that Piaget's work uncovers many hidden thought processes that (from Vygotsky's quote) are hidden from direct observation (Sullivan 1970). Ausubel would also agree with the following statement by Vygotsky (1965):

> Since instruction given in one area can transform and reorganize other areas of child thought, it may not only follow maturing or keep in step with but also precede it and further its progress. (p. 96)

Critics of the readiness concept have suggested ignoring it, because readiness cannot be measured directly, and concentrating on those factors in the learning situation that can be directly manipulated, such as reinforcement, organization of the learning task, and conditions of practice (for example, Gagné 1968). Ausubel has acknowledged the difficulty in measuring the person's present developmental stage, but he nevertheless feels that one can make fairly accurate inferences about existing cognitive readiness from knowledge of the learner's family, cultural, social-class, and educational backgrounds and from the use of diagnostic testing procedures. Furthermore, some control can be exercised over the readiness factor itself by providing a pertinent background of incidental experience or special preparatory learning activities at the desired level of functioning, perhaps through the use of advance organizers. Acknowledging the need for more research on readiness, Ausubel specifically recommends (1) studies indicating that certain kinds, components, and levels of subject matter which cannot be learned efficiently at one age level can be learned efficiently at another age level; (2) studies that by taking general or particularized readiness factors into account, achieve, thereby, superior learning and achievement; and (3) studies showing that more difficult kinds and levels of subject matter ordinarily not learnable at younger ages can be learned successfully and without inordinate effort if appropriate changes in teaching methods are made. Until the principle of readiness is particularized in each academic discipline with respect to the various subareas, levels of difficulty, and methods of teaching that can be most advantageously employed at each level of development, the principle will have little educational utility (Ausubel and Sullivan 1970).

In coordinating the concrete-abstract dimension (P) with instructional approaches (E), Ausubel suggested that the preoperational child's (P) dependence on concrete empirical experience (E) typically limits the acquisition of those primary concepts whose referents consist of perceptible and familiar objects (for example, "dog," "house"). Only with such concrete concepts are there both sufficient available examples and examples at a sufficiently low level of abstraction for the child to handle at his level of cognitive maturity (see Table 14).

The concrete operational child's (P) acquisition of concepts proceeds at a much higher level of abstraction and yields correspondingly more abstract concept meanings. He is able to cope with secondary concepts whose meanings he learns without actually coming into contact with the concrete empirical experience from which they are derived. Since such concepts can be learned by assimilation (E) or reception learning, he is merely presented with their criterial attributes, either definitively or by context. But he does not have to relate these attributes to particular examples of the concepts before they become relatable to his cognitive structure; he depends instead on the use of concrete empirical supports, that is examples of the attributes. The use of such props implies a much higher level of conceptualizing operation than the corresponding use of the exemplars of the concept itself. Nevertheless, the process of conceptualization is constrained by the particular nature of the input. Only the less complex kinds of secondary concepts, not too remotely removed from the child's own personal experience, can be acquired at this time.

The child at the stage of abstract logical operations (P) is capable of the highest level of concept acquisition. The criterial attributes of complex and higher-order concepts can be related to the cognitive structure without any concrete empirical props (E) whatsoever; and the emerging products of conceptualization are refined by verbalization to yield precise, explicit, and genuinely abstract ideas (B) (Ausubel and Sullivan 1970).

Ausubel emphasizes as a long-term educational objective the acquisition of a clear, stable, and organized body of knowledge which involves meaningful learning and retention. To attain this objective, the educational environment must be viewed differentially, or specifically, for example, the appropriateness of didactic and discovery learning atmospheres (E) for different learners. For the preoperational child (P), discovery learning may take precedence over reception learning. At later stages, reception learning along with "guided discovery" takes on continuing prominence.

Person	Environment
Preoperational	Discovery
Concrete operational and Abstract logical	Guided discovery reception

The *advance organizer* (E) is a more specific environmental technique that can facilitate meaningful verbal learning, that is, reception learning. At present, there are only short-term nondevelopmental studies utilizing this technique, and they are mostly geared to the secondary-school level (Ausubel 1968). The utility of Ausubel's ideas in this area rests ultimately on the extent to which they influence educational psychology and curriculum planning. The feasibility of classroom application of his theories is presently being tested by teacher-training specialists (Joyce and Weil 1972b), and the results appear to offer considerable promise.

Up to now, the chapter focus has been on Ausubel's theorizing in the *cognitive domain* (Ausubel 1963) without discussion of some of his ideas pertaining to the *affective domain* of educational objectives. Since his theory of ego development contains a B-P-E interactive perspective, it will be considered even though it has not been explicitly applied to education.

Personality development serves mainly as a nonspecific energizing function in learning and, unlike other motivational factors, it is an enduring and self-consistent individual difference dimension in learners (Ausubel 1960; Ausubel and Sullivan 1970). Ausubel describes the early ego-identification process and traces a chain of evidence linking this process to level of aspiration, that is, relative ambitiousness of goals, and to normal and neurotic anxiety. The central feature of his ego-development theory is that of satellization and nonsatellization (Ausubel 1952; Ausubel 1968; Ausubel and Sullivan 1970), which we discuss next.

SATELLIZATION VERSUS NONSATELLIZATION

Ausubel contends that whenever interpersonal and group life is characterized by differences in roles and status, and by dependence of one person on another person or group of persons, a basic form of interaction to consider is the identification of the dependent person with the superordinate person or group. This dependent relatioship includes such examples as dominance-subordination, leader-follower, and care-dependency. Ausubel (1952) distinguishes between two different kinds of identification, each of which involves a reciprocal relationship between a relatively dependent and subordinate individual, on the one hand, and a relatively independent or dominant individual (or group), on the other hand. He refers to these two identifications as satellization and nonsatellization (Ausubel 1952; 1968).

Satellization is one type of identification characteristic of early parent-child relationships (Ausubel 1952; 1968; Ausubel and Sullivan 1970). In the satellizing relationship, the subordinate party (child) renounces an independent, earned status of his own and accepts a status dependent on that of the superordinate party (parent). He identifies in a dependent sense with the parent's status, and the parent, as superordinate party, in turn accepts the child as an intrinsically valuable entity in his own personal orbit. The satellizer thereby acquires a vicarious or derived biosocial status that (1) is wholly a function of the dependent relationship and independent of his own competence or performance ability and (2) is bestowed upon him by the fiat of simple unqualified acceptance by a superordinate individual or group whose authority and power to do so are regarded as unchallengeable. This short summary implies that the satellizing child always experiences an intrinsically accepting parent (E).

Nonsatellization involves a different type of interpersonal relationship between the child and the parent or group. The subordinate party (nonsatellizer) acknowledges his dependency simply as a temporary, regrettable, and much-to-be-remedied fact of life requiring, as a matter of expediency, various acts of conformity and deference, but without really accepting a dependent and subordinate status as a person (Ausubel 1952; 1968; Ausubel and Sullivan 1970). In turn, he either could be rejected outright or could be accorded acceptance—not unqualifiedly as an individual for himself—but in terms of his current or potential competence and usefulness to the superordinate party. The act of identification, if it occurs at all, consists solely in the child's using the parent as an emulatory model so that he can learn the latter's skills and methods of operation and thus eventually succeed to his enviable status. And, accordingly, the only type of biosocial status the child can hope to enjoy in this relationship is a primary (earned) status that reflects his own degree of functional competence or performance ability.

The nonsatellizing type of identification occurs primarily for one or both of two reasons. Either the superordinate party does not extend unqualified intrinsic acceptance (the parent either rejects this child or values him basically for extrinsic, ulterior, self-enhancing purposes of his own), or the subordinate party is incapable of accepting a dependent role or is reluctant to do so. Ausubel contends that it would be reasonable to expect that children who are temperamentally more assertive, self-sufficient, independent, and thick-skinned would be less disposed to satellize than children with the opposite characteristics. It should be noted clearly the type of person-environment interaction that occurs in these two different forms of identification. The chart on page 203 is a shorthand summary of the person-environment interaction.

Differences related to culturally determined sex role are expected in Ausubel's theory, and he cites evidence that girls perceive themselves to be more highly accepted and intrinsically valued when compared with boys. For Ausubel, the outcome of satellizing or nonsatellizing has educational implications for achievement motivation in school.

Effects on achievement motivation. When school learning is considered, the wider significance of satellization versus nonsatellization in early personality development is seen in the outcomes associated with distinctive patterns of achievement motivation and with a distinctive mode of assimilating norms and values (Ausubel 1968). Ausubel (1968) distinguishes between two essentially different extrinsic components of achievement. One component, termed *affiliative drive,* is oriented toward vicarious or derived status. The other component, termed *ego-enhancement drive,* is concerned with achievement as a source of earned status. Ausubel (1968) believes that, in general, the nonsatellizer exhibits a much higher level of achievement in which the ego-enhancement component is predominant, whereas the satellizer exhibits both a lower level of achievement motivation and one in which the affiliative component tends to predominate prior to adolescence. It should be pointed out that Ausubel takes both a *comtemporanceous* and *developmental* view of the person in discussing achievement motivation.

Each of the cognitive, ego-enhancement, and affiliative components are normally represented in achievement motivation; however, their proportions vary, depending on such factors as age, sex, culture, social-class membership, ethnic origin, and personality structure. Affiliative drive is most prominent during early childhood when children largely seek and enjoy a derived status based on dependent identification with, and intrinsic acceptance by, their parents. During this period, their striving for achievement is one way of meeting their parents' expectations and, hence, of retaining the approval they desire. Actual or threatened withdrawal of approval for poor performance therefore motivates them to work harder to retain or regain this approval. Since teachers are largely regarded as parent surrogates, children are likely to relate to them in a similar fashion (Ausubel and Sullivan 1970).

Affiliative drive is thus an important source of motivation for achievement during childhood. However, children who are not accepted and intrinsically valued by their parents, and who therefore cannot enjoy any derived status, are motivated to seek an inordinate amount of earned status through high

P	E	B
Dependent	Intrinsic acceptance	Satellization
	Extrinsic acceptance or rejection	Nonsatellization
Nondependent		Nonsatellization

achievement. Thus, high levels of achievement motivation typically represent low affiliative drive that is more than compensated for by high ego-enhancement drive.

During late childhood and adolescence, affiliative drive both diminishes in intensity and is redirected from parents to peers. Desire for peer approval, however, may also depress academic achievement when such achievement is negatively valued by the peer group.

It can be seen from the discussion above that as the child grows older, significant normative fluctuations (as well as individual differences) in the balance between primary and derived status occur throughout the course of ego development. But, as already indicated, initial ways of relating to others tend to persist, especially if they occur at critical periods of socialization. Thus, although it is true that as the satellizing child grows older he strives increasingly for primary status, he will, even as an adult, continue to enjoy the residual sense of intrinsic worth which his parents earlier conferred on him and will continue to satellize in some aspects of his current interpersonal relationships.

Thus, Ausubel takes explicit account of person-environment interaction in his cognitive theory (differential appropriateness of reception and discovery learning in meaningful learning) and in the affective domain (theory of satellization).

Summary

Ausubel's theory of meaningful verbal learning was considered partly because it is a theory of classroom learning and partly because it explicitly considers person-environment interaction. Ausubel's theory was considered in relation to the theory of Vygotsky, which, in turn, permitted a comparative analysis of Ausubel and Piaget.

The greatest similarity between Ausubel and Piaget was in their use of stages in conceptualizing persons. The concrete-abstract dimensions proposed by Ausubel were considered, and certain differences from Piaget's stages were noted.

In a similar fashion, Ausubel's conceptions of different kinds of learning were compared with the taxonomy of cognitive objectives. Ausubel employs such concepts as rote versus meaningful learning, problem solving, and creativity to describe different levels of behavior.

In describing the educational environment, Ausubel distinguishes between reception learning and discovery learning, insisting that reception learning need not necessarily be entirely passive and that discovery learning may be inefficient in many instances. He also advocated the use of advance organizers in presenting material and distinguishes them from summary statements and overviews.

At the cognitive level, person-environment interaction is seen in terms of the appropriateness of discovery learning at the preoperational stage, while at higher stages guided discovery and reception learning are likely to be more effective. At the affective level, the importance of a matched environment was demonstrated by his maintaining that the process of satellization in personality development requires both the child's willingness to become dependent (P) and the parents' accepting him intrinsically (E). Educational implications of both forms of interactions were considered.

SUGGESTED READINGS

Ausubel, D. P. "Some psychological and Educational Limitations of Learning by Discovery." *The Arithmetic Teacher* 11 (1964): 290–302.

———. "The Use of Advance Organizers in the Learning and Retention of Meaningful Verbal Material." *Journal of Educational Psychology* 51 (1960): 267–272.

Ausubel, D. P., and Fitzgerald, D. "Organizer, General Background, and Sequential Verbal Learning." *Journal of Educational Psychology* 53 (1962): 243–249.

Joyce, B., and Weil, M. *Models of Teaching.* pp. 165–179. Englewood-Cliffs, N.J.: Prentice-Hall, 1972.

chapter 9

CONCEPTUAL LEVEL MATCHING MODEL

The Conceptual Level matching model (D. E. Hunt 1971) is derived from a theory of personality development (Harvey, Hunt, and Schroder 1961). To be helpful to teachers, a developmental theory should specify the educational needs of students at different stages of development and should distinguish between a child's immediate needs (contemporaneous) and his long-term requirements for growth (developmental). In this chapter, the Conceptual Level (CL) model is described as an approach that attempts to specify those environments most appropriate for a child at a given stage for both contemporaneous and developmental purposes. The educational relevance of the CL model will be illustrated in Chapter 11.

As noted in Chapter 6, Piaget's developmental theory has attracted the interest of educators because of its specific description of children's thinking at each stage. However, the theory does not specify the environment necessary for progression. Indeed, Piaget has deplored educational efforts to foster, or accelerate, progression, referring to them as the "American fallacy."

Before describing the CL model, it may be useful to consider again the distinction between a theoretical specification of the conditions necessary for development or change and the implementation of such specifications, which will be considered in the Chapter 11. It is quite true that developmental knowledge may be applied in the wrong way. However, this does not mean that specification of how persons develop should not be sought. Nutritional theories may specify the minimum and optimal dietary requirements for different persons of different ages, and such information is theoretically and practically valuable. Their value is not diminished by the fact that certain zealous parents make bad use of them. Similarly, a road may have much value but does not prevent some drivers from speeding and crashing.

A developmental theory, as Dewey suggested (1902), is like a map giving some general idea of the pattern of development. If the information is too general, it may have little value for teachers. This is often what happens when developmental theories are presented in teacher training. It is precisely the specific nature of Piaget's theory (about the person) and Skinner's theory (about behavior and environment) that has made them attractive to both psychologists and educators. We believe that the problem is not so much that psychological ideas may be wrongly applied, but that there are too few specific and valid psychological ideas to be applied.

Developmental theories are ways of thinking about how development occurs, about how the change from the "booming, buzzing confusion" of infancy to adult maturity takes place. The description of such a complex process will always be incomplete, selective, and arbitrary, so developmental theories will necessarily be tentative accounts. For a teacher concerned with how his students differ from one another, how a student may develop in years to come, and how these differences relate to his teaching, even a tentative account provides a useful background for the day-to-day activities. These theories will not prescribe exactly what the teacher should do but should be sufficiently specific to give a legible map.

A developmental theory describes the course of ideal development and specifies the environment most likely to produce developmental progression. A developmental theory also describes the person's present stage of development in contemporaneous terms—how he reacts now and to what he reacts. Both descriptions guide the planning of educational approaches.

The CL matching model illustrates how a theory of personality development provides educators with both a developmental perspective and a contemporaneous perspective. For example, a student might be at a dependent, conforming stage of development (or contemporaneous orientation). In dealing with such a student, a teacher may take into account his contemporaneous orientation and plan the immediate educational environment that will be most effective. The teacher may also bear in mind that efforts should be directed in the long run to the development of the student's independence.

Development does not occur overnight, nor does an observable change always occur during one school year. Similarly, a developmental perspective does not require that every move by the teacher be directed toward developmental growth, and it does not imply that unless all students have reached the highest stage of development at the end of the year, the teacher has failed. Such thinking would certainly exemplify the "fallacy" to which Piaget referred.

Maintaining a developmental perspective is as difficult for teachers as it is for parents. It requires the teacher to consider what a child is doing today in relation to what he may do in the future. It requires accepting the child for himself and disengaging his present behavior from its context to see it in terms of its potential for growth.

CL Theory

CL theory was first described as a theory of personality development and organization (Harvey, Hunt, and Schroder 1961). Since the original theory was described, the authors have stated more specific versions (Harvey 1967; D. E. Hunt 1966b; Schroder, Driver, and Streufert 1967). The CL matching model (D. E. Hunt 1971) described here is an attempt to extend the theory to education. Because CL theory has evolved explicitly in a B–P–E framework, the description begins with the conception of the person.

Conception of the Person

DEVELOPMENTAL ASPECTS

The development of a person is viewed on a dimension of conceptual complexity or interpersonal maturity. Although development is continuous under ideal conditions, this process can best be described in stages or segments, much as a motion-picture sequence could be represented by selecting still shots from the sequence. Development is considered on a dimension of Conceptual Level, which is a dimension of increasing conceptual complexity and interpersonal maturity. Figure 14 (which is similar to Figure 2) represents the CL dimension by means of three stages: A, B, and C. These stages are similar to those referred to in earlier publications (D. E. Hunt 1966) as Sub I Stage, Stage I, and Stage II, respectively.

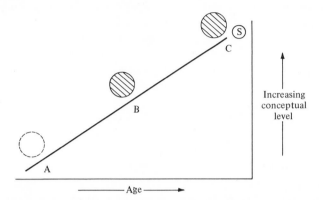

Figure 14   Development of Conceptual Level under Ideal Conditions

The sequence of stages can be summarized as proceeding from an immature, unsocialized stage (A) to a dependent, conforming stage (B) to an independent, self-reliant stage (C). The diagrams in Figure 14 are intended to represent this development. Clarification of cultural standards is shown by cross-hatching in the large circle in Stage B, and the self-definition in Stage C is designated by the smaller circle. From a developmental view, the stages can be described in terms of increasing interpersonal maturity and increasing understanding of one's self and others.

Progression from Stage A to Stage B requires the conceptual work of defining the external boundaries and learning the generalized cultural standards that apply to both self and others. This learning of rules and roles is the basic assimilation of cultural norms and expectations. The Stage B person shows features of moral realism, as described by Piaget (1932), in literal concern with rules and compliance to them. In the person's learning the "rules of the game," the rules *are* the game. His interpretations are likely to be categorical, all good or all bad.

This general standard incorporated in Stage B serves as the anchor for the self-defining work in progressing to Stage C. Self-definition occurs through a process of breaking away from the standard developed in Stage B. Learning about how one is distinctively one's self provides the basis for beginning to accept individual responsibility for outcomes. Stage C independence may appear initially in exaggerated form, but it is nonetheless the person's first awareness of his own feelings as cues for differential action.

Progressive conceptual development refers both to increasing interpersonal maturity, or increasing self-responsibility, and to increasing conceptual complexity, or effectiveness in processing information. Thus, the Stage C person is not only more independent than the Stage B person, but he is also superior in processing information, that is, more capable of distinguishing different elements and putting them together.

A consideration of Figure 14 raises a number of questions. Why is Stage C assumed to be desirable? Is the progression—unsocialized $\longrightarrow$ dependent $\longrightarrow$ independent—essential? Put another way, must everyone be dependent to become independent? What is the relation of stage to age? Why doesn't everyone reach Stage C? These questions will be considered in the remainder of the chapter, beginning with the last question.

The Conceptual Level model is an interactive theory of development that considers progression or growth to be determined *both* by the person's present developmental stage and by the environment he experiences. Figure 14 shows development under ideal conditions, but the environment may not always be ideal, so it is important to consider how the environment is viewed and what specific environment will produce development.

It is helpful to think of environments and developmental stages as being matched or mismatched, just as was done for contemporaneous person-environment combinations. A person and an environment are *developmentally* matched if the combination produces progression, and they are mismatched if the combination results in arrestation, or no progression. Thus, an environment is not generally good or bad for development but must be considered in relation to the developmental stage of the person.

Environments most likely to produce stage-specific development in Figure 14 were derived by asking the question, "Given the conceptual work required to progress from one stage to the next, what is the environment most likely to facilitate such work?" For example, for the Stage A person to progress to Stage B, he must understand and incorporate the cultural rules. Since rules are learned best when the rules are clear, the ideal environment to foster development to Stage B is a clear, consistent, highly structured one.

Following similar logic, the ideal environment for progression to Stage C is moderately structured, but it encourages self-expression and autonomy. These environments are summarized in Table 15, which is similar to Figure 7.

Stage C persons are assumed to benefit from environments that are highly autonomous; whether this will produce progressive development above Stage C is discussed elsewhere.

Cross (1966) investigated the parental environments associated with children at different stages. Cross selected a group of junior-high-school boys at

Table 15. Stage Specific Matched Environments

Desired Development	*Matched Environment*
Stage A→B	Highly structured, clear, and consistent
Stage B→C	Moderately structured, encouraging self-expression

Stage B and another group, equal in age and IQ, at Stage C to obtain information from their parents about the parental environments the two stage groups had experienced. From Table 15, it was expected that the parents of Stage C children would probably have emphasized the boys' independence and self-expression more than would parents of Stage B children. Parental interviews were coded for the interdependence of structure, or how much the parent took account of the boy and permitted him to help determine decisions. Interview responses were scored unilateral if the parent was in complete control, setting and imposing standards on the child with little or no deviation. Responses were scored interdependent if the parent influenced the child through factual information, and the child determined standards through interaction with the parent. As expected, Cross found that parents of Stage C boys were significantly more interdependent and less structured than were parents of Stage B boys. Since the two groups were of the same age and IQ, it was concluded that the unilateral training by the Stage B parents prevented the Stage B boys' progression to Stage C.

The necessity for the stage sequence in Figure 14 is more difficult to verify. It might seem from Figure 14 alone that longitudinal evidence should shed light on whether the A–B–C sequence actually occurs by observing whether each person progresses through each stage. However, since progression to the next stage is also determined by a matched environment (Table 15), if a person at Time 1 is at Stage A, he will not be expected to progress to the next stage at Time 2 unless he has experienced an appropriate environment. Nonetheless, longitudinal data on seventy-two adolescent boys (Hunt 1971) over a four-year period indicates a significant increase in CL during this time. This data is not conclusive evidence on the sequence of stages because, as Kessen (1960) has observed, one person's skipping a stage is negative evidence, but the longitudinal and cross-sectional evidence supports the sequence. The most compelling evidence for the A–B–C sequence is logical: Without the cultural standard assimilated in Stage B, there is no foundation on which to define one's self at Stage C.

Data do not permit a clear answer to the question of age-stage relation, either, except that from age ten to age eighteen, the proportion of Stage A persons decreases and the proportion of Stage C persons increases.

CONTEMPORANEOUS ASPECTS

In addition to its developmental significance, a person's Conceptual Level also indicates his capacity to process information effectively. Stage C is desirable because a person at this stage is more capable of adapting to a *changing* environment, is more tolerant of stress, and is capable of considering an experience from different viewpoints. (Note that if one defined the most desirable stage as ability to adapt to an unchanging, fixed environment, then Stage B would probably be best.)

Figure 15 summarizes diagrammatically the contemporaneous characteristics of variations in CL.

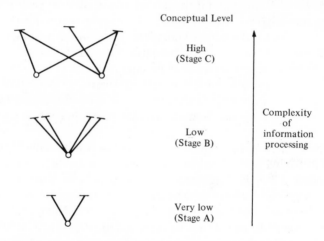

Figure 15   Contemporaneous Aspects of Conceptual Level

The high CL person (stage C) can form at least two concepts about the same elements of information (see Schroder, Driver, and Streufert 1967; and Schroder 1971 for more extensive treatment). An example of the adaptive significance of higher CL is a study by Suedfeld (1964) investigating resistance of influence after stress (a situation analogous to brainwashing). Experimental subjects were placed in sensory deprivation for twenty-four hours, followed by an attempt to indoctrinate them through a persuasive communication. High

CL persons were more capable of resisting indoctrination, that is, they were more stress tolerant than low CL students.

Validity for the contemporaneous aspects of CL also comes from Wolfe's finding (1963) that high CL persons are better able to look at a problem from a variety of viewpoints. Conceptual Level has also been related to moral muturity and ego development (Sullivan, McCullough, and Stager 1970) as well as to creativity and self-responsibility (D. E. Hunt 1971).

Conception of Behavior

Figure 15 can represent variation in behavior as well as variation in the person's capacity to process information. Behavioral variation in complexity (differentiation, discrimination, and integration) is similar to the cognitive taxonomy in that behavior of low complexity is exemplified by recall of facts or memory, while more complex (process) behavior is exemplified by analysis or synthesis. The findings of Claunch (1964), described in Chapter 1, are a case in point: When the required behavior on an examination is simple (objective test), there is no difference in CL groups, but when the behavior requires analysis and synthesis (essay), the high CL group is significantly superior.

CL is generally, though not strongly, related to academic achievement. The more interesting results appear when the content and the method for indexing achievement are considered. The correlation between CL and Grade Point Average (GPA) with the effect of intelligence (SAT) partialled out was inverse (the higher the CL, the lower the GPA, $r = -.56$) for engineering students while the CL-GPA correlation was positive ($r = .44$ and $.38$) for social-science and humanities students (Pohl and Pervin 1968). In the case of engineering, which presumably requires a more conventional orientation of memorization, CL is inversely related to achievement; while in social science and humanities, which presumably require more critical thinking, analysis, and generation of alternatives, the correlation is positive.

Finally, the study by Noy and Hunt (1972), described in Chapter 5, is a further example of the conception of behavior in CL terms. Here, behavior was seen as varying from recall to synthesis. Persons high in CL were superior to those low in CL when the behavior was at a more complex level.

Conception of Environment

The basic dimension of environmental variation is *degree of structure.* In high structure, the environment is largely determined by the training agent (parent, teacher), while the person himself (child, student) has little responsibility for what happens in the environment. In low structure, by contrast, the person experiencing the environment is at least as important in determining the environment as is the training agent.

In educational practice, low structure is exemplified by student-centered approaches, discovery learning, and presentation of examples before presentation of the principle (inductive teaching). In all these cases, the student is primarily responsible for organizing the material. High structure is exemplified by teacher-centered approaches, learning through lecture, and presenting the rule or principle before the examples. Here, responsibility lies with the teacher. In the Cross study, unilateral training is high in structure, while interdependent training is low in structure. Table 16 summarizes these variations in structure.

Table 16. Variations in Environmental Structure

	Low	High
Examples	Interdependent Student-centered Discovery Example-rule	Unilateral Teacher-centered Lecture Rule-example

Degree of structure was described in Chapter 4 as the major difference between the alternative high schools, and in Figure 7 as the environmental dimension. Degree of structure may be applied to environmental units varying in size and duration—from a single teacher statement, "Why do you think that happened?" (low structure, reflective), to an entire school described in Chapter 4 (high structure).

Degree of structure may be indexed by asking the student ("Do students have a chance to determine what goes on?"), asking the teacher ("Who is responsible for determining procedures?"), or by observation. Since structure is considered a dimension, the examples in Table 16 are extreme points on the dimension. Therefore, some environments may be at other points. For example, a particular educational environment may be best described as moderate in structure because it combines lecture statements with student questions.

Person-Environment Interaction

Figure 15 and Table 16 serve to coordinate person characteristics (CL) with environment characteristics (degree of structure) as shown in Figure 7. Given the characteristics of low CL persons (categorical, dependent on external standards, and incapable of generating their own concepts), one predicts that they will profit more from highly structured approaches. Given the character-istics of high CL learners (capable of generating new concepts, having internal standards to a high degree, and capable of taking on different views), it is predicted that they will either profit more from low-structured approaches or be unaffected by the degree of structure. Thus, the heart of the CL matching model is a generally inverse relation between CL and degree of structure: *"Low CL learners profit more from high structure and high CL learners profit more from low structure or, in some cases, are less affected by variation in struc-ture."* (Hunt, 1971, p. 44)

The first evidence for this matching model comes from an experiment in homogeneous classroom grouping (D. E. Hunt 1966b). Three stage groups were formed: Stage A, Stage B, and Stage C. To observe the different stage groups under the same conditions, each group was scheduled with the same English teacher, the same social-studies teacher, and the same science teacher. During this time, eight observers recorded their impressions of the three stage groups, qualitatively and by scale ratings. After six weeks, each of the three participating teachers also rated each group and responded to a structured interview aimed at obtaining his impressions of the groups and how he had reacted to them with educational procedures. Neither observers nor teachers were aware of the nature of the groups during the observation period.

CHARACTERISTICS OF STAGE A GROUP

As expected, the Stage A group was highest in noise level and interfering activities (due to short attention span). Observers described this group as "noisy, poorly disciplined, generally inattentive" and "extremely resistant to teacher." Teacher comments on this group were: "They get confused easily . . . they have less self-control than other groups." "They really don't care what is going on . . . it's hard to keep them interested in something for any length of time beyond ten minutes." "Majority of these people are not too interested in school, period."

CHARACTERISTICS OF STAGE B GROUP

As expected, the Stage B group obtained higher school grades relative to their intelligence than did the other two groups, even though this group was no higher in intelligence than the Stage C group. This tendency to overachieve (on objective tests) reflects their strong concern with cultural conformity. Therefore, if the goal of education is the acquisition of fixed, preestablished responses, then Stage B is the ideal.

The Stage B group's first rank in competitiveness agrees with theoretical expectations. Observers commented on this group as follows: "The dependence on each other's approval seemed to be quite high." "Questions were asked to impress the teacher ... group very orderly, quiet, and attentive." Teacher comments were: "Anxious to make a high grade ... never complain about the work being too heavy." "If I question them after they have made a statement, a lot of them do not have faith in their convictions, and as soon as you question them they just back down."

CHARACTERISTICS OF STAGE C GROUP

The Stage C group was highest on spontaneity as expected. Observers commented as follows: "The class interacted largely with itself and needed the teacher only as an arbiter ... did not seem to rely on the teacher's direction as much as the other two groups." "Interested in finding out information." "Did not ask questions to impress teacher and other students." Teacher comments follow: "They will stand up to their convictions more than [Stage B] ... they back up their feelings ... they will stick to what they believe." "We had a discussion and I mentioned statistical studies done on how smoking can produce cancer, and they were not willing to believe this without checking it for themselves whereas the [Stage B] group were willing to believe it."

EFFECTIVE TEACHING PROCEDURES FOR EACH STAGE GROUP

In an effort to determine the potential educational relevance of the groupings, each of the teachers was asked, "What did you find was the best way to work with this particular group?" It was not expected that teachers would respond with the stage-specific optimal environments summarized in Table 14; rather, if they accurately sized up the groups, they would probably describe functionally effective procedures. As mentioned, a highly structured environment may not foster progression for persons at Stage B, but it may nonetheless facilitate present functioning.

The teachers described the most effective procedures with the Stage A group as follows: "... more visual things, demonstration, showing them the actual thing by demonstration rather than by having them show me what they know about it." "I get them busy immediately with a writing exercise ... when it came to discussion the whole thing got out of hand, out of control." "More rote learning, the usual slow-group procedures, drilling, going over the same thing." One teacher discovered that discussions did not work with this group because they relied heavily on concrete evidence and were easily distracted—a further specific corroboration.

The teacher who was most effective with the Stage B group commented as follows: "This class is very competitive, so I put them in seats according to the order of scores on their tests . . . when you get a lot of competition, that's good, and they are very competitive." This teacher's emphasis on a student's position on a competitive standard (presumably a matched environment) suggests why he was so effective with this group. Over the long run (developmentally), the teacher should gradually introduce autonomous activities within the normative standard that are less competitively evaluated.

Table 17. *Homogeneous Classroom Grouping by CL*

	Stage A	Stage B	Stage C
Expected characteristics of stage group.	Egocentric, very concrete, impulsive, low tolerance for frustration.	Concerned with rules, dependent on authority, categorical thinking.	Independent, inquiring, self-assertive, more alternatives available.
Observed characteristics of classroom group.	"Noisy, poorly disciplined, inattentive"; "easily confused, less self-control, than others."	"Orderly, quiet, attentive"; "Questions asked to impress teacher"; "Do not have faith in their convictions."	"Did not rely on teacher's direction"; "Interested in finding out information"; "Stand up for their convictions."
Expected optimal environment for progression.	Highly structured, consistent environment providing many concrete, specific experiences.	Encouraging autonomy within normative standards.	Highly autonomous with opportunity for self-selected, individual activities and projects.
What teachers found worked best with group (optimal for current functioning).	"More visual things, showing the actual thing by demonstration rather than having them show me"; "Drilling, exercise, get them busy right away."	"Since they are so competitive, I put them in seats according to order of scores on tests." Use of debates.	"I let them know how I feel about something and they listen, evaluate, and discuss it." Debates ineffective.

The Stage C group should function most effectively in an environment that encourages individual activities. The teacher most effective with this group commented: "Many times I let them know how I feel about something and they'll listen to it, evaluate it, and discuss it." A summary of expected and observed classroom characteristics and expected and observed optimal environments appears in Table 17.

EXPERIMENTAL EVIDENCE FOR MATCHING MODEL

Using a matching model, McLachlan and Hunt (1973) investigated the interactive effects of learner CL and variations in structure. These variations were represented by a discovery (low structure) versus lecture (high structure) approach. Equal numbers of low and high CL students, matched on ability, were assigned to each of the two instructional methods. The content of the presentation consisted of a specially designed set of visual materials aimed at acquainting the student with the Picasso painting "Guernica." Students in both conditions were shown the same pictorial materials—a slide containing the entire picture and a series of component parts of the picture on separate slides. Students in the lecture method heard a short explanation of the meaning of each component slide, while students in the discovery method viewed each slide for a comparable length of time but were instructed to work out for themselves what the picture meant. Afterward, students were asked to give their own idea of the central meaning of the picture and of how the parts fitted together into this meaning (subjective integration). Figure 16 indicates the pattern of results for subjective integration.

Results indicated that the low CL students performed significantly better (p <.05) with high structure (lecture) than with low structure (discovery). Since no differences were noted for the high CL students, this pattern illustrates the compensatory ATI model suggested by Snow (Chapter 5).

In a companion study, Tomlinson and Hunt (1971) used the matching model to investigate the differential effects of rule-example order as a function of learner CL. Groups of low and high CL students were assigned equally to three treatment conditions varying in degree of structure. Low structure consisted of instruction that first presented the examples, with the rules presented at a much later time. Intermediate structure consisted of instructions in which the examples were presented first, followed almost immediately by the rule. In the high-structure method, the rule was presented before the examples. The rule, or principle, was Festinger's concept (1957) of "cognitive dissonance," and the examples were included in a brief excerpt from a story about two college boys. Students' concept learning was indexed by multiple criteria: definition of concept, recall of examples, and production of new examples. Figure 17 presents the composite scores recorded one week after instruction.

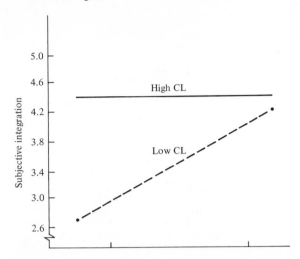

Figure 16   Subjective Integration as a Function of Discovery versus Lecture and Learner CL (After McLachlan and Hunt 1973)

Analysis of the results in Figure 17 indicated a highly significant CL X treatment effect (IQ effects having been removed by regression), and the expected pattern was borne out when comparing the mean scores. Under conditions of low and intermediate structure, the low CL groups were significantly lower (p <.05) than the high CL groups. The low CL groups under low and intermediate structure were also significantly lower (p <.05) than the low CL group under high structure. Although there was a tendency toward disordinal interaction, the difference between CL groups in the high-structure condition was not significant. Nonetheless, this tendency toward high CL decrement illustrates the preferential model suggested by Snow (Chapter 5).

Finally, a study by Tuckman (1968) should be noted, even though he used a somewhat different method for assessing CL. He investigated the interactive effects of learner CL with degree of structure, in this case nondirective teachers (low structure) versus directive teachers (high structure). He used the CL matching model to predict matching effects for low CL students with directive teachers and for high CL students with nondirective teachers. When the measures of teacher preference, satisfaction, and course grade were analyzed, he found that the primary effects occurred in one mismatched cell. Compared with the other three combinations, the high CL students with directive teachers rated these teachers lower and were less satisfied with them, thus providing an even clearer illustration of Snow's preferential model.

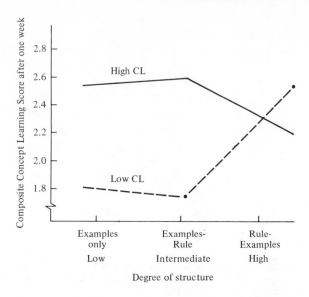

Figure 17   Concept Learning as a Function of Rule-Example Order and Learner CL (After Tomlinson and Hunt 1971)

Person-Environment Interaction in Educational Evaluation

If the expected person-environment interaction can be specified in advance, then the differential effects of educational intervention can be evaluated.

Experimental evidence in support of the CL model has been observed in the evaluation of the differential effectiveness of several summer Upward Bound programs (Hunt and Hardt 1967). Upward Bound was a precollege enrichment program sponsored by the U.S. Office of Economic Opportunity for culturally disadvantaged high-school students (essentially a "Head Start" for teen-agers) in which the students attended special programs on college campuses for six to eight weeks in the summer. The national evaluation of this program consisted of studying a sample of 21 of the total 214 programs. In these target programs, measures were administered to approximately 1,600 students at the beginning and end of the summer, so that change scores could be calculated. The objectives of the Upward Bound programs did not specifically include growth in Conceptual Level; rather they were objectives related to the goals of the program, for example, motivation for college.

Based on the rationale of the matching model, the twenty-one target programs were first classified into two groups, structured approach and flexible approach, as measured on the autonomy scale. These two groups were further classified into low and high CL on the basis of the predominant CL of the students in each program. Students' change scores were then considered in terms of the model by comparing the degree of change in matched programs (structured—low CL, flexible—high CL) against the change in mismatched programs (structured—high CL, flexible—low CL). For four of the seven measures (attitude to summer programs, motivation for college, possibility of college graduation, and interpersonal flexibility), students in matched programs showed significantly greater change than students in mismatched programs, and for two of the remaining measures (internal control and self-evaluated intelligence), there was a borderline tendency for students in matched programs to change more.

Not only did these results support the matching model, but they underlined the importance of considering differential effectiveness in evaluating program impact. In only one measure was there any significant change due to program approach alone. To conclude from this large-scale evaluation that the evaluation of any educational program (E) must include the nature of its effects (B) upon specific kinds of students (P) may seem obvious. Nevertheless, most programs of educational evaluation continue to operate on a general effects model, that is, which program is better? Not only do such programs waste millions of dollars, but they prevent any accumulation of useful knowledge that can accrue only when the differential effects are considered.

Summary

A Conceptual Level (CL) matching model based on a theory of personality development was described in B–P–E terms. Conceptual Level is only one of many personality dimensions with educational relevance, but it was discussed because it provides a basis for specifying matched person-environment combinations from both a contemporaneous and a developmental viewpoint.

Persons are characterized on the CL dimension that ranges from a very concrete level at which the person is unsocialized and capable of only very simple information processing to a complex stage where the person is self-responsible and capable of processing and organizing information in a complex fashion. CL may be viewed contemporaneously as an accessibility characteristic related to environmental degree of structure, or developmentally as a succession of stages related to long-term goals for developmental progression.

Degree of structure, the major environmental dimension, was exemplified by educational procedures high in structure (lecture, teacher-centered approaches) and low structure (discovery, student-centered approaches). Person-environment interaction is summarized in the basic matching principle: Low CL learners profit more from high structure and high CL learners profit more from low structure or, in some cases, are less affected than low CL learners by variations in structure.

Experimental evidence supporting this matching principle was summarized and an application of CL theory to homogeneous grouping described. It was emphasized that the matching model does not specify how to implement person-environment matching (homogeneous grouping, different schools, etc.) but specifies the nature of the match. Finally, it was noted that if different programs affect different learners, such differential effects must be assessed in any attempt to evaluate the effects of educational programs.

SUGGESTED READINGS

Chapman, S. L. G. "Education and the Permissive Society." *School Progress* September 1971, pp. 28–30.

Hunt, D. E. *Matching Models in Education.* Chapter 3. Toronto: Ontario Institute for Students in Education, 1971.

McLachlan, J. F. C., and Hunt, D. E. "Differential Effects of Discovery Learning as a Function of Student Conceptual Level." *Canadian Journal of Behavioural Science,* 5 (1973):152–160.

Noy, J. E., and Hunt, D. E. "Student-Directed Learning from Biographical Information Systems." *Canadian Journal of Behavioural Science* 4 (1972):54–63.

Tomlinson, P. D., and Hunt, D. E. "Differential Effects of Rule-Example Order as a Function of Learner Conceptual Level." *Canadian Journal of Behavioural Science* 3 (1971):237–245.

chapter 10

HUMANISTIC APPROACHES:

Rogers and Maslow

The psychological theories of Carl Rogers and Abraham Maslow contrast with most of the theories discussed earlier in their total emphasis on the individual's psychological health and well-being. Roger's theory has developed from psychotherapy and counseling. Maslow's theory, although based primarily on "normal" persons, has been influenced by theories of psychotherapy. To consider their theories raises the question of the similarity between psychotherapy and education. From a differential, interactive viewpoint, the question is, "Do these theories have something to contribute in working with certain students with certain approaches for certain purposes?" Therefore, since both Rogers (1969) and Maslow (1968a) have specifically described the applicability of their ideas to education, it seems worthwhile to consider their theories in the same chapter and to evaluate their possible contribution to educational practice within the B-P-E framework. Although these theories differ in certain respects, they are sufficiently similar to warrant considering them together under the general heading of humanistic approaches.

Like most terms, humanistic is misleading in that it implies other approaches are not humanistic. Indeed, many writers, including Rogers, have defined their position by stating what it is not. Despite these difficulties, we use the term humanistic to describe those approaches that are referred to by various terms: personalistic; student-centered; self-actualizing; affective; intrinsic; internal; individualistic; nondirective; and, perhaps most of all, relevant.

Irrelevance Of Traditional Education

The most widely publicized advocates of what might be called humanistic approaches in education have been destructively critical (Holt, Kohl, Postman, and Weingarten). These well-known criticisms against traditional education may be summarized by listing the opposite characteristics of humanistic approaches as the way to describe traditional practices: nonhumanistic; nonpersonalistic; teacher-centered; non-self-actualizing; cognitive; extrinsic; external; nonindividualistic; directive; and therefore, most of all, *irrelevant.* Commenting on educational practices in recent years, Floyd Robinson stated, "If future historians are to do us justice, surely they will be obliged to refer to our time as the Age of Irrelevance" (1970 p. 25).

The term relevance has been used to refer to the relevance of psychological theories to educational practice, but here it is used in a different sense, the relevance of education to real life. Like most issues, little is gained by posing the question in categorical terms, "Are present educational approaches relevant or irrelevant?" There is much need for improvement, but it is doubtful that much can be learned from the destructive critics who teach for one year and then retire to a lifetime of writing destructive comments on educational practice. Therefore, we will not review here the well-known criticisms of education, even though they might be regarded as "humanistic" by exclusion. Rather, we discuss those writers who offer constructive suggestions for applying humanistic approaches to education, principally Rogers and Maslow as well as Weinstein and Fantini (1970) and Brown (1971).

Even for these more constructive advocates of the humanistic approach, the temptation to introduce the ideas by describing the irrelevance of present practice, or what the approach is not, is very strong. Rogers, for example (1969), describes methods that are *not* employed as follows:

> When the leader concentrates on creating a facilitative climate, there are
> a number of traditional methods which he does not use and perhaps a very

brief mention of these could be useful. He does not set lesson tasks. He does not assign readings. He does not lecture or expound (unless requested to). He does not evaluate and criticize unless a student wishes his judgment on a product. He does not give required examinations. He does not take sole responsibility for grades. (p. 144)

In their book *Humanistic Education: A Curriculum of Affect,* Weinstein and Fantini (1970) list the causes of irrelevance in education:

1. Failure to match teaching procedures to children's learning styles.
2. The use of material that is outside or poorly related to the learner's knowledge of his physical realm of experience.
3. The use of teaching materials and methods that ignore the learner's feelings.
4. The use of teaching content that ignores the concerns of the learners. (pp. 21–22)

The next chapter describes a group of teachers who have in fact matched teaching procedures to learning styles, but nonetheless these points are worth noting. However, it seems important to note that the central unifying notion of humanistic applications to education lies in the negative notion of irrelevance. It is understandable that a new notion may emphasize the negative characteristics of the old and overstate the case for emphasis. However, it is also important to distinguish the persuasive appeal of the approach from its practical feasibility. Put another way, John Dewey made many of the suggestions that advocates of humanistic education are making today. It may be instructive to consider why these suggestions were not heeded while we are trying to put the present ideas of Rogers and Maslow into a perspective that may improve the quality of education.

As before, we summarize the theories before considering them in a B-P-E framework.

Maslow's Theory

Maslow (1968a) has characterized his humanistic psychology as a "Third Force" psychology distinct from the prevailing two theories of behaviorism and psychoanalysis, although it draws on each. In Maslow's words (1968a):

Classical academic psychology has no systematic place for higher-order elements of the personality such as altruism and dignity, or the search for truth and beauty. You simply do not ask questions about ultimate human values if you are working in an animal lab.

Of course, it is true that the Freudian psychology has confronted these problems of the higher nature of man. But until very recently these have been handled by being very cynical about them, that is to say, by analyzing them away in a pessimistic, reductive manner. Generosity is interpreted as a reaction formation against a stinginess, which is deep down and unconscious, and therefore somehow more real. Kindliness tends to be seen as a defense mechanism against violence, rage, and the tendency to murder. It is as if we cannot take at face value any of the decencies that we value in ourselves, certainly what I value in myself, what I try to be. This belief in the reality of higher human needs, motives and capacities, that is, the belief that human nature has been sold short by the dominant psychological theories, is the primary force binding together a dozen or so "splinter groups" into this comprehensive Third Force psychology.

Among the many educational consequences generated by this philosophy, to come closer to our topic now, is a different conception of the self. This is a very complex conception, difficult to describe briefly, because it talks for the first time in centuries of an essence, of an intrinsic nature, of specieshood, of a kind of animal nature. (pp. 686–687)

Readers unfamiliar with the enormous influence of behaviorism and psychoanalytic theory may find Maslow's comments unnecessarily defensive because the basic elements in the humanistic approach are so much in keeping with commonsense psychology. Behaviorism has been based largely on animal studies and psychoanalysis primarily on patients with psychological problems, Maslow's approach of studying relatively normal human beings as the basis for his theory was quite novel.

Maslow's theory, therefore, is a psychology of being, a psychology of health, that emphasizes and clarifies the human potential. It emphasizes what man may be and cites specific examples of these highest forms, which he refers to as peak experiences. Maslow, like Rogers, tries to be explicit in his values about the ideals of human nature and development. For Maslow, the ideal is the self-actualizing person, a state that occurs only when other, more primitive needs are met, as indicated in this quotation (1968b):

So far as motivational status is concerned, healthy people have sufficiently gratified their basic needs for safety, belongingness, love, respect and self-esteem so that they are motivated primarily by trends to self-actualization (defined as ongoing actualization of potentials, capacities and talents, as fulfillment of mission (or call, fate, destiny, or vocation), as a fuller knowledge of, and acceptance of, the person's own intrinsic nature, as an unceasing trend toward unity, integration or synergy within the person.

Much to be preferred to this generalized definition would be a descriptive and operational one which I have already published. These healthy people are there defined by describing their clinically observed characteristics. These are:

1. Superior perception of reality.
2. Increased acceptance of self, of others and of nature.
3. Increased spontaneity.
4. Increase in problem-centering.
5. Increased detachment and desire for privacy.
6. Increased autonomy, and resistance to enculturation.
7. Greater freshness of appreciation and richness of emotional reaction.
8. Higher frequency of peak experiences.
9. Increased identification with the human species.
10. Changed (the clinician would say, improved) interpersonal relations.
11. More democratic character structure.
12. Greatly increased creativeness.
13. Certain changes in the value system. (pp. 25–26)

In addition to these characteristics, the self-actualizing person is "growth-motivated." Self-actualization is the highest point on Maslow's hierarchy of needs (1968b), which consists of the following (listed in order): physiological needs, safety needs, longingness and love needs, esteem needs, and, finally, self-actualization.

Maslow places these needs in a hierarchy because he believes that a person may be characterized as concerned about a particular level and that if "lower-level" needs have not been gratified, he cannot experience events with higher-level concerns. Thus, to be self-actualizing, the person must have dealt with lower-level needs. Maslow does not think of these needs as a stage sequence as does Piaget, but rather he indicates the relations among the needs. In contrast to behaviorists, such as Skinner, who maintain that reinforcement increases the tendency for a behavior to occur, Maslow believes that when a need is gratified, the need then disappears. For example, when a mother kisses a child, the need for love and longingness is gratified and thus disappears. The healthy person who becomes self-actualizing is not preoccupied with esteem needs, concerns about being loved, and so forth, so he can be and become more himself. While lower-level needs may be gratified, self-actualization continues in a dynamic development.

Because the self-actualizing person is more open, he is more likely to have a "peak experience," which is Maslow's term for an intensely pleasurable experience of illumination, perfection, or insight. Maslow's ideas about the need hierarchy and peak experience have been based on the study of relatively normal, healthy individuals. During the past ten years, many studies conducted on self-actualizing persons used the Personal Opinion Inventory (POI) as the basis for measurement. Therefore, although Maslow's theory emphasizes the idiosyncratic human qualities, it has considerable empirical validity.

Rogers' Theory

Rogers' theory is a clear example of an internal theory that emphasizes the characteristics of the person more than the characteristics of the environment. He has referred to his approach as nondirective, or client-centered, to emphasize that the person himself, that is, the client, is the central point of concern. Like Maslow, Rogers believes firmly in the integrity and potential of the person. Given a generally accepting environment, therefore, the person will develop and grow to a fully functioning person. This growth process is facilitated, or made possible, by the person's self-acceptance; getting in touch with himself, or becoming more self-aware, and then using such self-knowledge as the basic ingredients for growth and development.

Since Rogers wrote originally in a counseling context with reference to a counselor and a client, his ideas may be easily translated to education by substituting teacher for counselor and student for client. His list of educational methods that are not to be used are derived from nondirective counseling and thus define what might be called nondirective teaching. Student-centered teaching is a more apt description because it conveys the notion of respecting and being sensitive to the student and his feelings rather than simply not doing anything.

The Rogerian recommendation for the counselor (teacher) to reflect the client's (student's) feelings does not involve merely repeating the statement, for example, "I feel bad today" "You feel bad today," as some critics have claimed. If this were the case, the client would benefit as much from listening to a tape recording of his voice. Rogers recommends that the counselor accept the client with "unconditional positive regard," such acceptance being conveyed through words, tone of voice, action, and whatever means will communicate such a feeling. It is this acceptance that the counselor is urged to convey rather than any kind of (directive) response to the client's statement.

Given such an accepting environment, the person is capable of using his internal resources to become more self-aware, to grow, and to develop. Because clients frequently have experienced less acceptance than "normals," it should not be expected that they will respond immediately to the counselor's acceptance. On the other hand, persons do not need to be clients to experience the growth-producing effects of being completely accepted. If Rogers' approach were stated in Maslow's terms, the recommendation is that the counselor meet the client's needs for love, longingness, and esteem through his unconditional positive regard so that the client is more likely to deal with himself as an entity.

Rogers described the fully functioning person as follows (1969):

He is able to live fully in and with each and all of his feelings and reactions. He is making use of all his organic equipment to sense, as accurately as possible, the existential situation within and without. He is using all of the data his nervous system can thus supply, using it in awareness, but recognizing that his total organism may be, and often is, wiser than his awareness. He is able to permit his total organism to function in all its complexity in selecting, from the multitude of possibilities, that behavior which in this moment of time will be most generally and genuinely satisfying. He is able to trust his organism in this functioning, not because it is infallible, but because he can be fully open to the consequences of each of his actions and correct them if they prove to be less than satisfying.

He is able to experience all of his feelings, and is afraid of none of his feelings; he is his own sifter of evidence, but is open to evidence from all sources, he is completely engaged in the process of being and becoming himself, and thus discovers that he is soundly and realistically social; he lives completely in this moment, but learns that this is the soundest living for all time. He is a fully functioning organism, and because of the awareness of himself which flows freely in and through his experiences, he is a fully functioning person. (p. 288)

Rogers views the counselor as a facilitator of growth and development, just as a teacher is a facilitator of learning, which is personal growth in Rogers' (1969) view. Following are the principles for facilitating learning:

1. Human beings have a natural potentiality for learning.
2. Significant learning takes place when the subject matter is perceived by the student as having relevance for his own purposes.
3. Learning which involves a change in self organization—in the perception of oneself—is threatening and tends to be resisted.
4. Those learnings which are threatening to the self are more easily perceived and assimilated when external threats are at a minimum.
5. When threat to the self is low, experience can be perceived in differentiated fashion and learning can proceed.
6. Much significant learning is acquired through doing.
7. Learning is facilitated when the student participates responsibly in the learning process.
8. Self-initiated learning which involves the whole person of the learner—feelings as well as intellect—is the most lasting and pervasive.
9. Independence, creativity, and self-reliance are all facilitated when self-criticism and self-evaluation are basic and evaluation by others is of secondary importance.
10. The most socially useful learning in the modern world is the learning of the process of learning, a continuing openness to experience and incorporation into oneself of the process of change. (pp. 157–163)

The Person's Responsibility in Choice

Rogers and Maslow agree on many points, but probably no point of agreement between them is stronger than their belief that the person himself must make his own decisions and must make his own choices. Maslow described the choice situation as follows (1968b):

> Therefore we can consider the process of healthy growth to be a never ending series of free choice situations, confronting each individual at every point throughout his life, in which he must choose between the delights of safety and growth, dependence and independence, regression and progression, immaturity and maturity. Safety has both anxieties and delights; growth has both anxieties and delights. We grow forward when the delights of growth and anxieties of safety are greater than the anxieties of growth and the delights of safety. (p. 47)
>
> The primal choice, the fork in the road, then, is between others' and one's own self. If the only way to maintain the self is to lose others, then the ordinary child will give up the self. This is true for the reason already mentioned, that safety is a most basic and prepotent need for children, more primarily necessary by far than independence and self-actualization. If adults force this choice upon him, of choosing between the loss of one (lower and stronger) vital necessity or another (higher and weaker) vital necessity, the child must choose safety even at the cost of giving up self and growth. (p. 52)

Maslow's belief that the individual's responsibility for choosing is a necessity is not based on the simple notion that every choice will be the correct one. Rather, it takes a special set of circumstances:

> ... such people [self-actualizing] when they feel strong, if *really* free choice is possible, tend spontaneously to choose the true rather than the false, good rather than evil, beauty rather than ugliness, integration rather than dissociation, joy rather than sorrow, aliveness rather than deadness, uniqueness rather than stereotypy." (1968b, p. 168)

Thus healthy people are more likely to be "good choosers."

> Another very likely hypothesis is this: what healthy people choose is on the whole what is "good for them" in biological terms certainly, but perhaps also in other senses ("good for them" here means "conducing to their and others' self-actualization"). Furthermore, I suspect that what is good for the healthy persons (chosen by them) may very probably be good for the less healthy people, too, in the long run, and is what the sick ones

would also choose if they could become better choosers. Another way of saying this is that healthy people are better choosers than unhealthy people. (p. 169)

Although Maslow criticized the behaviorists for basing their conclusions on animal research, he occasionally refers to animal experimentation, for instance, the experimental work by Dove in 1938 that supports the above hypothesis:

Chickens allowed to choose their own diet vary widely in their ability to choose what is good for them. The good choosers become stronger, larger, more dominant than the poor choosers, which means that they get the best of everything. If then the diet chosen by the good choosers is forced upon the poor choosers, it is found that they now get stronger, bigger, healthier and more dominant, although never reaching the level of the good choosers. That is, good choosers can choose better than bad choosers what is better for the bad choosers themselves. If similar experimental findings are made in human beings, as I think they will be (supporting clinical data are available aplenty), we are in for a good deal of reconstruction of all sorts of theories. So far as human value theory is concerned, no theory will be adequate that rests simply on the statistical description of the choices of unselected human beings. To average the choices of good and bad choosers, of healthy and sick people is useless. (1968b, p. 151)

In his last point, Maslow makes the identical criticism we made in Chapter 1 about the lack of precision of statistical averages.

In referring to the nondirective teaching example described in Chapter 5, Rogers commented as follows (1969):

It does not seem reasonable to impose freedom on anyone who does not desire it. Consequently it seems wise, if it is at all possible, that when a group is offered the freedom to learn on their own responsibility, there should also be provision for those who do not wish or desire this freedom and prefer to be instructed and guided. Miss Shiel recognized this problem and divided her sixth graders into two groups—one self-directed and one conventional. The fact that they had freedom to move back and forth between these two appraoches made this a very happy solution to the situation. (p. 134)

It would seem from the humanistic view, that the person is free to do almost anything except refuse to choose. He must choose, even if the choice involves choosing not to learn or choosing not to put himself in a position to grow. In their discussions about choice, Rogers and Maslow are dealing with an issue that is frequently either taken for granted in educational approaches or else not discussed, "Should students be allowed to choose or not?" Rogers and Maslow say that they should. From a differential developmental view, the issue is how persons can become better choosers by learning from their choices. To maintain that a bad choice made by the person himself is better than no choice or than a choice made for him is not always true because it disregards the reversibility of the decision. As Rogers suggests, when students' have the opportunity to move from one class to another with no penalty for choosing one way or the other, then student choice is certainly appropriate. However, if choosing one option eliminates many subsequent options, then giving the person the responsibility to choose may not be humanistic.

It is necessary to distinguish between the good feelings of self-responsibility that one experiences in making one's own choice and the wisdom of that choice. One intermediate solution is to give students provisional experience in the various environments, as suggested in Chapter 4, so that their decisions are more likely to be based on experience. It is obvious to say that students learn from their poor choices as well as from their mistakes; however, it is more difficult for the teacher (facilitator) to know when the consequences of a bad choice will be irreversibly negative or devastating.

Conception of the Person

CONTEMPORANEOUS

Maslow described persons who are primarily concerned at lower levels of the hierarchy—safety, love, belongingness, and esteem—as being deficiency-motivated and excessively dependent on the environment. By contrast, self-actualizing persons are growth-motivated and less dependent on the environment. This distinction implies a differential person-environment match. The deficiency-motivated person requires, and must seek, specific forms of environmental gratification, while the growth-motivated person is much less dependent on specific forms of environmental support and is more capable of exerting an effect on the environment.

Maslow noted the similarity of the growth-motivated person to "inner-directed" and the deficiency-motivated person to the "other-directed" person described by Riesman (1950). Deficit-motivated persons "*must* be sensitive to other people's approval, affection and good will" (1968b, p. 34). Maslow believed that such excessive dependence on others restricts the nature of interpersonal relations. The deficit-motivated person sees the other person only as a need-gratifier or in terms of his usefulness, rather than in terms of his unique personal qualities. He observed (1968b):

> One characteristic ... of need-gratifying relations to other people is that to a very large extent these need-gratifying persons are interchangeable. Since, for instance, the adolescent girl needs admiration per se, it therefore makes little difference who supplies this admiration; one admiration-supplier is about as good as another. So also for the love-supplier and the safety-supplier. (p. 36)

The implications for working with students with differing deficit-motivations as well as with growth-motivated students is clear. Student variation on the hierarchy is well illustrated by application of what Weinstein and Fantini (1970) call the "Faraway Island" technique. The procedure, designed to help students become more aware of their concerns in viewing other people, consists essentially of instructing students to think about what it would be like to live on an island for the rest of your life with only six other people whom you could select. These others should not be real people. The student is to describe them in general terms, giving special attention to their need-gratifying qualities. When responses of a disadvantaged group were compared with a private-school group, Weinstein and Fantini (1970) found that:

> This group [disadvantaged] seem to feel that the island society could easily revert to a state of nature, and its members wanted people around who would ensure control and regularity. The children in the private-school group expressed less need for control and perhaps less awareness of the survival needs: they seemed to trust themselves and those like them to keep life safe and under control. The data are true to Maslow's hierarchy of needs, according to which security and safety needs are prior to love and belonging needs. (p. 130)

At a more objective level, Shostrom (1962) developed the Personal Opinion Iventory (POI). This self-report questionnaire is designed to assess a person's orientation in terms of Maslow's hierarchy (other-support-oriented versus self-support, compulsive conformity versus freedom) and is primarily a method of identifying self-actualizing persons.

It is hardly surprising that Rogers has not proposed a systematic means for characterizing persons. Rogers believes in each person's uniqueness and the need for the facilitator (whether counselor or teacher) to try to tune in to this unique person, and, of course, any system of classification (even one as general as the Maslowian hierarchy) can be misused to provide inflexible stereotypes.

However, to evaluate change that occurred in client-centered therapy, Rogers developed "a tentative scale for the measurement of process in psychotherapy" (1958, 1961). Although these "strands," as Rogers called them, are meant to describe the change in successful psychotherapy, they do provide a fairly specific description of some characteristics of the person whom the Rogerian approach emphasized and are presented in Table 18.

Table 18.   Seven Areas on the Change Process of Client-Centered Therapy

Strand 1.   Relationship to Feelings and Personal Meanings 　　　Low Stage: Feelings are unrecognized or unexpressed. 　　　High Stage: Feelings are experienced freely in the immediate moment.
Strand 2.   Manner of Experiencing 　　　Low Stage: Individual is remote from experiencing. 　　　High Stage: Experience is an accepted inner referent.
Strand 3.   Degree of Incongruence 　　　Low Stage: Individual is unaware of contradictory self-statements. 　　　High Stage: Individual is able to recognize temporary moments of 　　　incongruence.
Strand 4.   Communication of Self 　　　Low Stage: Individual avoids revealing himself. 　　　High Stage: Individual experiences his self and is able to communicate 　　　his self-awareness.
Strand 5.   Manner in Which Experience Is Construed 　　　Low Stage: Individual has rigid constructs which he accepts as fact. 　　　High Stage: Constructs are recognized to be ways of construing a 　　　moment of experience and are open to change.
Strand 6.   Relationship to Problems 　　　Low Stage: Problems not recognized or perceived to be external to 　　　self, and individual is closed to change. 　　　High Stage: Individual lives his problem and seeks to cope with it.
Strand 7.   Manner of Relating 　　　Low Stage: Close relationships avoided as dangerous. 　　　High Stage: Individual risks being himself in the process of relating to 　　　others.

(From an excerpt by Pervin 1970)

CONCEPTION OF DEVELOPMENT

It should be emphasized that the central unit in Rogers' theory is the self, and change in self is the central process in successful psychotherapy. Rogers' ideas on development and change can be seen in the following summary description (1958) of the process of psychotherapy:

> The process involves a change in the self. From being a self which is not congruent with experience, the client moves through the phase of perceiving self as an object, to a self which is synonymous with experience, being the subjective awareness of that experience.
>
> There are other elements, too, involved in the process: movement from ineffective to effective choice, from fear of relationships to freely living in relationship, from inadequate differentiation of feelings and meanings to sharp differentiation.
>
> In general, the process moves from a point of fixity, where all these elements and threads are separately discernible and separately understandable, to the flowing peak moments of therapy in which all these threads become inseparably woven together. In the new experiencing with immediacy which occurs at such moments, feeling and cognition interpenetrable, self is subjectively present in the experience, volition is simply the subjective following of a harmonious balance of organismic direction. Thus, as the process reaches this point, the person becomes a unity of flow, of motion. He has changed; but, what seems most significant, he has become an integrated process of changingness. (p. 149)

Like Rogers, Maslow believes that most of the forces for growth are within the person. As indicated by Maslow's emphasis on the person's free choice, he conceptualizes the process of development in terms of conflict between defense and growth, or more specifically safety and growth. He believes in what he calls the "delight-in-growth." By this he means that when a person has experienced the enjoyment at a particular level, he then becomes ready to seek other "higher" concerns. Safety and security are always opposing such forces toward growth. Therefore, development will be probable if the growth forces are made more attractive, while concerns about safety, security, and defensiveness can be minimized. Maslow's summary of growth-through-delight, though similar to earlier descriptions of choice, is worth noting:

> Of course this formulation of growth-through-delight also commits us to the necessary postulation that what tastes good is also, in the growth sense, "better" for us. We rest here on the faith that if free choice is really free and if the chooser is not too sick or frightened to choose, he will choose wisely, in a healthy and growthward direction, more often than not. (1968b, p. 48)

Conception of Behavior

Humanistic approaches describe the goal of education as growth and development. They emphasize intrinsic learning as opposed to extrinsic learning.

Maslow (1968a), for example, criticizes "learning-theory" conceptions because of their arbitrary, impersonal approach. Similarly, Rogers refers to "nonsense-syllable learning," which he distinguishes from his objective of "significant, meaningful, experiential learning" (1969, p. 4) that has a quality of personal involvement, is self-initiated, pervasive, learner-evaluated, and in essence meaningful. Ausubel (Chapter 8) has also emphasized meaningful learning, but his emphasis is on the meaningful relations in logical terms, while Rogers's emphasis is upon meaningful relations between the person's feelings and what he learns. It is clear, therefore, that the practical suggestions flowing from a humanistic approach will be similar to those proposed by John Dewey discussed in Chapter 2.

Both Maslow and Rogers regard as unlikely the possibility that learning (growth and development) as defined above will occur in school. For example, Maslow wrote (1968a):

> For instance, if I were to list the most important learning experiences in my life, there come to mind getting married, discovering my life work, having children, getting psychoanalyzed, the death of my best friend, confronting death myself, and the like. I think I would say that these were more important learning experiences for me than my Ph.D or any 15 or 150 credits or courses that I've ever had. I certainly learned more about myself from such experiences. (p. 692)

The goal of education for Maslow would be to provide experiences for the person to become more self-actualizing and less dependent on the environment. For Rogers, the goal would be for the person to become more fully functioning. In addition, Rogers (1969) also favors process goals as described in Chapter 3:

> Teaching and the imparting of knowledge make sense in an unchanging environment. This is why it has been an unquestioned function for centuries. But if there is one truth about modern man, it is that he lives in an environment which is continually changing. The one thing I can be sure of is that the physics which is taught to the present day student will be outdated in a decade. The teaching in psychology will certainly be out of date in 20 years. The so-called "facts of history" depend very largely upon the current mood and temper of the culture. Chemistry, biology, genetics, sociology, are in such flux that a firm statement made today will almost certainly be modified by the time the student gets around to using the knowledge.
>
> We are, in my view, faced with an entirely new situation in education where the goal of education, if we are to survive, is the facilitation of

change and learning. The only man who is educated is the man who has learned how to learn; the man who has learned how to adapt and change, the man who has realized that no knowledge is secure, that only the process of seeking knowledge gives a basis for security. Changingness, a reliance on process rather than upon static knowledge, is the only thing that makes any sense as a goal for education in the modern world. (p. 104)

Weinstein and Fantini's subtitle *A Curriculum of Affect* (1970) typifies the humanistic concern with affective, rather than cognitive, objectives in education. The humanist's emphasis on the student's feelings and emotions as a legitimate concern of education is usually stated in exaggerated terms because most humanistic theorists believe that education has been excessively preoccupied with cognitive concerns. However, it is probably most accurate to say that Rogers and Maslow would agree with George Brown (1972) who stated that the problem is one of harmonizing affective with cognitive aspects. Here again, we realize that readers unfamiliar with the hallowed categories of affective and cognitive may wonder why all the fuss. Why not just work with the student? This is, of course, what Dewey meant by the "whole child," and it is what good teachers do without thinking about it. It remains to be seen whether the distinction between feeling and thinking will continue to be useful in the most effective application of psychological ideas to education and, especially, in teacher training. However, for now, the distinction should probably be regarded as a holding term that may be useful. Another way to state this issue is that we believe it is just as "humanistic" to be aware of, and modulate to, a student's learning style (which is usually regarded as cognitive) as it is to be aware of his feelings.

Conception of the Educational Environment

ROLE OF THE TEACHER

Maslow and Rogers disagree so fundamentally with traditional educational practice that they frequently use different terms to refer to the teachers: Maslow speaks of the teacher as a guide or Taoist helper (1968a, p. 693), while Rogers uses the term facilitator (1969, p. 164).

Maslow's view of the role of the teacher follows (1968a):

We speak then of a self, a kind of intrinsic nature which is very subtle, which is not necessarily conscious, which has to be sought for, and which has to be uncovered and then built upon, actualized, taught, educated. The notion is that something is there but it's hidden, swamped, distorted, twisted, overlayed. The job of the psychotherapist (or the teacher) is to help a person find out what's already in him rather than to reinforce him or shape or teach him into a prearranged form, which someone else has decided upon in advance, a priori. (p. 688)

He continues to describe how a teacher-guide can help in this "learning-to-be-a-person" process (1968a):

In the first place, unlike the current model of teacher as lecturer, conditioner, reinforcer, and boss, the Taoist helper or teacher is receptive rather than intrusive.

It is my strong impression that this is the way in which much of the world of education could function. If we want to be helpers, counselors, teachers, guiders, or psychotherapists, what we must do is to accept the person and help him learn what kind of person he is already. What is his style, what are his aptitudes, what is he good for, not good for, what can we build upon, what are his good raw materials, his good potentialities? We would be non-threatening and would supply an atmosphere of acceptance of the child's nature which reduces fear, anxiety and defense to the minimum possible. Above all, we would care for the child, that is enjoy him and his growth and self-actualization. (p. 693)

Therefore, obviously the teacher-guide must be as sensitive as possible to the student because he must decide when to choose the next step ahead. He cannot be pushed ahead, and in this sense, Maslow is in agreement with Piaget. However, Maslow (1968b) admits:

This is a ticklish task, for it implies simultaneously that we know what is best for him (since we do beckon him on in a direction we choose), and also that only he knows what is best for himself in the long run. This means that we must offer only, and rarely force. We must be quite ready, not only to beckon forward, but to respect retreat to lick wounds, to recover strength, to look over the situation from a safe vantage point, or even to regress to a previous mastery or a "lower" delight, so that courage for growth can be regained.

And this again is where the helper comes in. He is needed not only for making possible growth in the healthy child (by being "available" as the child desires) and getting out of his way at other times, but much more urgently, by the person who is "stuck" in fixation, in rigid defenses, in safety measures which cut off the possibilities of growth. (pp. 54–55)

Rogers (1969) described guidelines for a facilitator that may serve as principles for a facilitator-teacher in applying student-centered teaching:

1. The facilitator has much to do with setting the initial mood or climate of the group or class experience.
2. The facilitator helps to elicit and clarify the purposes of the individuals in the class as well as the more general purposes of the group.
3. He relies upon the desire of each student to implement those purposes which have meaning for him, as the motivational force behind significant learning.
4. He endeavors to organize and make easily available the widest possible range of resources for learning.
5. He regards himself as a flexible resource to be utilized by the group.
6. In responding to expressions in the classroom group, he accepts both the intellectual content and the emotionalized attitudes, endeavoring to give each aspect the approximate degree of emphasis which it has for the individual or the group.
7. As the acceptant classroom climate becomes established, the facilitator is able increasingly to become a participant learner, a member of the group, expressing his views as those of one individual only.
8. He takes the initiative in sharing himself with the group—his feelings as well as his thoughts—in ways which do not demand nor impose but represent simply a personal sharing which students may take or leave.
9. Throughout the classroom experience, he remains alert to the expressions indicative of deep or strong feelings.
10. In his functioning as a facilitator of learning, the leader endeavors to recognize and accept his own limitations. (pp. 164–166)

Although Rogers includes encounter groups, inquiry training, and simulation problems as specific suggestions, it may come as a surprise that he also includes programmed instruction as a method of building freedom. He sees it as a means of facilitating his own learning and filling in gaps by working at his own rate. He acknowledges that programmed learning can be misused, but it is a tribute to his own openness that he does not dismiss it simply because it seems mechanical and impersonal.

Weinstein and Fantini (1970) are perhaps the most specific in recommending educational procedures in the humanistic tradition. In addition to the "Faraway Island" technique referred to earlier, they suggest many specific procedures for identity education (especially pp. 66–161). Many procedures flowing from the humanistic view are intended to "loosen up" the student, to increase flexibility and creativity, and George Brown has suggested numerous procedures for this purpose (1971; 1972).

Conception of Person–Environment Interaction

Because Maslow has been more explicit in describing the person in his hierarchy, his theory is a little more amenable to person-environment, differential analysis. For example, Weinstein and Fantini's reported difference between the disadvantaged group and the private-school group in terms of concerns would have implications for differential educational approaches. Thus, growth-motivated persons (who are less dependent on the environment) might require less specific environmental matching than would deficit-motivated persons.

Maslow described what is close to the differential demands on the teacher-guide as follows (1968b):

> Defensiveness can be as wise as daring; it depends on the particular person, his particular status and the particular situation in which he has to choose. The choice of safety is wise when it avoids pain that may be more than the person can bear at the moment. If we wish to help him grow (because we know that consistent safety-choices will bring him to catastrophe in the long run, and will cut him off from possibilities that he himself would enjoy if only he could savor them), then all we can do is help him if he asks for help out of suffering, or else simultaneously allow him to feel safe and beckon him onward to try the new experience like the mother whose open arms invite the baby to try to walk. We can't force him to grow, we can only coax him to, make it more possible for him, in the trust that simply experiencing the new experience will make him prefer it. Only he can prefer it; no one can prefer it for him. If it is to become part of him, he must like it. If he doesn't, we must gracefully concede that it is not for him at this moment. (p. 54)

If these principles for a facilitator seem utterly unrealistic for a classroom teacher to apply, it should be noted that Rogers is not especially concerned (nor is Maslow, for that matter) with maintaining traditional educational procedures. Therefore, it is important to distinguish what specific aspects can be used and what suggestions require an entire restructuring of education. We conclude this section with some more specific suggestions.

Specific Educational Procedures

Since many teachers may find Rogers' own way of facilitating a class (1969, pp. 57–97) somewhat too nonspecific (essentially he works out in concert with the students the answer to the question of what they want to learn and then proceeds with it), his description of "methods of building freedom" (1969, pp. 129–144) is helpful. Rogers admits that giving students freedom in the sense that he recommends may produce frustration and confusion because students have been unaccustomed to such responsibility. Therefore, he recommends the use of contracts (used by the sixth-grade teacher whose work was described in Chapter 5) to provide a transition between completely free learning and meeting institutional demands. The student and teacher together work out the terms of the contract that involves both the goals and the means to these goals. Many undergraduate courses are utilizing such arrangement now, especially the option to choose between different modes of instruction.

Therefore, in Maslow's view, differential procedures involve making certain that the student's "lower" needs have been met. Although from Rogers' counseling work and the tone of his writing, it is obvious that he has a great sensitivity for working with each person in a distinctive, unique way, this very insistence on each person's uniqueness makes Rogers disinclined to make any prescriptions that involve characterizing persons. He acknowledges (1969) that some students may prefer more structured learning experiences:

> If students are free, they should be free to learn passively as well as to initiate their own learning. Perhaps, as programmed learning develops, this will offer another alternative. Those students who prefer to be guided on a carefully pre-determined path of learning may choose to take the programmed learning. Those who prefer to follow their own directions and initiate their own learning can meet as a group or follow any of the various patterns which have thus far been described. (p. 134)

However, as noted in commenting on the sixth-grade experiment in Chapter 5, one gets the feeling that the Rogerian approach is not altogether satisfied with giving students a choice when they choose the more structured alternative. As we discuss in the next section, a truly humanistic approach must be as accepting of the student who chooses a more structured learning environment as the one who chooses a less structured one, even though one may hope in the long run that the former student will develop more independence and self-responsibility.

Only occasionally has Rogers acknowledged that client-centered therapy is not the method of choice for all clients, for example, "the client who externalizes his problem, feeling little self-responsibility is much more likely to be a failure" (1957, p. 101). Occasionally, when Rogers deals with individual differences, his comments are surprising, such as when he proposes "a revolutionary program for graduate education" (1969, pp. 189–202) that begins with a rigorous selection of students:

> I would propose a rigorous selection system, which would weed out, so far as possible, those who seem unlikely to become creative scholars or practitioners. Part of my reasoning is that being refused admission to a

program is not a serious blow to a student's personality. It is a rejection which can be rationalized relatively easily. But once in the program, the student should not be rejected except for very grave cause. Instead, it should be the task of the staff to develop all the selected students as competent professional individuals.

I would like to suggest three criteria for selection. The first would be "intelligence," perhaps more specifically defined as a high degree of ability in problem solving. My reason for this criterion is simply that, in general, intelligence "pays off." Of two professional individuals completely equal in every other respect, the brighter one of the two is probably more likely to make a lasting contribution. (pp. 191–192)

Educational Relevance and Feasibility

HARMONIZING COGNITIVE AND AFFECTIVE APPROACHES

Floyd Robinson's essay (1970) on "Relevance for the school" provides a useful perspective for considering the possibility of keeping so-called cognitive objective within a humanistic framework. Following are excerpts in his argument:

> But what we tend to forget, or perhaps have never fully understood, is that it is precisely these structures of the rational mind which enhance the quality of affect. To establish this point I think we might start with the universally accepted proposition that what is uniquely human about human nature is the capacity for more highly developed states of consciousness than is possible in other living creatures. We have no reason to believe that our raw sensations are more acute than those of animals; rather, our superiority lies in the ability to modify these raw sensations in order to give a richer, more varied, more elaborate, more subtle internal feel to our existence. (p. 27) . . . it is in this act of stepping outside our primary states of consciousness, of becoming conscious of our own consciousness, that we acquire our individual freedom. For each shift away from primary consciousness changes and makes more subtle the emotion which we experience, so that when we have acquired a certain virtuosity in making such shifts we can call forth a variety of affect states at will. We can, then, in time, come to create an internal life of our own choosing, to "orchestrate" as it were the internal feel of our own existence. It seems to me that an education which can help people attain this state has done all that can be hoped for in the way of providing something that is personally relevant. (p. 28)
>
> One aspect of the paradox, then, is that the fullest development of the affective life rests upon the fullest development of the rational structures

of mind. And yet, as a deeper part of the paradox, it is necessary that we learn how to escape from our own structured intelligence. (p. 29)

Robinson's comments remind us that the cognitive is not all sterile and logical, but rather that it provides the basis for orchestrating a fuller experience.

IS NONDIRECTIVE TEACHING POSSIBLE?

The "ticklish task" to which Maslow referred when the teacher (in Dewey's terms) knows the road map of ideal development but cannot force the student to travel is a central problem in humanistic theories that avoid all direction on the part of the training agent/facilitator/guide. There is evidence from Rogers' own cases, which have been analyzed in terms of the counselor's effect on the client, that counselors cannot help having a directive or influencing effect. Murray (1956), for example, demonstrated that when client statements were categorized by the nature of concerns, these statements showed an orderly increase or decrease (much as a Skinnerian learning curve) as a result of what the counselor paid attention to (reinforced). When a client makes a complex statement, the counselor must be selective in responding to one or another aspect of the statement and selective about when he does this.

The facilitator cannot solve the problem by not responding. On the basis of their past experiences, students or clients may interpret nonresponse as negative. Therefore, although one can applaud the humanistic rationale, one must be cautious about accepting the idea that a teacher or counselor can be nondirective in dealing with another person. Since it is impossible to be nondirective, it may be more valuable to be explicit about one's values and what one hopes to accomplish with the student or client. Again, it should be noted that in practice Rogers himself demonstrates a capacity to respond to the other person's wishes with a bare minimum of direction. However, teachers attempting to apply nondirective teaching should be wary of making the mistake that some versions of discovery learning make, that the student is "free to discover" the answer in the teacher's head. The problem in nondirective teaching is more subtle, but it is epitomized by the teacher's grudging acceptance of a person who does not want to be free. As mentioned, the most critical test of a humanistic approach is its willingness to accept persons who do not make choices in accordance with the humanistic value orientation. In these cases, it would seem more valuable to be explicit about such a value orientation and admit that the approach may be less useful for certain students. We conclude with a more intensive consideration of this question.

ARE STUDENTS FREE TO CHOOSE NOT TO DO THEIR OWN THING?

With the present emphasis on independent study, open schools, free schools, student options, individual timetables, it is appropriate to note that, although some suggestions brought in by the application of humanistic approaches to education were necessary to redress an imbalance, it will be no improvement if educational procedures become completely unstructured and affectively oriented.

We noted in Chapter 9 that students with varying Conceptual Levels require or prefer different amounts of structure. Our entire point in presenting a differential analysis of humanistic education is to put it into perspective for those students and purposes for which it may be most useful. The current emphasis on "doing your own thing" is so ingrained as a cultural value that it may be difficult at first to see how this value, if forced on everyone, can be as unreasonable as requiring structured education for all. The best way to make this point is to cite statements made by students who attended a relatively open high school for a time and then chose to transfer to a more structured school. Following are some of their responses to the question, "What do you think is the best way for you to learn?"

> If a teacher makes you see things very clearly, that is obviously the best
>   way to learn. I like it when the teacher will stand up in front of the class
>   and explain things and get you to understand.
> I like rigid rules and a pattern set down.
> I like a teacher standing up there telling us what to do.
> I think I need to be pushed a bit in order to learn.
> I need that crack on the back . . . they are formal here but I like it because
>   you get your work done.
> I like order and respect for the teacher.
> I have to be told it has to be done, and if not, I won't do it. That's it and
>   then I won't learn anything.

The humanistic theorist's response to these students' preferences for less freedom may be that they have been "conditioned" to such structure by many years of traditional schooling. This may be partially true. However, it would seem that if the humanistic approach is to be truly humanistic, it must accept persons who really prefer less freedom. On the face of it, such persons do not seem to fit into the notions of Maslow and Rogers, who set so much store by internal determinants. This apparent disparity is much less important than that all students be accepted on their own terms, even if these are a continued preference for structure. Such acceptance is a major challenge for humanistic education.

Summary

Humanistic approaches as exemplified by the theories of Rogers and Maslow were considered in B-P-E terms. Rogers' theory of nondirective, or client-centered, counseling can be easily adapted to education by considering the teacher as the counselor and the student as the client. Maslow's theory has derived primarily from studies of normal persons, but it has also drawn from psychotherapy. Both theories emphasize the individual, his well-being, and his potential for developing into a better person. Because of their belief in the integrity of the individual, both theorists insist that the person himself must make choices, rather than have choices forced upon him.

Maslow conceptualizes persons in terms of a need hierarchy ranging from physiological needs, belonging and love needs, esteem needs to the highest level, self-actualization. All lower-level needs must be met before the person is capable of self-actualization. Rogers is less explicit about the differences between persons but sets the developmental goal as that of a fully functioning person.

Since both theories are developmental, the goal is that of developing, or becoming, a better person. Affective goals are emphasized as being more relevant. Both theorists have strong reservations about the likelihood of such growth being encouraged in conventional schools.

For Rogers, the prescribed general environment is that of unconditional positive regard. Providing such unqualified acceptance frees the person to use his potential for growth. Rogers only occasionally admits that this requires a self-responsible person. Maslow is somewhat more specific in stating the necessity for meeting whatever lower needs require gratification. Rogers describes the role of the teacher as a facilitator, while Maslow refers to him as a Taoist guide.

The chapter concluded by posing three questions that confront humansitic approaches: (1) coordinating affective with cognitive goals; (2) acknowledging that no one can be truly "nondirective" in interacting with another; and (3) accepting persons who by their choices may not agree with humanistic ideals, that is, persons who really prefer a more structured environment.

SUGGESTED READINGS

Brown, G. I. *Human Teaching for Human Learning.* New York: Viking Press, 1971.

Maslow, A. H. "Some Education of the Humanistic Psychologist." *Harvard Educational Review* 38 (1968):685–696.

Rogers, C. R. *Freedom to Learn.* Columbus, Ohio: Charles E. Merrill Publishing Co., 1969.

Weinstein, G., and Fantini, M. D. *Toward Humanistic Education: A Curriculum of Affect.* New York: Frederick A. Praeger, 1970.

chapter 11

FROM PSYCHOLOGICAL THEORY TO EDUCATIONAL PRACTICE

This chapter considers how psychological ideas, such as those described in Chapters 6 through 10, are applied to educational practice. The major purpose in the coordination of psychology and education is to improve the quality of education through the implementation of psychological ideas. Psychological theories may be enriched through their application to educational problems, but the ultimate purpose for implementing psychological ideas is to further understanding of and solutions for human problems. As Lewin said, "There is nothing so practical as a good theory."

Psychological theories have not always been applied to educational problems with maximum effectiveness. Some theories may be inadequate or irrelevant, while other theories are poorly understood. In any case, there is room for improvement. If psychological ideas are to be implemented in educational practice, more attention must be paid to the process of implementation. There is an important difference between a psychological principle and the implementation of that principle. Understanding a child's needs, for example, neither assures that they will be met nor indicates how they will be met.

Because a theory of implementation is required, this chapter describes criteria for evaluating the likelihood of a psychological idea being adopted in educational practice. In addition, two implementation strategies—traditional and teacher-centered—are described, and two illustrations of teacher-centered implementation considered.

Before discussing the process of how new ideas are adopted, it should be made clear that all innovation is not inherently good, that is, change for the sake of change alone may be detrimental. In fact, a psychologist might make a valuable contribution by pointing out that a current educational practice may be as effective or more effective than newer practices under consideration. This point should be borne in mind in the following discussion.

What Is Implemented?

The *psychological idea* is the basic unit to be implemented. The idea may be a specific principle, such as "learning is less likely to extinguish under conditions of partial reinforcement," or a more general idea, such as student-directed learning. An excellent example of specifying psychological ideas in educational terms is found in "Teaching Concepts in the Classroom" (Clark 1971). Clark summarizes the results of several hundred studies on concept learning and translates the findings into educational terms. The term psychological idea may describe a variety of principles, laws, or concepts.

The central idea in Piaget's theory, for example, is that children experience and apprehend events in terms of their present cognitive stage. The major idea in Skinner's theory is that behavior can be controlled by manipulating the conditions of reinforcement. These ideas, as well as those proposed in Chapters 8, 9, and 10, are distinctly psychological in contrast to other ideas, such as language laboratories and team teaching, which are not psychological ideas. However, the criteria for evaluating psychological ideas that are proposed in the next section should apply to nonpsychological ideas as well.

Criteria for Evaluating Ideas in Terms of Implementation

Why is one idea adopted into educational practice and another not adopted? The first thing to note is that the criteria for evaluating the implementability of an idea in education will *not* be the same as the criteria for determining the scientific value of an idea. This is not to say that the objective validity of an idea is not important proof of its value, but it is not the only criterion. Tests of statistical significance applied to results collected in controlled experiments are only one measure of validity.

The following quotation (D. E. Hunt 1970) elaborates on this:

> Of course, the prime consideration is whether the principle is sufficiently well established to attempt implementation, and such validity should not be ignored. However, at the risk of seeming cynical, it seems unlikely that the validity of an educationally relevant psychological principle will have very much to do with whether or not it is accepted in educational practice. Validity of a principle is probably a necessary, but certainly not a sufficient, condition to insure its adoption. Assuming that the matching principle is sufficiently well established, it seems probable that one of the major determinants of its acceptability will be the degree to which it is congruent with the "implicit matching principles" that teachers have in their heads. If one accepts this formulation, then the task of implementing a matching model should begin with an investigation of what "theory of matching" the educational decision-maker is now using, because from what we know of attitude change and adoption of new procedures, the suggested matching prescriptions should not be too far out of line with those held by the person who will be implementing the prescription. (p. 80.)

Therefore, an idea should be evaluated in terms of how it fits in with what the teacher thinks. The following criteria aim to relate the psychological idea to its implementation in educational practice:

	Criteria	
	1. Objective validity	
Psychological idea	2. Potential relevance	Educational implementation
	3. Comprehensibility	
	4. Practicality	

In a comparison of two ideas, the one chosen for implementation should be evaluated higher on some if not all four criteria. Whether an idea must meet all criteria is not certain, but the relative importance of each criterion is considered in the following discussion.

OBJECTIVE VALIDITY

A psychologist's primary criterion for an idea is its validity. Validity may be *theoretically* determined by the logical coherence and theoretical consistency of an idea or *empirically* determined by experimentation. In the analysis of controlled experiments, statistical tests are used to decide whether different experimental conditions cause significantly different outcomes.

Differences in the meaning of the term significant, as in the statement, "Method A produced significantly more learning than Method B," account for much of the misunderstanding between psychologists and educators (Bakan 1966). The term "significance" means to the psychologist a conventionally accepted scientific procedure for deciding whether the results of an experiment were produced by chance or not. It does not give any indication of what the layman usually means by significance. Statistical significance may be related to practical significance, but this is not necessarily the case. In evaluating a psychological idea for its implementability, it is as important for the psychologist to understand what is meant by practical significance as it is for the educator to understand what is meant by statistical significance.

A full treatment of this complex problem is beyond the scope of this discussion, partly because there are clear signs that psychologists are changing their ideas about criteria of validity. At the heart of the issue is whether psychology is a science and can evaluate ideas using scientific methods. One of the most rigorous scientific procedures is to replicate, or repeat, an experiment that has produced significant results. When an experiment is repeated with another experimenter, or with other subjects, or especially with a different task, the results of the second study sometimes do not confirm those of the first.

Does this happen because psychology is a young science (and therefore should not expect clear proof at this stage) or because the scientific method is inappropriate to the study of the complexities of human interaction? Probably neither is entirely accurate, but it would seem that the inclusion of criteria other than statistical significance and replication would be one solution to the problem of validity. We do not propose to abandon evaluation by objective validity, or the use of significance tests; we only propose that such evaluation be tempered by other criteria, such as common sense. The most comprehensive procedure for evaluating a psychological idea is that of construct validity (Cronbach and Meehl 1955). See D. E. Hunt (1971, pp. 71–78) for an example of this procedure.

If validity is only one aspect, the question arises of whether validated ideas are more likely to be implemented than nonvalidated ideas, but this problem has not been studied by psychologists. Likelihood of implementation could be investigated by an experiment which involved ideas differing in their scientific validity and procedures of varying incentives to observe which was more important, validity or reward for implementation.

To propose additional criteria for evaluating an idea does not mean that educators should ignore the objective validity of an idea. They are not likely to express their concern by asking, "Has this idea been proven?" because they assume that the psychologist would not be proposing the implementation of an unproven idea. However, the educator does not necessarily require the same kind of proof as that required by the psychologist.

Some ideas are stated in such general terms that they cannot be validated. S. B. Sarason (1971) refers to these as "untestable abstractions" and gives these examples:

> The classroom should not be a dull and uninteresting place but one which brings out the *creativity* in children. . . . The *potential* of the children is not being realized. The classroom should be a place where self actualization is constantly occurring. *Sarason, 1971,* (p. 25)

Educators are not likely to question such untestable abstractions because they typically *sound* as if they had been proven. The ready acceptance of psychological ideas stated in the form of untestable abstractions is perhaps the most important reason for requiring tests of objective validity. If the idea is untestable, it cannot be validated.

POTENTIAL RELEVANCE

As described in Chapter 1, the potential educational relevance of a psychological idea may be considered by using the B-P-E way of thinking, as summarized in Table 19.

Table 19. *Dimensions of Relevance*

	Low relevance	*High relevance*
E	Independent variable	Way of teaching
P	Experimental subjects	Students
B	Dependent variable	Learning outcome

For example, the more closely the experimental treatments resemble actual ways of teaching, the more similar the experimental subjects are to actual students, and the more closely the dependent variables approximate desirable learning outcomes, the more likely it is that the validated psychological idea will have educational relevance.

A more traditional view of relevance is found in Table 20 from Hilgard (1964).

Table 20 contains implicit dimensions of relevance as well as sequenced strategy for implementation, which we will discuss in the next section.

Jackson (1970) recently criticized educational psychologists for using the term "educational treatment" rather than "way of teaching." He also feels that teachers are probably inarticulate about describing their ways of teaching and concludes, "Let us, therefore, be appropriately cautious as we talk about the future promise of educational research for those who work in classrooms" (p. 23).

For the psychologist who hopes that his work may produce some effect on educational practice during his lifetime, Jackson's admonition may be very frustrating. Cronbach's statement (1966) nicely captures this frustration:

> The educational psychologist is torn between two responsibilities. His responsibility as educational specialist is to give schools advice on matters where the evidence is pitifully limited. His responsibility as scientist is to insist on careful substantiation of claims for each educational innovation. In education, unfortunately, there is great furor about whatever is announced as the latest trend, and the schools seem to careen erratically after each Pied Piper in turn. This giddy chase keeps them almost beyond earshot of the researcher standing on his tiny, laboriously tamped patch of solid ground, crying in a pathetic voice, "Wait for me! Wait for me!" (p. 91)

There are no easy solutions, but it is a prophecy of despair to state that psychological principles are too specific and irrelevant to affect practice. An obvious approach is for the psychologist to work more in the classrooms so that he can better understand how teachers view relevance. One task that needs doing is a careful sifting of the research work conducted by psychologists to determine its potential relevance in terms of the dimensions listed in Table 19.

How psychologists and educators interpret the potential relevance of an idea will obviously be colored by other criteria: for the psychologist, objective validity; and for the educator, intuitive reasonableness and practicality. However, the dimensions in Table 19 may provide the basis for a dialogue between the psychologist and educator about relevance.

COMPREHENSIBILITY AND INTUITIVE REASONABLENESS

Although an idea may have been complex in its formulation and validation, it must eventually be stated in terms that are understood by the person responsible for its implementation. As indicated in an earlier quotation, most teachers have some "implicit theory of matching," even though it may not be well

Table 20. Steps in Research on Learning—
Pure Research to Technological Development

Not directly relevant	Relevant subject and/or topics	School-relevant subjects and topics	Laboratory classroom, and special teacher	Tryout in "normal" classroom	Advocacy and adoption
Step 1	Step 2	Step 3	Step 4	Step 5	Step 6
Animal mazes, eyelid conditioning, pursuit learning, etc.	Human verbal learning concept formation, etc.	Mathematics, reading, typing, etc.	Programmed instruction; language laboratory in early stages	Results of step 4 tried in regular setting	Manuals and textbooks prepared; teacher training undertaken

(After Hilgard 1964)

articulated, and the likelihood of a teacher's implementing a differential idea will be determined by its congruence with the teacher's implicit theory and present practice that is, its intuitive reasonableness. As E. M. Rogers (1962) puts it in discussing the adoption of innovations:

> Old ideas are the main tools with which new ideas can be assessed. One cannot deal with an innovation except on the basis of the familiar and the old-fashioned. The rate of adoption of a new idea is affected by the old idea that it supersedes. Obviously, however, if a new idea were completely congruent with existing practice, there would be no innovation. (p. 127)

As the last sentence suggests, a new idea may be *too* compatible if it is perceived as identical to the old idea; thus, there is usually an optimal distance between the new idea and the old idea (D. E. Hunt 1971, p. 74).

That new ideas may be so compatible and intuitively reasonable as to be uninteresting is illustrated by an experience that one of the authors had in describing the CL stage theory to a twelfth-grade class in psychology. Care was taken to make the presentation as comprehensible as possible with frequent examples. At the conclusion, one girl raised her hand and remarked, "Is that supposed to be a theory? I already knew that!" Many psychologists might be quite disappointed by such a reaction should their ideas be perceived by teachers as too reasonable or too compatible with current practice. However, intuitive reasonableness forms the basis for the teacher-centered implementation.

PRACTICALITY

Educators are understandably concerned with the practicality of an idea. Can I use it? Will it fit into existing structures and constraints? We made the point initially that the statement of a differential idea, for example, the higher the student CL, the less structure required, does not tell us anything about *how* to implement this matching principle. It might be implemented within classes, between classes, or between schools. Despite efforts to distinguish matching ideas from their implementation, educational decision-makers find it difficult to grasp the idea of matching without immediately relating it to a specific practice, such as homogeneous grouping or individualized instruction. Some expectations that ideas be practical under existing conditions are unreasonable, for example, every idea must be applicable in a self-contained classroom. However, other expectations, such as recognition of the constraint of complusory education to sixteen, are quite reasonable, at least for the present.

Cronbach (1967) has suggested three means for implementing differential educational practices, as shown in Table 21.

Table 21. Patterns of Educational Adaptation to Individual Differences

Educational goals	Instructional treatment	Possible modifications to meet individual needs
Fixed	Fixed	1a. Alter duration of schooling by sequential selection. 1b. Train to criterion on any skill or topic, hence alter duration of instruction.
Options	Fixed within an option	2a. Determine for each student his prospective adult role and provide a curriculum preparing for that role.
Fixed within a course or program	Alternatives	3a. Provided remedial adjuncts to fixed "main track" instruction. 3b. Teach by different methods.

(From Cronbach 1967)

An even more comprehensive taxonomy of the size of the unit of adaptation has been provided by Lesser (1971) as follows:

Diversity of instructional strategies: variation in the learning situation.
1. Differentiation by school type.
2. Differentiation by tracks within school.
3. Differentiation by sections within track.
   a. Classes organized by general ability.
   b. Classes organized by ability in particular subjects.
4. Differentiation within a class.
   a. Ability groups within class.
   b. Grouping for remediation.
   c. Computer-aided instruction and other mechanical devices. (pp. 534–536).

Lesser's system is based on the size of unit in the implementation. As Cronbach states (1967):

A distinction needs to be made regarding the scale of adaptation. Branched programming is a microadaptation; a new decision is made every few minutes. The decision to put a six-year-old into lessons that generate reading readiness, instead of giving him a primer, is a macroadaptation; the decision prescribes several weeks of treatment. The choice of scale merits a good deal of thought. The finer scale is more responsive, but not necessarily superior, since each microdecision is made with less information. Microdecisions keep such a multiplicity of treatments in play that it becomes impossible to evaluate every branching rule with care. Macrotreatments, being fewer, can be designed on the basis of theory and can be empirically validated. (p. 28)

The psychologist concerned with the implications of an idea for differential educational practice can consider his idea in terms of these various procedures. However, he should not expect that the idea itself will determine the size of the unit to be implemented. For example, the matching of teaching method to learning style prescribed by the CL matching model can be implemented by homogeneous classroom grouping, as will be described, but it can also be implemented within an entire school, as described at the conclusion of Chapter 4 (D. E. Hunt 1972). Gibbons (1970) has provided a thorough classification system of individualized instructional programs.

Although one benefit for the psychologist working in schools is to learn, among other things, the practical constraints, these constraints should not determine exclusively what the psychologist does. Jackson (1970) questioned the advisability of studying person-environment interactions because teachers would not be able to apply them. Ignoring the question of the validity of Jackson's premise, it still holds that psychologists must study some problems for their own sake rather than for their immediate payoff. Otherwise, the argument suggests that one should not try to understand the needs of a child if educational arrangements to meet these needs are not presently available. Such an argument confuses understanding with implementation (we may know more than we can apply) and also implicitly assumes that the self-contained classroom led by a teacher will be the only form of educational arrangement in the future (cf. Joyce 1967).

OTHER CRITERIA

These four criteria are not, of course, the only criteria. S. B. Sarason (1971) has elegantly described the importance of the school culture as a determinant of the implementation of new ideas. Thelen (1967) points out the importance of the general culture.

There is a close connection between the state of affairs in the larger society of the nation and the smaller society of the community or even of the school. This is understandable because the smaller segments are part and parcel of the larger; dialogue at the level of national government is animated by the same attitudes, prejudices, and values that nourish local dialogue. The words at the two levels may be about different topics, but the emotional dynamics are the same.

What this means in practice is that successful innovations of new practices in schools have to satisfy not only the criterion of educational plausibility or soundness; they must also catch the mood of the public. For example, teaching machines are currently failures because they do not teach the "higher mental processes" such as critical thinking—but the public is willing to buy them. At the same time, "self-directed study," which can be valuable for the child's education, has been driven underground by the national drive toward standardization, automation, and routine-teaching procedures applicable to everyone. (p. 3)

Some readers may feel that sociological or cultural factors are the major factors for determining the adoption of an idea into practice. These certainly are important factors, but we prefer to consider the implementation in terms of all levels of the educational environment listed in Table 9 rather than deal with only one level of concern. The Zeitgeist and culture of the school are important, but so is a teacher's way of thinking.

Criteria for validating categories. Bruner, Goodnow, and Austin (1956) described several means of validating a category; however, as ways of thinking, they illustrate the variety of criteria for evaluating an idea. One may take *recourse to an ultimate criterion.* For example, one may try out the idea to find out if it works. *Testing by consistency* is the second method of validating or evaluating whether the idea fits in with one's other ideas. *Testing by consensus,* or evaluating by consensual validation of a reference group, is a third method. Finally, one may *test by affective congruence*—does it "feel" right?

Characteristics of innovation in other fields. Much more has been written about implementation and innovation in agriculture and industry than in education. Based primarily on industry, agriculture, and medicine, E. M. Rogers (1962) has set forth five characteristics of innovations that are somewhat similar to our own four criteria described above.

1. *Relative advantage* is the degree to which an innovation is superior to ideas it supersedes. (p. 124)
2. *Compatibility* is the degree to which it is consistent with existing values. (p. 127)
3. *Complexity* is the degree to which an innovation is relatively difficult to understand and use. (p. 130)
4. *Divisibility* is the degree to which an innovation may be tried on a limited basis. (p. 131)

5. *Communicability* is the degree to which the results of an innovation may be diffused to others. (p. 132)

Strategies of Implementation

TRADITIONAL IMPLEMENTATION STRATEGY

Hilgard (1964) has summarized the traditional strategy as follows:

> Abstractly, the steps of innovation are clear enough: Provide (a) a sound research-based program, validated in tryout, (b) the program packaged in such a way as to be available, as in good textbooks, supplementary readings in the form of pamphlets, films, programs for teaching machines, and guides for the teacher, (c) testing materials by which it can be ascertained if the objectives of the program have indeed been realized, with appropriate normative data on these evaluative instruments, (d) in-service training of the teacher to overcome the teacher's resistance to something new and to gain his enthusiastic acceptance of the program as something valuable as well as to train him in its use, and (e) support for the program from the community, school boards, parents, and others concerned with the schools. (p. 414)

Miles (1964) has provided a useful description of the dimensions of innovation strategies in education as follows:

> Any given strategy is thought of here as being ultimately aimed at getting an innovation installed in a "target" system (usually a local school system and its immediate community environment, or a college or university). Strategies may be initiated by the target system itself, or by other systems in the environment of the target system, such as state departments of education, mass media, foundations, and government agencies.
>
> In either case, the strategy may involve the use of existing structures, or the creation of new structures. "Existing" and "new" must of course be defined with reference to the time at which the innovation is introduced.
>
> We thus have four ways in which a strategy may be initiated. Chronologically, we may then think of a series of stages which occur prior to the actual adoption of an innovation by a target system. These stages include: (1) design—the innovation is invented, discovered, made up out of whole cloth, produced by research and development operations, etc.; (2) awareness-interest—the potential consumers of the innovation, that is, members of the target system, come to be aware of the existence of the designed innovation, become interested in it, and seek information about its characteristics; (3) evaluation—the consumers perform a kind of mental trial of

the innovation, and form pro/con opinions about its efficacy in accomplishing system goals, its feasibility, and its cost; (4) trial—the target system engages in a (usually) small-scale trial of the innovation, in order to assess its consequences. If these are favorable, the innovation tends to be adopted, and the strategy is complete. Note that, whether the initiation of a strategy comes from the target system itself or from the environment of the target system, this typology always assumes the strategy to be aimed at adoption of the innovation in the target system. (pp. 19–20)

Note that the "traditional" strategy draws heavily on industrial models that "install" innovations like refrigerators. However, educationally relevant ideas are neither like refrigerators to be installed and plugged in nor are they like the practice of using hybrid corn to be diffused. Implementation in education must take into account at the outset the person who will be implementing the idea—the teacher. Such a strategy is described in the next section.

TEACHER-CENTERED IMPLEMENTATION STRATEGY

Fox and Lippitt (1964) illustrate how one might proceed with a teacher-centered strategy.

It was hypothesized that teachers might be encouraged to make changes in their classrooms in at least two ways—(1) by collaboration with the research team in gathering and interpreting data about the state of affairs in the teacher's own classroom, leading to innovation designed to modify the situation; or (2) by examining the innovation efforts of other teachers to meeting situations similar to ones believed to exist in one's own class. In this second case, the challenge is one of adaptation—modifying the original innovation in ways that will fit the unique situation faced by the client teacher. The adoption of new ideas or innovative procedures developed by one's colleagues, or reported in the professional literature, becomes in itself an innovating activity for that teacher and that class. (p. 272)

As we have indicated repeatedly, the B-P-E model serves as a guide in following a teacher-centered implementation strategy, since the first step is to determine the teacher's perception of students (P), environment (E), and behaviors (B).

Teacher's conception of students. The procedures used by Fox and Lippitt are quite helpful in taking into account the teacher's implicit theory of matching. Fox and Lippitt began the implementation of classroom practices by first asking the teacher to describe her perception of the students in ways described earlier in Chapter 2.

Teacher's conception of environment. Fox and Lippitt (1964) have also provided a method for finding out how a teacher perceives classroom practices (environments):

> She was also asked to suppose that a visiting teacher from Russia had engaged her in conversation about school practices in this country. She was to assume that her visitor knew very little about American teaching practice. He was particularly interested in learning about mental health in classroom teaching, and what Teacher "A" considered to be good mental health practices and good mental conditions in the classroom. She listed as many ideas as she could for the visitor, each on a blank 3 X 5 card. Cards were then grouped, and placed in rank order. A similar set of cards was produced around the practices and condition conducive to effective learning. Teacher "A" was then asked to describe any connections or relationships she saw between the mental health variables and the learning conditions. (p. 277)

Teacher's conception of behavior. Similar procedures could be used to find out about a teacher's ideas of behavior, desirable and undesirable. As mentioned in Chapter 7, such procedures are the first step in introducing behavior modification into the classroom.

Having described these procedures, we may illustrate the teacher-centered strategy by the following examples.

An Example of Implementation: Conceptual Level Matching Model[1]

To illustrate the principles and criteria in this chapter, we describe some recent experiences with implementing the central idea in the CL matching model. The idea to be implemented is that the higher the student's Conceptual Level, the less structure he requires to process information effectively. One practical application of the model was described in Chapter 9, in which students were placed in classes homogeneous for CL. We have recently had experience with three schools, two open-concept elementary schools and one junior-high school, in which some form of matching has been implemented. We begin describing in narrative form one of these implementation activities.

[1] This implementation was reported in D. E. Hunt et al. 1972.

The first example concerns a teaching team of five teachers who were working together in a new open-concept elementary school. The five teachers were assigned to work with approximately 165 Grade 5 and Grade 6 students in whatever ways would be most effective for the students. As in most open schools, physical facilities were quite flexible so that the teachers could arrange their interactions with the students in a variety of forms. As these teachers became better acquainted with each other and with their students, they began to discuss ways in which they might arrange the learning situations more effectively. In their discussions, the teachers all agreed that the students varied considerably in terms of the best way of teaching them, some thriving when allowed to work by themselves and others needing much more teacher structure and support. It is important to note that it was *after* they had made the observation in environmentally relevant terms (degree of structure) that they considered how such students (persons) might be described. They described the students as varying in independence. The teachers were therefore familiar with student differences that could be translated into different teaching procedures, which was important because it meant that they were not concerned with categorizing the students for categorization's sake, but only with how such categories could be transformed into decisions about more effective educational practice.

A member of the professional development staff in the school district was working with the team at this time, and he was aware of the CL matching ideas. He brought these ideas to the attention of the team, and after they had read material similar to that in Chapter 9, they asked to meet with members of our psychology group to discuss our common interests. Before our first joint meeting with the teaching team, they continued to meet to discuss problems, such as "What is the difference between an independent student and a dependable student?" to sharpen their understanding of the student types.

That the request for liaison and establishing the relation came from the teacher team can hardly be overemphasized. It is possible for psychologists to develop a good working relation with teachers who have not initiated the contact, but considerable time is required for teachers to consider whether or not they wish to become involved.

At the first meeting with the teaching team, we listened to their ideas about educational aims and objectives. They were agreed that they wanted (1) to make the educational experience a pleasant one, (2) to help students think and solve problems, and (3) to encourage students to be more independent. When we began a discussion of student types, it was in terms of independent and dependent students rather than in the language of Chapter 9—Stage A, Stage B, and Stage C. We discovered in our first meeting that this team had some very strong (and legitimate) feelings about classifying students in any way that would imply a value judgment. They were remarkably sensitive to the importance of considering differences among students that would permit "meeting each student's needs" more effectively without stigmatizing him through the classification. Thus, dependent and independent are less value laden, compared with such descriptions as low and high CL, although these terms, too, are evaluative.

When we discussed their understanding of what independent and dependent students were like, it became clear that their comprehension of these student types was almost entirely rooted in the different environments that would be most effective for different types. For example, they described an independent student as one who could profit from a great deal of freedom and opportunity to work on his own. As we found in other experiences, it is essential that the teachers understand the students in environmentally relevant terms. For teachers who are less clear about these student differences, it might be more effective simply to describe students *only* in environmentally relevant terms, that is, students might be described as "needing structure and support" or "needing opportunities for individual work," terms which are also less value laden.

Members of this team were quite articulate about the differences they could see among their students, and they could begin to understand specific procedures that would be more effective in working with these different students. Note that up to this point there has been no explicit use of the matching idea —the higher the student CL the less structure is required—although the idea has been implicit in all discussions.

After the discussion of the teachers' conceptions of person and environment, the principal, who was also present at the meeting, asked about the validity of the CL matching model. We discussed objective validity (D. E. Hunt 1971), emphasizing the importance of distinguishing between developmental and contemporaneous perspectives. Next, we talked about some of the options for implementation. Since an open-concept school provides innumerable variations in arrangements, there were many alternatives available. For example, students could be grouped by learning style alone (the term which we quickly came to use to describe dependence-independence), or by learning style half the time for certain courses and by other groupings for other courses.

Following this first joint meeting, the school staff met together to discuss their reactions. At our next joint meeting, they asked if it would be possible for us to classify the students for the following year so that learning style groups could be formed. We agreed, and two of our staff members went about the job of assessing the students. Since the implementation was to take place the following year, it was necessary to assess students in Grade 4 who were then working with another team of teachers, and this required that we discuss some of the matching ideas with the Grade 4 team. The experience brought to the surface some feelings of inter-group rivalry and competition, which we have seen in every school where we have worked with only one team. Rivalry between teams would be less likely to happen if matching were implemented for a whole school rather than for only one teaching team; however, such a schoolwide arrangement would be out of keeping with our idea about teacher-centered implementation (unless requested by all teachers).

Although our emphasis in this example is on liaison with the teachers, we might comment about a practical assessment problem in going from learning styles to classroom-size groups. Once the 165 students were assessed, the distribution of scores on the CL dimension had a possible range from 0 to 3. From Chapter 9, you will recall that evidence suggests that three CL, or learning-style, groups be distinguished. For purposes of implementation, how-ever, it was necessary to classify the students into *five* classroom-size groups of approximately thirty-five each since there were five teachers. Therefore, some ground rules were necessary for making this transition. If we think of Group 1 as very dependent and Group 5 as independent, there was rather little difference between, for example, Groups 2 and 3, a similarity we pointed out to the teachers when we made the final groupings. This is shown in Table 22.

Table 22.   From Theory to Practice: Homogeneous Groups

Psychological "language" and groups	Conceptual Level				
	Low CL (Stage A)	Moderately Low CL (Stage B)		High CL (Stage C)	
Educational "language" and groups	Learning Style				
	Group 1 Very de-pendent	Group 2 Moderately dependent	Group 3 Middle	Group 4 Moderately independent	Group 5 Very independent

Once these five groups were assembled on paper with approximately thirty-five students in each group, we met with the team to discuss their reactions. It was exciting to hear their reactions to the students' placement in learning styles. They felt that the groups were extremely reasonable and made good sense. One teacher remarked, "I don't think I could have begun next year if we didn't have these groups."

We had noted earlier in our discussions that there was no point in grouping students unless the educational approach was appropriately modified to their learning style, and the teachers agreed. The matter of specific teaching assign-ment was handled through discussion. Since they were able to discuss issues openly with one another, the teachers were able to work out their assignments quickly. Again, the psychologist could have proceeded to assign the teachers to the groups by matching teaching styles and environments to be provided for each learning style. However, for obvious reasons, we felt that a teacher-determined option was preferable. Therefore, each teacher came to the meeting with an understanding of which group he was going to work with. On looking at the groups of students, for instance, one teacher who was to be working with the very dependent group said, "This will be a very exciting group to work with . . . we may have a few fights, but it will be a lot of fun."

We spent this meeting discussing any changes the teachers might want to make in the groups. There were one or two instances where teachers recommended a change because they felt a particular student would profit more from one teacher than from another, and where these suggestions did not change the learning style appreciably, students were moved from one group to another. There were a few cases in which the teachers raised questions about the accuracy of the learning-style classification. Our psychological team reviewed the data on classification to reconsider the bases for classification. In two cases, the students were moved from one group to another. However, generally, there was a great deal of agreement. The final grouping of students, therefore, was based on a combined discussion in which the teachers had the opportunity to change the groups. There was not a single instance in which the teachers suggested changing a student because the teacher himself did not get along well with or like a particular student.

Once the groups were fixed, the discussion turned to a number of feasibility problems that occur in grouping. How will the grouping be explained to the students? How will the grouping be explained to the parents? We discussed these matters in some detail and also considered whether or not there would be the opportunity to change students from one group to another during the year. Obviously, if one maintains a developmental perspective, there is the possibility of developmental growth which should be included in whatever arrangements are used. Table 23 summarizes how the terms were translated.

Table 23. *Translating Psychological Terms into Educational Practice*

Psychological idea or term	Educational translation
Matching	Meeting a student's needs
Conceptual Level	Learning style
Low CL	Student who needs structure
High CL	Student who needs less structure
Variation in structure	Teaching methods
Paragraph Completion Test	Questionnaire
Developmental perspective	Providing support for growth
CL grouping	A way to help students become more independent and increase their self-esteem

When the fall classes began, the program was explained to the parents using the following summary sheet:

LEARNING STYLES AND TEACHING METHODS

Students differ in how they learn, or in their *learning styles*. For example, some learn better by listening to the teacher, some by discussions, and others by working on their own. To say that students differ in their learning styles does not mean that a student needs only one approach (exclusively) but that, generally speaking, he has one way of learning which for him is better than others.

Similarly, teachers use a variety of approaches, or *teaching methods*. For example, they may lecture, they may discuss, or they may let the student discover for himself. That is not to say that lecture, discussion, and independent study are the only methods, but they illustrate the variety in ways of teaching. No teacher uses one method exclusively, but he tries to use the method most likely to work with a specific class.

Grouping students by learning style enables the teacher to use that teaching method most likely to work for the majority of students in that class. To say that the teacher will try to match the teaching method to the class learning style does not mean that only one approach is used. For example, a teacher working with a class whose predominant learning style is for independent learning will not always assign them to work on their own. The teacher will use a variety of approaches with each class and will ask students in each class to give their opinions and ideas about teaching methods throughout the year. Therefore, the learning style of the class is only to give the teacher some general idea about what teaching method is likely to work best.

Regardless of the class learning style, all classes will learn the same material. It is the *way they learn* which will differ, not what or how much they learn. Grouping by learning style is simply a procedure to make it more likely that the teacher can meet the needs of the students.

If the CL matching model is to be educationally effective, the ideas of degree of structure of the environment must be translatable into specific procedures. This is obviously a central point in implementation, and as implied in Chapter 4, it is the weakest link in the model.

A final point: the issue of value judgments in classifying students was dealt with by describing them in somewhat neutral terms ranging from needing more structure to needing less structure. However, if one follows a developmental theory, it is impossible for grouping to be entirely value-free. For, if some value is placed on developmental growth, then there will always be some value in being higher on the developmental scale.

An Example of Implementation: Moral-Education Project

Our second example of implementation is taken from a moral-education project carried out by the second author in cooperation with a moral philosopher (Sullivan and Beck 1972). Both of the project directors had been working in the area of moral development and its relation to contemporary social issues. We had been experimenting with programs in value education for eleventh- and twelfth-graders in several schools for three years.

For the first part of the project, both directors abandoned their ivory towers and took on the role of teachers. During initial meetings with the students, we discussed moral theories and principles, using an elementary text as a stimulus. These discussions were necessary to establish a common vocabulary among the students and overcome communication problems resulting from a diversity of moral reasoning. After going through the text, the students selected topics of contemporary social significance; some of the topics were suggested by the students and others by us. The topics ranged over a number of areas, including abortion, capital punishment, drugs, and pollution.

Our evaluations of our programs were based on Kohlberg's Moral Judgment Scale (see Chapter 3). Apropos of *process* versus *content* in educational objectives, it will be seen that this instrument is oriented in several ways toward thinking *processes,* and we were much more interested in the process than in the particular content of our students' thinking.

The objective validity of the instrument is partially established cross-sectionally in several cross-national studies (for example, in Canada see Sullivan, McCullough, and Stager 1970) and also in the longitudinal follow-up of the original sample. Let us briefly schematize here the stages discussed in Chapter 3.

Level I   *Premoral*
  Stage 1 Obedience and punishment orientation
  Stage 2 Naively egoistic orientation
Level II   *Conventional Role Conformity*
  Stage 3 Good boy–nice girl orientation
  Stage 4 Authority and social order maintenance orientation
Level III   *Autonomous Morality of Principles*
  Stage 5 Contractual legalistic orientation
  Stage 6 Conscience or principle orientation.

We were interested in developmental change, and we did a pretest at the beginning of the course and two follow-ups. The first follow-up occurred at the end of the course and the second follow-up one year later. As will be seen shortly, this long-term developmental orientation has important implications in our work, and we are not at all interested in contemporaneous short-term measures. Of the three levels of moral judgment outlined above, one most often finds the premoral stages among elementary-school children, the conventional role conformity stages in most high-school students, and a smattering of autonomous morality stages in high-school and college students.

In our classroom work, we utilized Kohlberg's model to get a general idea of our student's levels and stages of moral reasoning. Most of our eleventh-grade students reasoned at the conventional level with a mixture of Stage 3 and Stage 4 thinking. There also were some with Stage 2 and Stage 5 orientations. Our goal was to move the students from the conventional orientation to the postconventional stages exemplified in the Level 3 morality of self-accepted moral principles. In other words, we were trying to encourage progress to the higher level of moral reasoning. If the program were implemented in the elementary school, "conventional" moral stages would probably be the objective, since many of the students would be developmentally at the "premoral" level. In other words, our goals would vary because we are *developmentally* oriented and we use in our evaluation a *developmental* theory. In the broadest sense, it can be said, that our matching model involves a curriculum pitched at level 3(E) to students (P) who are at level 2.

Figure 18 summarizes the analysis of one of our classes (Pickering School) right through the one-year follow-up post-test. The results shown in the figure and tests of significance between the experimental and control groups indicate no significant difference between the groups on Stage 5 usage on the pretest and first post-test. The second post-test shows a rather radical jump for the experimental groups which was statistically significant. We assume this change in our students started with our course and developed at an accelerated pace the following year. We intend to analyze other classes in our project in the same way.

The next step in our project will be to get ourselves out of the classroom and to have regular teachers use our approach. Although Kohlberg's stages are intuitively reasonable and comprehensive for our purposes, this does not necessarily mean that teachers will find this to be the case. We are presently working on a teacher's manual of Kohlberg's stages and dealing with the evaluative connotation of the stages.

The feasibility of using this approach is contingent on many factors. One factor is the sophistication of the teacher with regard to the educational objectives. The teacher here is an important educational environment (E). The teacher's moral level and its effects on classroom discussion and the ultimate

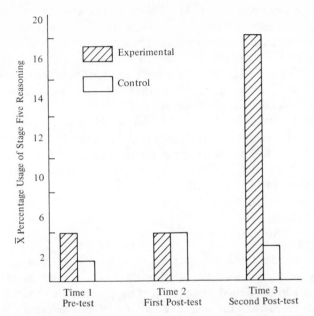

Figure 18 Percentages of Stage 5 Usage for Each Group at Each Test Time

attainment of development objectives represents a complex problem of matching.

There is usually a selective process operating in education, and ordinarily teachers who are successful in professional educational circles have conventional moral values. This is not an indictment of the teaching profession, since there are many good reasons that support conventional morality. The school is an agent of socialization and part of its mandate is to help parents and society in general inculcate conventional moral norms. Their conventions are the collection of wisdom that all new teachers need to know to succeed in their task. We conjecture from limited data that a predominant number of teachers remain for the most part in the conventional stages (3 and 4) of morality.

In the classroom where moral and ethical issues are being discussed, we think it is important to have teachers at a postconventional level of morality, so as to stimulate higher levels of moral reasoning in students. This does not necessarily mean the teacher must be a moral rebel or a danger to school order. In most instances, postconventional moral arguments recognize the need for conventions, but they base the merits of the conventions on sound reasoning rather than on some unquestioned authority source. Discussions on contemporary social issues also may take the students and the teacher into areas where there are no clear authoritative sources. The teacher must be willing to indicate to the students his own fallibility in such matters, if and when they arise in a classroom discussion. It would seem difficult for Stage 4 conventional "law and order" teachers to put themselves into this kind of role because of a latent fear that the teacher who does not have all the answers must relinquish his classroom authority. Since the structure of the class usually leaves the teacher in a controlling position, he typically modulates the level of the classroom discussion. If the teacher emphasizes maintenance of "law and order" and "authority," the discussion is not likely to venture into levels where authority is questioned on rational grounds.

Summary

This chapter has dealt with the question of why some psychological ideas are adopted in educational practice and others are not adopted, as well as means of improving the likelihood of implementing psychological ideas. Although psychologists emphasize the objective validity of an idea, four other criteria were suggested for determining the value of implementing an idea: potential relevance (which was considered in B-P-E terms), comprehensibility and intuitive reasonableness, practicality, and cultural factors.

To illustrate the application of these five criteria, a teacher-centered approach to implementation was described that began with understanding the teacher's implicit theory of matching, that is, using a B-P-E model as a basis for coordinating teacher's views with idea to be implemented. Teacher-centered implementation strategies were contrasted with more conventional strategies of implementation.

Two specific examples of the implementation of a psychological idea were described. Each one emphasized the necessity for understanding between the psychologist and the teacher, and the analysis of the educational process in B-P-E terms that are comprehensible to both parties was seen as an essential feature of this reciprocal relationship.

SUGGESTED READINGS

Hilgard, E. R. "Perspective on the Relationship Between Learning Theory and Educational Practices." In *Theories of Learning Instruction,* 63rd NSSE yearbook, Edited by E. R. Hilgard, pp. 402–415. Chicago: National Society for the Study of Education, 1964.

Rogers, E. M. *Diffusion of Innovations.* Chapter 5. New York: Free Press, 1962.
Thelen, H. A. *Classroom Grouping for Teachability.* Especially Chapter 1. New York: John Wiley & Sons, 1967.

chapter 12

B-P-E ANALYSIS:

How-to-do-it

Since the major purpose of this book has been to provide a new way of thinking, its value can be judged by the reader's experience in applying the model to his own situation. If Lewin's test of a "good" theory is to be accepted, then the test of the B-P-E model is the increased understanding it provides to psychologists and educators in viewing their own, and each other's work. Ways of thinking do not change easily, however, and many readers may close the book, return to the "real world" of their work without actually giving B-P-E thinking a try, and thus miss the real point of the book. You may come to the conclusion after applying B-P-E thinking to your own situation that it is not helpful, but you cannot know this unless you "try it on for size."

Although we have provided many earlier examples of application, we conclude with a short "how-to-do-it" chapter to encourage as many readers as possible to try it out. We have found in presenting this approach to classes, professional development meetings, and other groups that the model has proved quite valuable not only for educational psychologists, teachers, and administrators but also for counselors, teacher training staff, and the students themselves. Therefore, we describe some general procedures for applying the model and then indicate how persons in a variety of psychological and educational settings have found it useful to apply it to their specific area of work.

Despite lip service to being flexible and considering a variety of viewpoints, most of us suffer from hardening of the categories. In the present case such resistance takes the form of considering the B-P-E model as being self-evident and obvious ("I already knew that.") or impossibly complex ("It may be true but it's much too complicated to help me in my work."). Teachers frequently resist applying B-P-E thinking because they see it as only stating an impossible ideal in their own classroom ("Your theory may be all right for an ideal, but it doesn't apply to my situation because I can't treat each one of my students differently."). Educational administrators are likely to resist it because they see their job as requiring *general* principles to run an organization which cannot be adapted to individuals. Research psychologists may be the most resistant group for reasons we have indicated ("ATI has not paid off," "Individual differences are error variance," and so on). We do not expect to melt all these resistances with a final defrosting persuasive appeal.

However, readers who have come this far deserve a clear understanding of how to apply the model so that they do not reject trying it because of a misconception. It should be clear by now that we realize fully that a teacher cannot accommodate to every student nor can an administrator initiate educational programs which will be matched to every student. B-P-E analysis may involve specifying the theoretical ideal described in Chapters 6 through 10 when considering psychological theories. However, one may equally well analyze a specific situation such as a classroom, an educational program, or a counselor-client interaction in B-P-E terms. Thus, B-P-E analysis applies to the *actual* as well as to the ideal. It also indicates the disparity between actual and ideal, but one should not feel because his present situation does not measure up to the ideal that the B-P-E way of thinking does not "apply."

B-P-E thinking may provide useful insights by indicating what is missing as we noted in the Skinner omission of the person in the theory (Chapter 7). In addition, there may be value in obtaining a better understanding of one of the single components, for example, the teacher's reflecting on his conceptions of his students, a teacher training staff member's reflecting on how he conceptualizes different ways of teaching. Application of B-P-E, therefore, requires self-reflection, and its value will largely depend on the person's openness and desire for more systematic information about himself and his work.

The major advantage of B-P-E analysis is to put questions into a form which is most likely to provide an effective answer. Person-environment interactions are complex, but they cannot be ignored as a nuisance. They must be included in the initial form of the question, and B-P-E analysis provides a way for posing questions in such a differential form. The specific nature of the B-P-E components depends on who is asking the question. Thus, a teaching strategy is E to a classroom teacher (for example, which one shall I use?), but to the staff member of a teacher training institution, a teaching strategy is B since he is concerned with how to produce it in teacher trainees. This difference is illustrated in Table 24.

Table 24.   B-P-E analysis from different viewpoints

From Viewpoint of:	Environment (E)	Person (P)	Behavior (B)
Teacher	Way of teaching	Student type	Effect
Teacher trainer	Training intervention	Teacher trainees	Teaching skill
Principal	Teachers	Students	Objective
Superintendent	Programs	Groups of students	Objective
Researcher	Independent variable	Subjects	Dependent variable
Evaluator	Program	Different students	Criterion
Counselor	Counseling approach	Client	Goal of counseling
Student	Learning environment	Self-assessment	Desired outcome

Although the components may differ, Table 24 also illustrates a further advantage in B-P-E analysis, the application of B-P-E principles from another domain. For example, the matching principle describing P-E interactions in Chapter 9 was discussed primarily in terms of student-teaching method interaction in the classroom, but it has also been applied to P-E interactions in psychotherapy (McLachlan, 1972) and teacher training (Reid, in progress). Therefore, posing otherwise different questions in the common framework of B-P-E components may facilitate the interchange of knowledge.

We describe the steps in applying B-P-E analysis generally and then discuss how these steps would be used in each of the specific viewpoints in Table 24.

General Procedure

B-P-E analysis may be summarized in terms of the following steps:

1. State the question.
2. Translate question into a B-P-E diagram.
3. Describe differences in each component.
4. Collect information about components and their interrelation.

1. STATE THE QUESTION

B-P-E analysis is applicable to questions such as, "How can I better understand my teaching and its effect?" which involve a more systematic *description* of what is going on or has occurred as well as to questions such as, "What approach is likely to be most effective for this student to learn a concept?" which involves a *prescription* for action. When initially stating the question, however, one should not be concerned with whether it is descriptive or prescriptive, since this will become clear in later steps.

Following are a few examples of initial form of questions.

Teacher: "What will happen if I spend less time on this topic?" "What is the best way for me to teach this topic?" "How can I gain a better understanding of my teaching?" "How can I understand the relevance of this research report for my teaching?"

Teacher trainer: "How should I use my facilities for micro-teaching?" "How should I assign trainees to supervising teachers?" "How much time should be devoted to the trainees' learning systems of interaction analysis of classroom behavior?"

Principal: "Is there any way to maximize learning effectiveness through teacher-student arrangements?" "How will students be assigned to independent study?" "What arrangement will best capitalize on the diversity of teaching styles of my teachers?"

Superintendent: "How should educational alternatives be provided?" "Should this program be adopted?" "What are the major in-service training needs?"

Researcher: "What subjects should I select for the experiment?" "What experimental treatment should be used?" "What design should I use?" "What dependent variables should I observe?"

Evaluator: "How can the evaluation design reflect differential effects of program on different students?" "How many criteria should be employed?" "What kind of control group should be used?"

Counselor: "What kind of clients do I work with most effectively?" "What is the most effective treatment for this client?" "How can I determine therapeutic goals for a specific client?"

Student: "Which educational alternative should I select?" "Do I learn only when I am satisfied?" "How can I tell when I have learned something?"

Ideally, at this point the reader should try to state one or two questions himself so that he can follow through the next steps. Some questions may turn out to be unanswerable on further analysis, but this also is worth knowing.

2. TRANSLATE QUESTION INTO A B-P-E DIAGRAM

Throughout the book we have inserted B-P-E diagrams so that this step should by now be somewhat familiar. Using B-P-E diagrams may seem initially cumbersome, but they help to assure that the question will be stated in differential form. For example, the question "How shall I teach this topic?", requires first that the purpose (B) be specified. Next, the nature of the students must be stated. Therefore, this question might be stated as follows:

E	P	B
?	Grade 10 students	To understand the concept of cause-effect relations

Restated in sentence form, the question is "What instructional approach should be applied to grade 10 students to help them understand the concept of cause-effect relations." In most cases, the B-P-E diagram will consist of two "knowns" and one "unknown." The above example is in the form, "Given P and B, determine E." This form of the question is a person-centered approach as recommended in Chapter 2. Another example of this form (Given P and B, determine E) is the question often posed to the school psychologist. "What kind of approach is best for this student?" This question form is further illustrated by Cronbach's (1967):

> I suggest that we set out to invent interactions. Specifically, *we* ought to take a differential variable we think promising and design alternative treatments to interact with that variable. (p. 32)

To determine the E when P and B are known requires conceptualizing the person in terms of accessibility characteristics which are translatable into specific environmental prescriptions.

The question, "What kind of trainee can benefit most from this program?" would look like this:

E	P	B
Micro-teaching	?	Teaching skill

Here the question becomes "What kind of student is most likely to learn teaching skills through micro-teaching?" This example represents the form, "Given E and B, determine P." This form is similar to the personnel selection model in which persons are selected for environments rather than the other way round as in the first example.

The most straightforward form is the question "What are the likely effects of this program on these students?"

E	P	B
Sensitivity training	Highly organized executives	?

The form of "Given E and P, determine B" is the classic form for prediction in a psychological experiment. It is also the form in which evaluation questions are most often posed.

Although B-P-E diagrams usually leave one component to be prescribed, there are cases where all three components are known, and interest centers on describing and clarifying the B-P-E interaction. For example, a counselor may listen to a tape to reflect on what happened.

E	P	B
Counseling approach	Type of client	Effect

This form may also be helpful in analyzing a research report (see Table 11) or a psychological theory (Chapters 6–10).

Finally, there may be questions which are translated into two unknowns.

For example, "What are the most reasonable goals for this student and how can these best be accomplished?"

E	P	B
?	Student	?

This question is related to the specification of person-specific goals (particularistic objective as described by Lesser and discussed in Chapters 3 and 5) and specific approaches most likely to produce this effect. This is the ultimate in individualized instruction.

3. DESCRIBE DIFFERENCES IN EACH COMPONENT

The next step is to describe the variations in P, E, and B in terms related to the questions. If the question involves limited resources (E), then only those variations, should be described. The discussion in Chapters 2, 3, and 4 suggested references should guide this step in the analysis. The first question above might be described as follows:

E	P	B
?	Formal operational	To understand cause-effect relations
?	Concrete operational	

Describing the variation in person in Piagetian terms assumes that this description (1) is relevant to the B (cause-effect relations) and (2) can be differentially related to different instructional approaches. As the diagram above illustrates, the description of each component should be stated in a way most likely to provide a system of coordinating components. Put another way, it should be derived from a theory or model.

Table 11 in Chapter 5 illustrates an example of how teacher-student interaction was analyzed for its effect on student achievement gain. In the next section we consider how such information might be used to guide decisions.

Since the third and fourth steps become considerably more specific depending on the nature of the question, we postpone any further specific examples until the discussion of a specific application of B-P-E analysis.

4. COLLECT INFORMATION ABOUT COMPONENTS AND THEIR
INTERRELATION

Once the B-P-E diagram has been completed and the component specified, the
next step is to obtain the specific description for each component, and the
interrelation among them. For example, if a counselor is interested in learning
more about the specific effect of a counseling approach on a specific client, he
might collect information by taking notes on the transcript of an interview and
collating them. If a school principal were interested in using information from
Table 11 for maximizing the arrangements between student and teachers, then
he might use this as follows: If a limited number of "self-controlling teachers"
(E) are available, then these might be more efficiently allocated to "opposers"
(P), while "strivers" (P) could be assigned to almost any kind of teacher. This
is an example of how an empirical description may provide some guides for
prescription.

If the question is purely descriptive, then this step will involve simply
collecting information, that is, the teacher who is interested in learning more
about his teaching will simply collect information on his ways of teaching and
their effect on different students. Collecting information in this case is simply
aggregating, organizing, and noting the differential effects. If, however, the
question is stated with an "unknown," then it is more likely that a theory or
an earlier set of evidence will be required in order to derive the prescription.
For example, in answering the question of how to teach the students to
understand cause-effect relations it will be likely that a different teaching
method would be derived for students at the formal operational level than
those at the concrete operational level, as we described in Chapter 6.

Specific Suggestion for Application

TEACHERS

A teacher might want to explore the question, "How can I gain a better
understanding of my teaching?" which would be translated as follows:

E	P	B
Different ways of teaching	Different types of students	Effects

In specifying components, the teacher may describe students in his own terms by placing each student's name on a card and then sorting his class into groups according to how as he sees them. To specify the variations in students, the teacher should make an effort to describe the student specifically in accessibility channels. Next, the teacher would describe different effects (B) by asking the question "What are those things students do that make me feel I am succeeding?" Finally, the teacher will attempt to specify his ways of teaching or environments. As the teacher reflects on his own ways of teaching, he may find it useful to consider more explicit "Models of Teaching" (Joyce and Weil, 1972b) to stimulate his thinking about the variety of educational environments he radiates. As these authors comment:

> If the teaching profession is to become able to examine alternative kinds of educational approaches and various ways of achieving them, it seems essential that approaches to education be described in operational terms and that languages be developed which can be used to compare and contrast them. (p. 314)

Some teachers are put off by either B-P-E or analytic models of teaching because they feel such analytic precision is necessarily dehumanizing. These analytic models are simply ways of systematizing what is already going on; teachers use implicit models of teaching whether they acknowledge it or not, and to be self-reflective about such activity should improve the quality of teaching without destroying its spontaneity. As Joyce and Weil (1972b) comment:

> ... it may be that in order to be most effective, a teacher must develop his own particular models which blend with his particular style or his natural behavior patterns in such a way that he is able to engage in a kind of unique magic of his own making. (p. 316)

For the teacher, therefore, B-P-E analysis offers a means of describing and organizing his activities systematically so that he will be more open to suggestions from others and can more effectively communicate with them.

A geography teacher who read an early draft of this text found B-P-E analysis helpful in providing different instructional approaches to different students. In attempting to teach his students about the relation between climate and soil, he observed that some students were having difficulty in understanding this concept from the text. He had noticed earlier that these students frequently had difficulty with textual or verbal material, but on further consideration, he observed that they were capable of reading maps or charts. Once the students were considered in two groups with different accessibility characteristics—a verbal group and a spatial group—it was then a simple matter to develop an alternative approach for the spatial group. He devised a set of map overlays which the spatial group used rather than the text, and found that they were able to comprehend the relation between soil and climate very well by this method. His B-P-E diagram:

E	P	B
Text	Verbally oriented students	To understand relation between climate and soil
Map overlays	Spatially oriented students	

TEACHER TRAINER

The B-P-E model has two important implications for the training of teachers. First, the specification of the environments teachers radiate to students to produce certain effects (E:P $\longrightarrow$ B) provides a language for describing what teachers do. Once described, then the teacher training program has a rational basis for developing experiences for teacher trainees. As described in the "Model for analyzing the training of training agents" (Hunt, 1971), teaching effectiveness is defined as:

> the capacity to radiate a wide variety of environments, to select from this variety a specific environment to be radiated toward a particular person or group of persons (with the aim of producing a particular behavioral outcome), and to shift from one environment to another under appropriate circumstances. (Hunt, 1971, p. 52).

This definition leads to specific training objectives which can be aimed for in a teacher training program. For example, the trainees should learn skill in discrimination (discriminating between various educational environments, discriminating between various kinds of students, and discriminating between various behaviors). Next, they need to learn skill in radiating environments (to radiate a variety of environments, or to present the same lesson in a variety of instructional forms; to radiate that environment which will produce a specific behavior; and to radiate that environment which will produce a specific behavior from a particular person). Finally, trainees should acquire skill in flexible modulation from one environment to another. Of course, these are difficult goals to obtain, but unless some such specification is made of what is to be trained, then the training of teachers becomes very haphazard. (See Table 25.)

A specific description of how to use Table 25 in planning teacher training programs is found in Hunt (1971, Chapter 4). Trainees can be assessed in terms of these skill components and assigned to treatments accordingly.

The second contribution of the B-P-E model to planning programs in teacher education is to apply the matching principle to the program:

> The training of teachers, like the education of children, requires adaptation of individual differences. Teacher trainees vary enormously in skill level and in personality, yet most programs for training teachers are designed for an average trainee, with few options to accommodate trainee variation. A teacher training program, which provides alternative experiences modulated to trainee differences, is not only more likely to produce an efficient direct effect, but it will also be indirectly beneficial in providing the teacher trainee with an experiential example of what is meant by individualizing instruction and 'meeting the needs of the child.' (Hunt, 1971, p. 67)

The teacher trainer's question, "How should I use facilities for micro-teaching in the training program?" begins with the diagrams indicated earlier. Then, the teaching skill (B) is specified and the alternative training procedures to micro-teaching indicated. Salomon and McDonald (1970) found reaction to video feedback differed with differences in trainee self-esteem: High self-esteem trainees paid more attention to their teaching performance and improved in their self-evaluation while low self-esteem trainees paid more attention to the physical cues of their appearance and were less favorable in their attitudes towards teaching after self viewing. These results might be diagrammed as follows:

E	P	B
Self viewing after micro-teaching	High self-esteem	More positive
	Low self-esteem	Less positive

The diagram might be used to determine which trainees will benefit more from micro-teaching, but does not provide information as to what alternative train-

Table 25. Training Objectives

Objective	Definition of Objective		
Skill in discrimination	To discriminate between environments $E_x/E_y/E_z$	To discriminate between behaviors $B_1/B_2/B_3$	To discriminate between persons $P_I/P_{II}/P_{III}$
Skill in radiating environments	To radiate a variety of environments $E_x:$ $E_y:$ E_z	To radiate that environment which will produce a specific behavior $E_x: \longrightarrow B_1$ $E_y: \longrightarrow B_2$	To radiate that environment which will produce a specific behavior from a particular person $E_x: \ P_I \longrightarrow B_1$ $E_y: \ P_{II} \longrightarrow B_1$
Skill in flexible modulation from one environment to another		To shift from one environment to another under appropriate circumstances (Time 1) $E_x: \ P_1 \longrightarrow B_1$ (Time 1) $E_y: \ P_1 \longrightarrow B_3$	

(After Hunt, 1971, p. 53)

ing procedure to use for those low self-esteem trainees. This example illustrates the form in which B-P-E diagrams may help a teacher trainer, and they emphasize the importance of providing alternative procedures. For example Reid (in progress) is investigating alternative training procedures varying in the amount of staff support, supervision, and structure. Trainees varying in Conceptual Level (Chapter 9) experienced two forms of training: "independent study" in which they were given the description of the teaching skill and encouraged to learn it on their own and a another group given a good deal of staff explanation and support in learning the teaching skill. It is expected that high CL trainees will profit more from the independent training while low CL trainees will profit more from the guided approach but these results have not yet been completely analyzed. The following diagram summarizes predictions:

E	P	B
Guided study	Low CL trainees	Acquisition of teaching skilll
Independent study	High CL trainees	

PRINCIPAL

Principals of junior-high and secondary schools often face the problem of using the teaching resources most effectively. In B-P-E terms he must develop the most effective combinations of ways of teaching (E) with different kinds of students (P) to facilitate learning (B). If different ways of teaching can be specified, they can serve as the basis for coordinating such allocation of resources.

Although the variations in ways of teaching may be as complex as the sixteen models in Table 10 in Chapter 4, we have used a much simpler version of instructional variations: an "environmental cafeteria" consisting of three instructional modes, lecture, discussion, and discovery. These can be offered to students as follows:

E	P	B
Lecture	Student	Performance satisfaction
Discussion		
Discovery		

Thus, a student can be given a miniature experience in these three modes so that he can then select the one he wants. This form of self-selection has been used with many university courses.

Note, however, that the specification of different instructional modes also provides the basis for describing teaching styles so that teachers also can be given an option. For example, a teacher might try out each of these three approaches, and then express a preference for one or more of them. For the principal, therefore, such specification can serve to effect a better match between the teacher's preferred style with the student's learning style.

How much freedom of choice is given to students and teachers, and how much is determined by the principal is not answered by B-P-E analysis since this will depend at least partly on the distribution of teaching and learning styles available. However, B-P-E analysis will describe teachers and students in ways which will be much more likely to be coordinated.

SUPERINTENDENT

Superintendents and directors of education confront the question of how to arrange for educational alternatives to students, and how to select staff who will provide such specific alternatives. The alternative schools described in Chapter 4 are a good example of how a differential approach can be implemented at the school level (Chapman, 1970). A superintendent need not necessarily adopt the arrangement of differential schools for different types of students, or the "family of schools" concept, but he must cope with how to provide an arrangement for coordinating teaching resources with student needs. As with the principal, B-P-E analysis does not define which arrangement (alternative schools, programs within schools) to use, but it organizes the information so that a solution is more likely to be found.

RESEARCHER

We have described numerous examples of how the B-P-E way of thinking influences research design and the conclusions from research investigations, especially in Chapter 5 and Chapter 9, so that how to apply B-P-E analysis in research should be clear. What deserves reemphasis, however, is that the B-P-E approach to research in psychology and education is neither a solution nor a specific research design.

It is a paradigm for posing research questions and for accumulating information from research. Thus, when "negative results" occur, the conclusion is not that "B-P-E has not paid off," but rather to record the nature of the results in relation to the subjects (P) and treatments (E) so that a more orderly accretion of knowledge is possible. B-P-E analysis thus strikes at the heart of the present general-effects research model which strives for principles and generalizations for "people-in-general." When a particular finding is "not replicated," the principle is discarded, or else a frequency count made of the number of positive and negative findings. B-P-E analysis would require a more systematic summary of experimental results which emphasized the specific person-environment combinations producing certain results, and those which failed to do so.

B-P-E analysis is also helpful to the reader of research reports and journal articles, and the reader is encouraged to construct B-P-E diagrams for the next few research reports he reads.

EVALUATOR

First it seems important that evaluators be encouraged to take a developmental prospective as suggested in Chapter 2 and attempt to conduct educational longitudinal studies using the same students if possible. There is simply no substitute for such longitudinal work to gain an understanding of the impact of programs. There are many difficulties with continuing to study the same students, yet the advantages seem clear.

At the conclusion of Chapter 9, reference was made to differential evaluation effects in Upward Bound programs, and a diagram of these effects provides the best example of how B-P-E analysis may be used in the evaluation of educational programs.

E	P	B
Structured summer program	Primarily students needing structure	Increased positive attitude, motivation for college, and interpersonal flexibility
Flexible summer program	Primarily students not requiring structure	

COUNSELOR

One of our colleagues has used the B-P-E analysis to reflect on his implicit theory of counseling. He began by describing his own list of counseling objectives (B) which included: (1) expression of feelings and emotions, (2) self-understanding, and (3) behavioral change. Next he listed the types of clients he had worked with as he saw them: (1) emotionally inhibited or repressed, (2) rudderless or lost existentially, and (3) socially inhibited or inadequate. Finally, he listed those general therapeutic methods or approaches he used: (1) Gestalt therapy, (2) neoanalytic therapy, (3) bioenergetics, (4) Rogerian therapy, (5) rational-emotive approaches, (6) transactional analysis, and (7) behavior modification. Finally he organized the therapeutic techniques in relation to types of clients to describe those combinations which he felt to be most effective. Also, he made some kind of estimate of his own capability and comfort with various therapeutic approaches, and perhaps came to a more systematic understanding of why he was better able to work with certain kind of clients than with others.

We recommend this kind of individual B-P-E analysis before one attempts to organize various theories and techniques as they are described in the literature. Once you have your own B-P-E diagram organized, it then provides a foundation or an anchor from which to think about how others have viewed the various combinations. It is as true in counseling and psychotherapy as it is in teaching that most approaches are suggested as the general solution for all problems and all clients which is, of course, absurd. The differential analysis provides a way of distinguishing the specific values of a particular approach for specific clients for specific purposes. Approaches can then be more systematically integrated or, as indicated earlier, such B-P-E analysis provides the basis for a kind of synthesized eclecticism.

STUDENT

A student may be particularly interested in which alternative to select, "What educational alternative am I most suited for?" This is a question which is particularly cogent for university and high school students who are offered options in various modes of instruction but little opportunity for self-assessment. We recommend the "environmental cafeteria" approach described earlier for this question. We have encouraged students to experience educational environments which are systematically different and note their reactions both to how much they learn and how they feel about what they learn. To profit from the potential self-knowledge in an "environmental cafeteria," one must try to remain open to all alternatives, even though they seem unpleasant. For example, if a student is particularly biased against more humanistic approaches such as those described in Chapter 10, he is unlikely to allow himself to experience such approaches. However, students (and everyone else, for that matter) should be encouraged to sample a variety of instructional approaches so that he can learn more about these approaches as well as about himself.

Thus, at its most general level B-P-E analysis can be applied by any individual to his day-to-day activities. For example, each of us can consider the kinds of environments that we radiate to others in our interpersonal activities, the kinds of persons we interact with and the effects we have on them. We can also turn the B-P-E analysis the other way and use it to think about our own reactions to specific kinds of environments, and learn more about ourselves in this way.

Summary

This concluding chapter described how to apply B-P-E analysis because it is intended as a practical guide to persons in psychology and education. The general procedure in B-P-E analysis suggested was: (1) to state the question, (2) to translate the question into a B-P-E diagram, (3) to describe the variation in each component, and (4) to collect information about the components and their interrelation. Specific examples in B-P-E analysis were described for teachers, teacher trainees, principals, superintendents, researchers, evaluators, and students. Finally, it was noted that B-P-E analysis may be useful at a more general level as a systematic means of increasing one's self-knowledge and self-awareness.

REFERENCES

Adler, M. *Some Implications of the Theories of Jean Piaget and J. S. Bruner for Education.* Toronto: Board of Education for the City of Toronto, Research Service, 1963.

Aebli, H. "Piaget and Beyond." *Interchange* 1, vol. 1, no. 1 (1970), pp. 12–24.

Allport, G. W. "What Units Shall We Employ?" In *Assessment of Human Motives,* edited by G. Lindzey, pp. 239–262. New York: Holt, Rinehart & Winston, 1958.

Almy, H.; Crittenden, B.; and Miller, T. *Young Children's Thinking.* New York: Teachers College Press, Columbia University, 1966.

Alpert, D., and Bitzer, D. L. "Advances in Computer-Based Education." *Science* 167 (1970):1582–1590.

Anderson, R. C. "Educational Psychology." *Annual Review of Psychology* 18 (1967):- 129–164.

Argyris, C. "Some Unintended Consequences of Rigorous Research." *Psychological Bulletin* 70 (1968):185–197.

287

Ausubel, D. P. *Ego Development and Personality Disorders.* New York; Grune & Stratton, 1952.

————. "The Use of Advance Organizers in the Learning and Retention of Meaningful Verbal Material." *Journal of Educational Psychology* 51, (1960):262–272.

————. "Learning by Discovery: Rationale and Mystique." *Bulletin of the National Association of Secondary School Principals* 45 (1961):18–58.

————. *Learning Theory and Classroom Practice.* Bulletin No. 1. Toronto: Ontario Institute for Studies in Education, 1967.

————. *The Psychology of Meaningful Verbal Learning.* New York: Grune & Stratton, 1963.

————. "Some Psychological and Educational Limitations of Learning by Discovery." *The Arithmetic Teacher* 11, (1964):290–302.

————. *Educational Psychology: A Cognitive View.* New York: Holt, Rinehart & Winston, 1968.

————. *Readings in School Learning.* New York: Holt, Rinehart & Winston, 1969.

Ausubel, D. P., and Fitzgerald, D. "Organizer, General Backround, and Sequential Verbal Learning." *Journal of Educational Psychology* 53, (1962):243–249.

Ausubel, D. P., and Robinson, S. G. *School Learning: An Introduction to Educational Psychology.* New York: Holt, Rinehart & Winston, 1969.

Ausubel, D. P., and Sullivan, E. V. *Theory and Problems of Child Development.* 2d ed. New York: Grune & Stratton, 1970.

Bakan, D. "The Mystery-Mastery Complex in Contemporary Psychology." *American Psychologist* 20 (1965):186–191.

————. "The Test of Significance in Psychological Research." *Psychological Bulletin* 66 (1966):423–437.

Baldwin, A. L. "The Study of Child Behavior and Development." In *Handbook of Research Methods in Child Development,* edited by P. H. Mussen, pp. 3–38. New York: John Wiley & Sons, 1960.

————. *Theories of Child Development.* New York: John Wiley & Sons, 1967.

Bandura, A., and Walters, R. H. *Social Learning and Personality Development.* New York: Holt, Rinehart & Winston, 1963.

Becker, W. C. "Consequences of Different Kinds of Parental Discipline." In *Review of Child Development Research,* edited by M. L. Hoffman and L. W. Hoffman, vol. 1, pp. 169–208. New York: Russell Sage, 1964.

Bell, R. Q. "A Reinterpretation of the Direction of Effects in Studies of Socialization." *Psychological Review* 73 (1968):81–95.

Bereiter, C., and Englemann, S. E. *Teaching Disadvantaged Children.* Englewood Cliffs, N.J.: Prentice-Hall, 1966.

Bernstein, E. "What Does a Summerhill Old School Tie Look Like?" *Psychology Today,* vol. 2, no. 5 (1968), pp. 37–41.

Bettelheim, B. "How Much Can Man Change?" *New York Review of Books,* September 10, 1964, vol. 3, pp. 1–4.

Bloom, B. S. "Testing Cognitive Ability and Achievement." In *Handbook of Research on Teaching,* edited by N. L. Gage, pp. 379–397. Chicago: Rand McNally & Co., 1963.

————. *Stability and Change in Human Characteristics.* New York: John Wiley & Sons, 1964.

————. "Some Theoretical Issues Relating to Educational Evaluation." In *Educational Evaluation: New Roles, New Means,* 68th NSSE Yearbook, edited by R. W. Tyler, pp. 26–50. Chicago: University of Chicago Press, 1969.

Bloom, B. S., et al. *Taxonomy of Educational Objectives.* New York: David McKay Co., 1956.

Bracht, G. H. "Experimental Factors Related to Aptitude-Treatment Interactions." *Review of Educational Research* 40 (1970):627–646.

Bracht, G. H., and Glass, G. V. "External Validity of Experiments." *American Educational Research Journal* 5 (1968):437–474.

Broudy, H. S. "Research and the Dogma of Behavioral Objectives." Paper presented at American Educational Research Association meeting, 1969, at Los Angeles, California.

Brown, G. I. *Human Teaching for Human Learning.* New York: Viking Press, 1971.

————. "Growth of a Flexible Self Through Creativity and Awareness." In *Perspectives for Reform in Teacher Education,* edited by B. R. Joyce and M. Weil, pp. 89–115. Englewood Cliffs, N.J.: Prentice-Hall, 1972.

Bruner, J. S. *The Process of Education.* Cambridge, Mass.: Harvard University Press, 1960.

————. "The Course of Cognitive Growth." *American Psychologist* 19 (1964):1–15.

Bruner, J. S., and Oliver, R. R. *Studies in Cognitive Growth.* New York: John Wiley & Sons, 1966.

Bruner, J. S.; Goodnow, J. J.; and Austin, G. A. *A Study of Thinking.* New York: John Wiley & Sons, 1956.

Brunswik, E. *Perception and the Representative Design of Psychology Experiments.* Berkeley: University of California Press, 1956.

Burger, H. G. "Behavior Modification, an Operant Psychology: An Anthropological Critique." *American Educational and Research Journal* 9 (1972):343–360.

Carlson, R. "Where Is the Person in Personality Research?" *Psychological Bulletin* 75 (1971):203–219.

Carroll, J. B. "Instructional Methods and Individual Differences." In *Learning and Individual Differences,* edited by R. M. Gagné, pp. 40–44. Columbus, Ohio: Charles E. Merrill Publishing Co., 1967.

Chapman, S. L. G. "Education and the Permissive Society." *School Progress* September 1971, pp. 28–30.

Clark, D. C. "Teaching Concepts in the Classroom: A Set of Teaching Prescriptions Derived from Experimental Research." *Journal of Educational Psychology* 62 (1971):253–278.

Claunch, N. "Cognitive and Motivational Characteristics Associated with Concrete and Abstract Levels of Conceptual Complexity." Ph.D. dissertation, Princeton University, 1964.

Cremin, L. A. *The Transformation of the School: Progressivism in American Education.* New York: Afred A. Knopf, 1964.

Cronbach, L. J. "The Two Disciplines of Scientific Psychology." *American Psychologist* 12 (1957):671–684.

————. "Piaget Rediscovered." In *Piaget Rediscovered: A Report of the Cornell Conference on Cognitive Studies and Curriculum Development,* edited by R. E. Ripple and D. Rockcastle, pp. 73–77. Ithaca, N.Y.: School of Education, Cornell University, March 1964.

————. "The Logic of Experiments on Discovery." In *Learning by Discovery: A Critical Appraisal,* edited by L. S. Shulman and E. R. Kaislar, pp. 76–92. Chicago: Rand McNally & Co., 1966.

————. "How Can Instruction Be Adapted to Individual Differences." In *Learning and Individual Differences,* edited by R. M. Gagné, pp. 23–44. New York: Macmillan Co., 1967.

————. "Heredity, Environment, and Educational Policy." *Harvard Educational Review* 39 (1969):338–347.

Cronbach, L. J., and Meehl, P. E. "Construct Validity in Psychological Tests." *Psychological Bulletin* 52 (1955):281–302.

Cronbach, L. J. and Snow, R. E. *Project on Individual Differences in Learning Ability as a Function of Instructional Variables.* U.S. Office of Education Annual Report No. 2. Stanford, Calif.: School of Education, Stanford University, 1968.

————. *Individual Differences in Learning Ability as a Function of Instructional Variables.* U.S. Office of Education Final Report. Stanford, Calif.: School of Education, Stanford University, 1969.

Cronbach, L. J., and Suppes, P., eds. *Research for Tomorrow's School.* New York: Macmillan Co., 1969.

Cross, H. J. "The Relation of Parental Training Conditions to Conceptual Level in Adolescent Boys." *Journal of Personality* 34 (1966):348–365.

Crutchfield, R. S. "Conformity and Character." *American Psychologist* 10 (1955):- 191–198.

Dewey, J. *The Child and the Curriculum.* Chicago: University of Chicago Press, 1902.

————. *Democracy in Education.* New York: Macmillan Co., 1916.

Duckworth, E. "Piaget Rediscovered." In *Piaget Rediscovered: A Report of the Cornell Conference on Cognitive Studies and Curriculum Development,* edited by R. E. Ripple and D. Rockcastle. Ithaca, N.Y.: School of Education, Cornell University, March 1964.

Eisner, E. W. "Educational Objectives: Help or Hindrance?" *School Review* 75 (1967):250–266.

Erikson, E. H. "Identity and the Life Cycle." *Psychological Issues,* vol. 1, no. 1 (1959).

Featherstone, J. *Schools Where Children Learn.* New York: Liveright Publishing Corp., 1971.

Ferster, C. B., and Skinner, B. F. *Schedules of Reinforcement.* New York: Appleton-Century-Crofts, 1957.

Festinger, L. *A Theory of Cognitive Dissonance.* New York: Row Peterson, 1957.

Flavell, J. H. *The Developmental Psychology of Jean Piaget.* Princeton, N.J.: D. Van Nostrand Co., 1963.

Flavell, J. H., and Wohlwill, J. F. "Formal and Functional Aspects of Cognitive Development." In *Studies in Cognitive Development: Essays in Honor of Jean Piaget,* edited by D. Elkind and J. H. Flavell, pp. 67–120. New York: Oxford University Press, 1969.

Fox, R. S., and Lippitt, R. "The Innovation of Classroom Mental Health Practices." In *Innovation in Education,* edited by M. Miles, pp. 271–297. New York: Teacher's College, Columbia University, 1964.

French, E. G. "Effects of the Interaction of Motivation and Feedback on Task Performance." In *Motives in Fantasy, Action, and Society,* edited by J. W. Atkinson, pp. 400–408. Princeton, N.J.: D. Van Nostrand Co., 1958.

Furth, H. *Piaget for Teachers.* Englewood Cliffs, N.J.: Prentice-Hall, 1970.

Gagné, R. M. "Instructions and the Conditions of Learning." In *Instructions: Certain Temporary Viewpoints,* edited by L. Siegel, pp. 291–313. San Francisco: Chandler Publishing Co., 1967.

_____. "Contributions of Learning to Human Development." *Psychological Review* 75 (1968):177–191.

Gagné, R. M., and Rohwer, W. D. "Instructional Psychology." *Annual Review of Psychology* 20 (1969):381–418.

Gesell, A. "Maturation and the Patterning of Behavior." In *A Handbook of Child Psychology,* edited by C. Murchison, pp. 209–235. Worcester, Mass.: Clark University Press, 1933.

Gesell, A., and Ilg, F. L. *Infant and Child in the Culture of Today.* New York: Harper & Bros., 1934.

Getzels, J. "A Social Psychology of Education." In *Handbook of Social Psychology,* edited by G. Lindzey and E. Aronson, vol. 5, pp. 459–537. 2d ed. Reading, Mass.: Addison-Wesley Publishing Co., 1968.

Gibbons, M. "What Is Individualized Instruction?" *Interchange,* vol. 1, no. 2 (1970), pp. 28–52.

Gill, K. "Whither an English Curriculum for the Seventies?" *English Journal* 60 (1971):447–457.

Ginsberg, H., and Opper, S. *Piaget's Theory of Intellectual Development: An Introduction.* Englewood Cliffs, N.J.: Prentice-Hall, 1969.

Glaser, R. "Schooling and Education." In *The Great Ideas Today,* edited by R. M. Hutchins and M. J. Adler, pp. 100–145. Chicago: Encyclopedia Britannica, 1969.

_____. "Individuals and Learning: The New Aptitudes." *Educational Researcher.* Vol. 1, no. 6 (1972), pp. 6–13.

Goodlad, J. I. *School, Curriculum, and Individual.* Waltham, Mass.: Blaisdell Publishing Co., 1966.

Goodlad, J. I., and Anderson, R. H. *The Non-graded Elementary School.* New York: Harcourt, Brace & World, 1963.

Grace, G. L. "The Relation of Personality Characteristics and Response to Verbal Approval in a Learning Task." *Genetic Psychology Monographs* 37 (1948):-73–103.

Grant, M. Q.; Warren, M.; and Turner, J. K. *Community Treatment Project. An Evaluation of Community Treatment for Delinquents.* CTP Research Report No. 3, California Youth Authority, 1963.

Gulpers, H. "An Experimental Acceleration of the Concept of Density." Master's thesis, University of Toronto, 1968.

Hall, E. "A Conversation with Jean Piaget and Barbel Inhelder." *Psychology Today,* vol. 3, no. 12 (1970), pp. 25–32.

Hanley, A. M. "Review of Research Involving Applied Behavior Analysis in the Classroom." *Review of Educational Research* 40 (1970):597–625.

Harvey, O. J. "Conceptual Systems and Attitude Change." In *Attitude, Ego-Involvement, and Change,* edited by C. W. Sherif and M. Sherif, pp. 201–226. New York: John Wiley & Sons, 1967.

Harvey, O. J.; Hunt, D. E.; and Schroder, H. M. *Conceptual Systems and Personality Organization.* New York: John Wiley & Sons, 1961.

Hewitt, F. M. "A Hierarchy of Educational Tasks for Children with Learning Disorders." *Exceptional Children* 31 (1964):207–214.

Hidi, S. Ego Development and Motivation. Master's thesis, University of Toronto, 1971.

Hilgard, E. R. "Perspective on the Relationship Between Learning Theory and Educational Practices." In *Theories of Learning Instruction,* 63rd NSSE Yearbook, edited by E. R. Hilgard, pp. 402–415. Chicago: National Society for the Study of Education, 1964.

Hoffman, L. W., and Lippitt, R. "The Measurement of Family Life Variables." In *Handbook of Research Methods in Child Development,* edited by P. H. Mussen, pp. 945–1014. New York: John Wiley & Sons, 1960.

Hofstadter, R. *Anti-intellectualism in American Life.* New York: Vintage Books, 1963.

Holland, J., and Skinner, B. F. *The Analysis of Behavior.* New York: McGraw-Hill Book Co., 1961.

Holt, J. "Comment on Bettelheim, B. 'How Much Can Man Change?' " *New York Review of Books,* October 22, 1964, vol. 3, pp. 23–24.

Hovland, C. I. "The Generalization of Conditioned Responses. I. The Sensory Generalization of Conditioned Responses with Varying Frequencies of Tone." *Journal of General Psychology* 17 (1937):125–148.

Hunt, D. E. "A Model for Analyzing the Training of Training Agents." *Merrill Palmer Quarterly* 12 (1966a):137–156.

————. "A Conceptual Systems Change Model and Its Application to Education." In *Experience, Structure, and Adaptability,* edited by O. J. Harvey, pp. 277–302. New York: Springer Publishing Co., 1966*b*.

————. "Adaptability in Interpersonal Communication Among Training Agents." *Merrill Palmer Quarterly* 16 (1970):325–344.

————. *Matching Models in Education.* Toronto: Ontario Institute for Studies in Education, 1971.

————. *Alternative Approaches in Two York County Secondary Schools.* Grants-in-aid Project, Ontario Department of Education. Toronto: The Department, 1972.

Hunt, D. E., and Hardt, R. H. "The Role of Conceptual Level and Program Structure in Summer Upward Bound Programs." Paper presented at Eastern Psychological Association meeting, April 1967, at Boston, Massachusetts.

Hunt, D. E.; Greenwood, J.; Brill, R.; and Deineka, M. "From Psychological Theory to Educational Practice: Implementation of a Matching Model." Paper presented at American Educational Research Association meeting, April 1972, at Chicago, Illinois.

Hunt, J. McV. *Intelligence and Experience.* New York: Ronald Press Co., 1961.

Hutt, M. L. "A Clinical Study of 'Consecutive' and 'Adaptive' Testing with the revised Stanford Binet." *Journal of Consulting Psychology* 11 (1947):93–103.

Inhelder, B. "Some Aspects of Piaget's Genetic Approach to Cognition." *Monographs of the Society for Research in Child Development,* 27 (1962):19–33.

Jackson, P. W. *Life in Classrooms.* New York: Holt, Rinehart & Winston, 1968.

————. "Is There a Best Way of Teaching Harold Bateman?" *Midway* 10 (1970): 15–28.

James, W. *Talks to Teachers on Psychology, and to Students on Some of Life's Ideals.* New York: W. W. Norton & Co., 1958.

Jensen, A. R. "How Much Can We Boost IQ and Scholastic Achievement?" *Harvard Educational Review* 39 (1969):1–123.

Joyce, B. R. *Man, Media and Machines.* Washington, D. C.: National Educational Association, 1967.

————. *Alternative Models of Elementary Education.* Waltham, Mass.: Blaisdell Publishing Co., 1969.

Joyce, B. R., and Harootunian, B. *The Structure of Teaching.* Chicago: Science Research Associates, 1967.

Joyce, B., and Weil, M., eds. *Perspectives for Reform in Teacher Education.* New York: Prentice-Hall, 1972*a*.

————. *Models of Teaching.* New York: Prentice-Hall, 1972*b*.

Kagan, J. "On the Need for Relativism." *American Psychologist* 22 (1967):131–142.

Kelly, G. A. *The Psychology of Personal Constructs.* New York: W. W. Norton & Co., 1955.

Kelman, H. C. "Processes of Opinion Change." *Public Opinion Quarterly* 25 (1961): 57–79.

————. "The Problem of Deception in Social Psychological Experiments." *Psychological Bulletin* 67 (1967):1–11.

Kessen, W. H. "Research Design and the Study of Developmental Problems." In *Handbook of Research Methods in Child Development,* edited by P. H. Mussen, pp. 36–70. New York: John Wiley & Sons, 1960.

————. "Stage and Structure in the Study of Children." *Monographs of the Society for Research in Child Development* 27 (1962):65–82.

————. "Questions for a Theory of Cognitive Development." *Monographs of the Society for Research in Child Development* 31 (1966):55–70.

Kibler, R. J.; Barker, L. L.; and Miles, D. T. *Behavior Objectives and Instruction.* Boston: Bacon, 1970.

Kliebard, H. M. "Curricula Objectives and Evaluation: Reassessment." *High School Journal* 51 (1968):240–247.

Kohlberg, L. "The Development of Modes of Moral Thinking and Choice in the Years 10 to 16." Ph.D. dissertation, University of Chicago, 1958.

————. "Moral Development and Identification." In *Child Psychology,* 62d NSSE Yearbook, edited by H. Stevenson, pp. 277–332. Chicago: University of Chicago Press, 1963.

————. "Development of Moral Character and Moral Ideology." In *Review of Child Development Research,* edited by M. Hoffman and L. Hoffman, vol. 1, pp. 383–431. New York: Russell Sage, 1964.

————. "Moral Education in the Schools." *School Review* 74 (1966):1–30.

————. "Stage and Sequence: The Cognitive-Development Approach to Socialization." In *Handbook of Socialization Theory and Research,* edited by D. A. Goslin, pp. 347–480. Chicago: Rand McNally & Co., 1966.

Kohnstamm, G. A. "Experiments on Teaching Piagetian Thought Operations." Paper presented at Conference on Guided Learning, January 1966, at Cleveland, Ohio.

Krathwohl, D.; Bloom, B. S.; and Masia, B. B. *Taxonomy of Educational Objectives: Handbook II Affective Domain.* New York: David McKay Co., 1964.

Kuhn, T. *The Structure of Scientific Revolutions.* University of Chicago Press, Chicago, 1964.

Langer, J. *Theories of Development.* New York: Holt, Rinehart & Winston, 1969.

Laurendeau, M., and Pinard, A. *Causal Thinking in the Child.* New York: International Universities Press, 1963.

Lesser, G. "Postscript: Matching Instruction to Student Characteristics." In *Psychology and Educational Practice,* edited by G. Lesser, pp. 530–550. Glenview, Illinois: Scott, Foresman & Co., 1971.

Lewin, K. *Principles of Topological Psychology.* New York: McGraw-Hill Book Co., 1936.

————. "Comments Concerning Psychological Forces and Energies, and the Structure of the Psyche." In *Organization and Pathology of Thought,* edited by D. Rapaport, pp. 95–153. New York: Columbia University Press, 1951.

————. *Field Theory and Social Science.* New York: Harper & Bros., 1951.

Loevinger, J. "The Meaning and Measurement of Ego Development." *American Psychologist* 21 (1966):195–206.

_____. *Theories of Ego Development: Clinical-Cognitive Psychology.* Edited by L. Breger. Englewood Cliffs, N.J.: Prentice-Hall, 1969.

McDonald, F. J. "The Influence of Learning Theories on Education (1900–1950)." In *Theories of Learning Instruction,* 63rd NSSE Yearbook, edited by E. R. Hilgard, pp. 402–415. Chicago: National Society for the Study of Education, 1964.

Mandler, G., and Sarason, S. B. "A Study of Anxiety and Learning." *Journal of Abnormal and Social Psychology* 21 (1952):336–341.

Maslow, A. H. "Some Education of the Humanistic Psychologist." *Harvard Educational Review* 38 (1968a):685–696.

_____. *Toward a Psychology of Being.* 2d ed. New York: Van Nostrand Reinhold, 1968b.

Mayer, M. *The Schools.* New York: Doubleday & Co., 1961.

McClintock, C. G. "Personality Syndromes and Attitude Change." *Journal of Personality* 26 (1958):479–493.

McLachlan, J. F. C., and Hunt, D. E. "Differential Effects of Discovery Learning as a Function of Student Conceptual Level." *Canadian Journal of Behavioural Science,* 5 (1973):152–160.

McLachlan, J. F. C. "Benefit from Group Therapy as a Function of Patient-therapist match on Conceptual Level" *Psychotherapy: Theory, Research and Practice,* 9 (1972):317–323.

Messick, S. "The Criteria Problem in the Evaluation of Instruction: Assessing Possible, Not Just Intended Outcomes." In *The Evaluation of Instruction: Issues and Problems,* edited by M. Wittrock and D. C. Wiley. New York: Holt, Rinehart & Winston, 1971.

Miles, M., ed. *Innovation in Education.* New York: Teachers College, Columbia University, 1964.

Mischel, W. *Personality Assessment.* New York: John Wiley & Sons, 1968.

Montessori, M. *The Secret of Childhood.* London: Longmans Green, 1939.

Moore, O. K. "Autotelic Responsive Environments and Exceptional Children." In *Experience, Structure, and Adaptability,* edited by O. J. Harvey, pp. 169–216. New York: Springer Publishing Co., 1966.

Mosher, R. L., and Sprinthall, N. A. "Psychological Education: A Means to Promote Personal Development During Adolescence." *The Counseling Psychologist,* vol. 2, no. 4 (1971), pp. 3–82.

Murray, E. J. "A Content-Analysis Method for Studying Psychotherapy." *Psychological Monographs,* vol. 70, no. 13 (1956).

Neill, A. S. *Summerhill.* New York: Hart Publishing Co., 1960.

Noy, J. E., and Hunt, D. E. "Student-Directed Learning from Biographical Information Systems." *Canadian Journal of Behavioural Science* 4 (1972):54–63.

Ojemann, R. H., and Pritchett, K. "Piaget and the Role of Guided Experiences in Human Development." *Perceptual and Motor Skills* 17 (1963):927–940.

O'Leary, K. D.; Becker, W. C.; Evans, M. B.; and Saudargas, R. A. "A Token Reinforcement Program in a Public School: A Replication and Systematic Analysis." *Journal of Applied Behavior Analysis* 2 (1969):3–13.

Palmer, T. B. "An Overview of Matching in the Community Treatment Project." Paper presented at Western Psychological Association, 1968, San Diego, California.

Pascal, C. E., and McKeachie, W. J. "Offering Course Options: Personality, Option Preference, and Course Outcomes." Paper presented at American Educational Research Association meeting, 1970, at Minneapolis, Minnesota.

Pervin, L. A. "Performance and Satisfaction as a Function of Individual-Environment Fit." *Psychological Bulletin* 69 (1968):56–68.

―――. *Personality: Theory, Assessment and Research.* New York: John Wiley & Sons, 1970.

Peters, R. S. "Must an Educator Have an Aim?" In *Philosophy of Education,* edited by W. K. Frankena. New York: Macmillan Co., 1965.

Piaget, J. *The Moral Judgment of the Child.* London: Routledge & Kegan Paul, 1932.

―――. *The Psychology of Intelligence.* Totowa, N.J.: Littlefield, Adams & Co., 1960.

―――. "Cognitive Development in Children: Piaget Papers." In *Piaget Rediscovered: A Report of the Conference on Cognitive Studies and Curriculum Development,* edited by R. E. Ripple and D. N. Rockcastle, pp. 7–20. Ithaca, New York: School of Education, Cornell University, March 1964.

―――. "Psychology and Philosophy." In *Scientific Psychology,* edited by D. V. Wolman and E. Nagel pp. 28–43. New York: Basic Books, 1965.

―――. *Science of Education and the Psychology of the Child.* New York: Viking Press, 1971.

Pohl, R. L., and Pervin, L. A. "Academic Performance as a Function of Task Requirements and Cognitive Style." *Psychological Reports* 22 (1968):1017–1020.

Polanyi, M. *Personal Knowledge: Towards a Post-Critical Philosophy.* New York: Harper & Row Publishers, 1962.

Popham, W. J. "Probing the Validity of Arguments Against Behavioral Goals." Paper presented at American Educational Research Association meeting, 1968, at Chicago, Illinois.

Razran, G. "Stimulus Generalization of Conditioned Responses." *Psychological Bulletin* 46 (1949):337–365.

Reid, R. Accessibility characteristics as guides for individualizing teacher education: acquisition of basic teaching skills. Doctoral dissertation in progress, University of Toronto.

Riesman, D. *The Lonely Crowd.* New Haven: Yale University Press, 1950.

Robinson, F. "Some Relevance for the School." In *Teacher Education: A Search for New Relationships,* pp. 25–33. Toronto: OISE, 1970.

Rogers, C. R. "The Necessary and Sufficient Conditions of Therapeutic Personality Change." *Journal of Consulting Psychology* 21 (1957):95–103.

―――. "A Process Conception of Psychotherapy." *American Psychologist* 13 (1958): 141–149.

―――. "Toward a Science of the Person." In *Behaviorism and Phenomenology:*

Contrasting Bases for Modern Psychology, edited by T. W. Wann. Chicago: University of Chicago Press, 1964.

———. *Freedom to Learn.* Columbus, Ohio: Charles E. Merrill Publishing Co., 1969.

Rogers, E. M. *Diffusion of Innovations.* New York: Free Press, 1962.

Rosenshine, B., and Furst, N. "Research on Teacher Performance Criteria." In *Research in Teacher Education,* edited by B. O. Smith, pp. 37–72. Englewood Cliffs, N.J.: Prentice Hall, 1971.

Rosenthal, R. "Teacher Expectations and Their Effects upon Children." In *Psychology and Educational Practice,* edited by G. S. Lesser, pp. 64, 89. Glenview, Illinois: Scott, Foresman & Co., 1971.

Royce, J. R. *The Encapsulated Man.* New York: D. Van Nostrand Co., 1964.

Salomon, G. "Heuristics for the Generation of Aptitude-Treatment-Interaction Hypotheses." Paper presented at American Educational Research Association meeting, 1971, at New York.

Salomon, G. & McDonald, F. J. "Pretest and Posttest Reactions to Self-viewing one's Teaching Performance on Video Tape," *Journal of Educational Psychology,* 61 (1970):280–86.

Sanford, R. N. "Will Psychologists Study Human Problems?" *American Psychologist* 20 (1965):192–202.

Sarason, I. G., and Smith, R. E. "Personality." *Annual Review of Psychology* 22 (1971):393–446.

Sarason, S. B. *The Culture of the School and the Problem of Change.* New York: Allyn & Bacon, 1971.

Schaefer, E. S. "A Circumplex Model for Maternal Behavior." *Journal of Abnormal and Social Psychology* 59 (1959):226–235.

Scheffler, I. *The Language of Education.* American Lecture Series. Springfield, Ill.: Charles C. Thomas, Publisher, 1960.

Schroder, H. M. "Conceptual Complexity and Personality Organization." In *Personality Theory and Information Processing.* edited by H. M. Schroder and P. Suedfeld, pp. 240–273. New York: Ronald Press Co., 1971.

Schroder, H. M.; Driver, M. J.; and Streufert, S. *Human Information Processing.* New York: Holt, Rinehart and Winston, 1967.

Schroder, H. M.; Karlins, M.; and Phares, J. *Education for Freedom.* New York: John Wiley & Sons, 1973.

Shaver, J. P., and Oliver, D. P. "The Effect of Student Characteristics-Teaching Method Interactions on Learning to Think Critically." Paper presented at American Educational Research Association, 1968, at Chicago, Illinois.

Shostrom, E. L. *Personality Orientation Inventory.* Educational Testing Service, 1962.

Shulman, L. S. "Reconstruction of Educational Research." *Review of Educational Research* 40 (1970):371–396.

Siegel, G. M. "Interpersonal Studies of Normal Adults and Retarded Children." Planning Paper #29, Division of Speech Pathology and Audiology, University of Minnesota. Minneapolis, Minnesota: The University, 1966.

Sigel, L. E. "The Piagetian System and the World of Education." Merrill Palmer

Institute, 1968.

Simon, A., and Boyer, E. G. "Mirrors for Behavior." *Classroom in Action Newsletter* vol. 3, no. 2 (1968).

Sinclair-de-Zwart, H. "Developmental Psycholinguistics." In *Studies in Cognitive Development: Essays in Honor of Jean Piaget,* edited by D. Elkind and J. H. Flavell, pp. 315–336. New York: Oxford University Press, 1969.

————. *Acquisition du Language et Developpement de le Pensee.* Paris: Dunod, 1967.

Skinner, B. F. *The Behavior of Organism: An Experimental Analysis.* New York: Appleton-Century-Crofts, 1938.

————. *The Technology of Teaching.* New York: Appleton-Century-Crofts, 1968.

Smedslund, J. "The Acquisition of Conservation of Substance and Weight in Children." *Scandinavian Journal of Psychology* 2 (1961):85–87, 156–160, 203–210.

————. "Educational Psychology." *Annual Review of Psychology* 15 (1964):251–276.

Solomon, D.; Rosenberg, L.; and Bezdek, W. E. "Teacher Behavior in Student Learning." *Journal of Educational Psychology* 55 (1964):23–30.

Snow, R. E. "Brunswickian Approaches to Research on Teaching." *American Educational Research Journal* 5 (1968):475–489.

————. "Research on Media and Attitude." *Bulletin of the School of Education-Indiana University* 46 (1970):63–89.

Snow, R. E.; Tiffin, J.; and Seibert, W. F. "Individual Differences and Instructional Film Effects." *Journal of Educational Psychology* 54 (1965):315–326.

Stake, R. E. "Objectives, Priorities, and Other Judgment Data." *Review of Educational Research* 40 (1970):181–212.

Stern, G. G. "Environments for Learning." In *The American College.* edited by N. Sanford, pp. 690–730. New York: John Wiley & Sons, 1961.

————. *People in Context: Measuring Person-Environment Congruence in Education and Industry.* New York: John Wiley & Sons, 1970.

Stuempfig, D. W., and Maehr, M. L. "Effects of Conceptual Structure and Social Quality of Feedback on Persistence. *Child Development* 4 (1970):1183–1190.

Suedfeld, P. "Attitude Manipulation in Restricted Environments: Conceptual Structure and Response to Propaganda." *Journal of Abnormal and Social Psychology* 68 (1964):242–247.

Sullivan, C. E.; Grant, M. Q.; and Grant, J. D. "The Development of Interpersonal Maturity: Application to Delinquency." *Psychiatry* 20 (1957):373–385.

Sullivan, E. V. *Piaget and the School Curriculum: A Critical Appraisal.* The Ontario Institute for Studies in Education Bulletin No. 2. Toronto: The Institute, 1967.

————. "Piagetian Theory in the Educational Milieu: A Critical Appraisal." *Canadian Journal of Behavioural Science* 1 (1969):129–155.

————. "The Issue of Readiness in the Design and Organization of the Curriculum: A Historical Perspective." *Educational Technology* 10 (1970):39–48.

————. "Developmental and Contemporaneous Individual Differences and Their Role in Curriculum-Decision Making and Teacher Training." In *Perspectives for Reform in Teacher Education,* edited by B. Joyce and M. Weil, pp. 164–203. Englewood Cliffs, N.J.: Prentice-Hall, 1972.

Sullivan, E. V., and Beck, C. "Moral Education." In *Must Schools Fail?* edited by N. Byrne and J. Quarter, pp. 126–141. Toronto: McClelland & Stewart, 1972.

Sullivan, E. V.; McCullough, G.; and Stager, M. "A Developmental Study of the Relation Between Conceptual, Ego, and Moral Development." *Child Development* 41 (1970):399–412.

Szeminska, A. "The Evolution of Thought: Some Applications of Research Findings to Educational Practice." *Monographs of the Society for Research in Child Development* 30 (1965):47–57.

Thelen, H. A. *Classroom Grouping for Teachability.* New York: John Wiley & Sons, 1967.

Thompson, G. G., and Hunnicutt, C. W. "The Effect of Repeated Praise or Blame on the Work Achievement of 'Introverts' and 'Extroverts'." *Journal of Educational Psychology* 35 (1944):257–266.

Tomlinson, P. D., and Hunt, D. E. "Differential Effects of Rule-Example Order as a Function of Learner Conceptual Level. *Canadian Journal of Behavioral Science* 3 (1971):237–245.

Torrance, E. P. "Different Ways of Learning for Different Kinds of Children." In *Mental Health and Achievement: Increasing Potential and Reducing School Dropout,* edited by E. P. Torrance and R. D. Strom, pp. 253–262. New York: John Wiley & Sons, 1965.

Traub, R. E. "Some Implications for Educational Evaluation." In *Means and Ends in Education,* Occasional Papers #2, edited by B. R. Crittenden. Toronto: Ontario Institute for Studies in Education, 1969.

Tuckman, B. W. *A Study of the Effectiveness of Directive vs. Nondirective Vocational Teachers as a Function of Student Characteristics and Course Format.* U.S. Office of Education Final Report, 1968.

Turiel, E. "An Experimental Test of the Sequentiality of Developmental Stages in the Child's Moral Judgments." *Journal of Personality and Social Psychology* 3 (1966):611–618.

Vale, J. R., and Vale, C. A. "Individual Differences and General Laws in Psychology: a Reconciliation," *American Psychologist* 25 (1969):1093–1108.

Van de Riet, H. "Effects of Praise and Reproof on Paired-Associate Learning in Educationally Retarded Children." *Journal of Educational Psychology* 55 (1964):139–143.

Vygotsky, L. S. *Thought and Language.* New York: M. I. T. Press, 1965.

Wallach, M. S. "Creativity and the Expression of Possibility." In *Creativity and Learning,* edited by J. Kagan. Boston: Houghton Mifflin Co., 1967.

Warren, M. Q., and Community Project Staff. "Interpersonal Maturity Level Classification. Juvenile," California Youth Authority, 1966.

Washburne, C., and Heil, L. N. "What Characteristics of Teachers Affect Children's Growth?" *School Review* 68 (1960):420–426.

Webb, E. J.; Campbell, D. G.; Schwartz, R. D.; and Sechrest, L. *Unobtrusive Measures: Non-reactive Research in the Social Sciences.* Chicago: Rand McNally & Co., 1966.

Weinstein, G., and Fantini, M. D. *Toward Humanistic Education: A Curriculum of Affect.* New York: Frederick A. Praeger, 1970.

Werner, H. "Process and Achievement: A Basic Problem of Education and Development Psychology. *Harvard Educational Review* 7 (1937):353–368.

Whiting, J. W., and Child, I. L. *Child Training and Personality.* New Haven: Yale University Press, 1953.

Wittrock, M. C., and Wiley, D. C., eds. *The Evaluation of Instruction: Issues and Problems.* New York: Holt, Rinehart & Winston, 1970.

Wohlwill, J. F. "From Perception to Inference: A Dimension of Cognitive Development." *Monographs of the Society for Research in Child Development* 27 (1962): 87–106.

––––––. "The Place of Structural Experience in Early Cognitive Development." *Interchange* vol. 1, no. 2 (1970), pp. 13–27.

Wolfe, P. "The Role of Conceptual Systems in Cognitive Functioning at Varying Levels of Age and Intelligence." *Journal of Personality* 31 (1963):108–123.

Woodring, P. "Reform Movements from the Point of View of Psychological Theory." In *Theories of Learning and Instruction,* 63rd NSSE Yearbook, edited by E. R. Hilgard, Part I. Chicago: University of Chicago Press, 1964.

Worthen, B. R. "Discovery and Expository Task Presentation in Elementary Mathematics." *Journal of Educational Psychology* 59 (1968) (Monogr. Suppl. 1).

Zigler, E. "Social Class and Socialization Process." *A Review of Educational Research* 40 (1970):87–110.

Index